GLOBALIZATION, POVERTY AND INEQUALITY

Between a Rock and a Hard Place

RAPHAEL KAPLINSKY

polity

First published in 2005 by Polity Press

Polity Press
65 Bridge Street
Cambridge CB2 1UR, UK

Polity Press
350 Main Street
Malden, MA 02148, USA

ISBN: 0-7456-3553-9
ISBN: 0-7456-3554-7 (pb)

A catalogue record for this book is available from the British Library and has been applied for from the Library of Congress.

Typeset in 10.5 on 12 pt Sabon
by Servis Filmsetting Ltd, Longsight, Manchester
Printed and bound in Great Britain by MPG Books Ltd, Bodmin, Cornwall

For further information on Polity, visit our website: www.polity.co.uk

Contents

Figures

Tables

A Guide to the Reader

In a disciplinary sense this is a crossover book. Elements of the analysis are drawn from development economics, from economic geography, from international political economy, from sociology, from management studies, from production engineering, and from the literature on the management of innovation. Consequently most readers will sometimes find themselves confronted by unfamiliar literature and unfamiliar jargon. At the same time, the text is designed to be accessible to a wide audience, including fellow researchers, policy-makers, development professionals and students. For this reason I offer a guide to assist the selective reader. In addition each of the chapters incorporates summary boxes in almost all sections. These are designed both to assist non-specialist readers and to provide a route to the rapid reader. In this way it is hoped that both specialists and non-specialists can more easily find their way through the text.

The ultimate objective of the book is to explain the relationship between globalization, poverty and inequality, and to consider the policy implications of this analysis for low-income economies. At a minimum, therefore, those wanting to absorb the key argument should focus on the first, second and final chapters, in which the central propositions are stated, the empirical material is summarized and the conclusions are presented.

Readers who wish to understand in greater detail how and why I have reached these conclusions should read chapters 6 and 7. These chapters are focused at the macro-level and consider the workings of the global economy at large. Much of this discussion is backed by original empirical material and quantitative analysis, as is the analysis of globalization in three sectors in chapter 5. I am particularly concerned that these chapters should be read by those who have an expertise in more micro-related concerns such as micro-economics, production engineering and innovation management. This is because, in my experience, professionals with these more narrowly focused skills often tend to ignore the wider implications of their own expertise.

Conversely, the discussions in chapters 3 and 4 provide an introduction to the principles of management, production engineering and innovation management. I believe that this should be of particular concern to those readers with a specialism in macro-issues and who often consider the firm, or the chain and cluster of firms – entities which respond seamlessly to changes in economic policy – as a black box.

Student readers are at the forefront of my concern. I have attempted to keep jargon to a minimum, and wherever possible I have tried to provide an overview and literature review of key fields. Thus, for example, chapters 1 and 8 comprise a synoptic view of globalization, in historical perspective; chapter 2 summarizes the empirical material on global poverty and inequality and discusses the ambiguity of data and the various meanings attributed to poverty; chapters 3, 4 and 5 outline some of the key principles in the literature on innovation, on global value chains and on industrial districts and clusters; chapters 6 and 7 explain the underlying principles of the terms of trade and the theory of comparative advantage. In each case I have tried not only to present these ideas in accessible form, but also to draw the links between them and, where appropriate, to carry forward the discussion on to a new plane.

Acknowledgements

Polity Press has been an extremely supportive publisher, working with admirable professionalism. I have had only one problem, however, and this concerns the authorship of this book. I had wanted to have the book credited to 'Raphael Kaplinsky (and others)', but this ran against publishing conventions. My reason for wanting this form of ascription is that almost all of the discussion in this book, in one form or another, draws on the ideas of others. In some cases it results from close research collaboration, in others from extended discussions over the years, and in yet others to specific acts of assistance. I have also of course gained from access to a series of high-quality research reports emanating from the institutions in which I work, and the networks in which I participate, not all of which have been published.

It is invidious to try and name everyone who has contributed in one way or another to the preparation of this book, because I am bound to leave some out. For these omissions I apologize. Those that I remember are as follows.

For assistance with the project as a whole I am indebted to my wife Cathy, who allowed me to bounce various ideas around, who tolerated my periods of introspection and who encouraged me to make the personal part of the professional; Mike Morris, who nagged me for some time to get on with it, and who gave detailed comments on some of the chapters; Jeff Henderson and an anonymous Polity reviewer, who provided comments on the text as a whole; Howie Rush, for his understanding and generous support during the writing of the book; and David Evans, who at various times answered technical questions and read some of the draft chapters. My son, Ben, was a source of awkward and probing questions at various stages of the book's evolution, and these spurred me to try and make it more accessible to non-specialists – I am afraid that I am unable to write to a legal agenda!

Various sets of the analysis are drawn from collaborative work. On autos, I owe thanks to Justin Barnes and Mike Morris; on furniture to Jeff Readman; on the analysis of global prices to Amelia Santos-Paulino; on innovation management to Justin Barnes, John Bessant and Mike Morris; and on industrial districts to Andrew Grantham. In each case I have referenced our joint publications, but this is only a small indication of the benefits of our various collaborations.

Others helped with specific inputs. Andrew Grantham and Jeff Readman not only provided detailed comments on some of the chapters, but also were a continuous source of unselfish assistance on many points of detail. Shaun Gannon, Rob Fitter and Jenny Kimmis willingly assisted me (or so they said!) with the materials used in chapters 1 and 8, chapter 3, and chapter 6 respectively. Branco Milanovic offered generous assistance when I was writing on income distribution, as did Martin Ravallion. William Martin and Jim Lennon provided me with some of the data used in Chapter 6. Tom Rawski supplied me with useful unpublished data on China, and Wing Lim helped me update the data on Chinese education and training. Sanjaya Lall was a generous source of data on changing patterns of global production and trade, Gary Hamilton illuminated my understanding of the role played by global buyers, Parvin Alizadeh was an important stimulant for my understanding of the restrictive assumptions of Ricardo, and Carlotta Perez set my thinking right on the links between financial and productive capital. Dave Kaplan provided insightful comments on chapters 1, 2 and 6, Hubert Schmitz on chapter 8, and Jorge Katz on chapter 6. Mike Barnard helped me to avoid pitfalls on early European history when my mind wandered, and Mike Boulter got me thinking about the personal and the professional. Finally, on points of detail, I am indebted to Theo Mars for a useful brief on dialectics, to Henry Bernstein for the important insight on the distinction between the residual and relational explanations for poverty, and to Dave Francis for helping me to make the book more accessible to a wider audience. Unwitting graduate students at the Institute of Development Studies, Sussex University, Manchester University and the London School of Economics provided a similar (unconscious) service.

So much for the detail. There is also a range of people who have assisted me more generally. My colleagues at both the Institute of Development Studies at the University of Sussex and the Centre for Research in Innovation Management have been a constant source of stimulation and support – I often found myself writing for their attention. I have also gained greatly from participating in the global value chains group, and especially from Gary Gereffi and Tim Sturgeon.

I have been assisted in many practical ways throughout the writing of this book (and at other times) by Paula Lewis, who was unfailingly willing. Ellen McKinlay and David Held at Polity could not have been more helpful, and I am grateful to Caroline Richmond for her constructive editorial comments.

To all these people I offer my thanks. If only they would collectively agree to take responsibility for all the errors and misunderstandings I would be even more grateful. But that would be pushing my luck too far.

* * *

The author and publishers wish to thank the following for permission to reproduce copyright material:

Figure 3.5   Reproduced by permission of Santiago Acosta-Maya.

Figure 1.5   From R. E. Baldwin and P. Martin, *Working Paper 6904*, Cambridge, MA: NBER, 1999. Reproduced by permission of the authors.

Figure 6.5   From R. Bell, 'Competition issues in European grocery retailing', *European Retail Digest*, 39, 2003. Reproduced by permission of *European Retail Digest*.

Table 7.2   From J. G. Carson, *US Weekly Employment Update*, New York: Alliance Bernstein, 2003. Reproduced by permission of Alliance Capital Management.

Tables 1.1 and 1.3; figures 1.6 and 1.8   Calculated or adapted from CEPR, *Making Sense of Globalization: A Guide to the Economic Issues*, London: Centre for Economic Policy Research, 2002. Copyright, European Communities, 2002. Reproduced by permission of CEPR.

Figure 6.15   From Y. R. Cheong and X. Geng, 'Global capital flows and the position of China: structural and institutional factors and their implications', in J. J. Teunissen (ed.), *China's Role in Asia and the World* Economy, The Hague, FONDAD, 2003. Reproduced by permission of FONDAD.

Table 2.3   From A. C. Cornia and J. Court, 'Inequality, growth and poverty in the era of liberalization and globalization', *Policy Brief No. 4*, Helsinki: Wider, 2001. Reproduced by permission of UNU-WIDER.

Table 6.3   From R. Cotterill, *Continuing Concentration in Food Industries Globally: Strategic Challenges to an Unstable Status Quo*,

Storrs, CT: University of Connecticut, Food Marketing Policy Centre, 1999. Reproduced by permission of FMPC.

Figure 5.10   From P. Dicken, *Global Shift: Reshaping the Global Economic Map in the 21st Century*, London: Sage, 2003. Reproduced by permission of Sage Publications Ltd.

Figure 5.2   From P. Gibbon, 'At the cutting edge? Financialisation and UK clothing retailers' global sourcing patterns and practices', *Competition and Change*, 63, pp. 289–308. Reproduced by permission of Taylor & Francis Ltd. http://www.tandf.co.uk/journals.

Figure 7.8   From R. Hira, 'Implications of offshore sourcing', mimeo, Rochester Institute of Technology, 2004. Reproduced by permission of the author.

Box 4.1   IDS, *Policy Brief No. 10*, Brighton: Institute of Development Studies, 1997. Reproduced by permission of Institute of Development Studies.

Table 1.2; figure 6.7   From IMF, *World Economic Outlook*, 2002. Reproduced by permission of IMF.

Figures 3.1 and 3.2   Reproduced by permission of International Coffee Organization.

Figure 6.14   From G. H. Jefferson et al., 'Ownership, productivity change, and financial performance in Chinese industry', *Journal of Comparative Economics*, 28, 2000, pp. 786–813. Reproduced by permission of Elsevier.

Figure 7.2; table 7.1   Reproduced by permission of Macquarie Bank.

Figure 6.12   From A. Maizels, T. Palaskas and T. Crowe, 'The Prebisch–Singer hypothesis revisited', in D. Sapsford and J. Chen (eds), *Development Economics and Policy: The Conference Volume to Celebrate the 85th Birthday of Professor Sir Hans Singer*, Basingstoke: Macmillan, 1998. Reproduced by permission of Palgrave Macmillan Publishers.

Figure 6.3   From M. Martin and V. Manole, 'China's emergence as the workshop of the world', mimeo, Washington, DC: World Bank, 2003. Reproduced by permission of the authors.

Figure 6.3   From W. Martin, 'Developing countries' changing participation in world trade', *World Bank Research Observer*, 18, 2003, pp. 159–86. Reproduced by permission of Oxford University Press.

Figure 2.6   From B. Milanovic, 'The two faces of globalization: against globalization as we know it', *World Development*, 31, 2003, pp. 667–83. Reproduced by permission of Elsevier.

Figure 2.7   From B. Milanovic, 'The Ricardian vice: why Sala-i-Martin's calculations of world income inequality are wrong', Social Science Research Network, 2002. Reproduced by permission of the author.

Box 4.1   From K. Nadvi, 'Industrial clusters in developing countries', special issue of *World Development*, 27, 1999, pp. 1605–26. Reproduced by permission of Elsevier.

Figure 1.9   From M. Obstfeld and A. Taylor, *Global Capital Markets: Integration, Crisis and Growth*, Cambridge: Cambridge University Press, 2004. Reproduced by permission of Cambridge University Press.

Figure 7.6   Adapted from: OECD, 'Trade balances for goods and services $ billion, national accounts basis', *OECD Economic Outlook*, issue 2, 2004, © OECD, 2004. Reproduced by permission of OECD.

Figure 7.9   Adapted from OECD, 'Standardised unemployment rates/ Taux de chômage standardisés', *Main Economic Indicators/ Principaux indicateurs économiques*, issue 1, 2005, © OECD, 2005. Reproduced by permission of OECD.

Figure 7.5   From T. G. Rawski, 'Recent developments in China's labor economy', mimeo, University of Pittsburgh, Department of Economics, 2004. Reproduced by permission of the author.

Figures 2.2 and 2.4   From X. Sala-i-Martin, *Working Paper 8933* and *Working Paper 8904*, Cambridge, MA: NBER, 2002. Reproduced by permission of the author.

Tables 4.1 and 4.2   From H. Schmitz, 'Global competition and local cooperation: success and failure in the Sinos Valley, Brazil', *World Development*, 27, 1999, pp. 1627–50. Reproduced by permission of Elsevier.

Table 7.5   From UNCTAD, *World Investment Survey*, Geneva and New York: United Nations. Reproduced by permission of UNCTAD.

Table 6.1; figure 6.1   From UNIDO, *Handbook of Industrial Statistics, 1990*. Vienna: UNIDO, 1990. Reproduced by permission of the United Nations Industrial Development Organization.

Figure 1.4; table 6.2   From UNIDO, *Industrial Development Report 2002/2003: Competing through Innovation and Learning*, Vienna: UNIDO, 2002. Reproduced by permission of United Nations Industrial Development Organization.

Table 5.1; figure 5.3   From USITC, *Textiles and Apparel: Assessment of the Competitiveness of Certain Foreign Suppliers to the U.S. Market*, Washington, DC: United States International Trade

Commission, 2004. Reproduced by permission of the United States International Trade Commission.

Figure 6.11   From A. Wood, 'Openness and wage inequality in developing countries: the Latin American challenge to East Asian conventional wisdom', *World Bank Economic Review*, 11, 1, 1997, pp. 33–57. Reproduced by permission of Oxford University Press.

Figures 1.2 and 2.1   From World Bank, *Globalization, Growth and Poverty: Building an Inclusive World Economy*, Washington, DC: World Bank, 2002. Reproduced by permission of the World Bank.

Tables 2.1 and 8.1   From World Bank, *Policy Research Report*, 2002. Reproduced by permission of the World Bank.

Tables 3.2 and 8.2; figure 7.7   From World Bank, *World Development Indicators*, 2004. Reproduced by permission of the World Bank.

Tables 5.2, 5.5, 5.6 and 6.4; figure 1.3   From WTO, *International Trade Statistics*, Geneva: World Trade Organization, 2004. Reproduced by permission of the World Trade Organization.

Figure 6.4   From N. Wrigley, 'Transforming the corporate landscape of US food retailing: market power, financial re-engineering and regulation', *Tijdschrift voor Economische en Sociale Geografie*, 93, 1, 2002, pp. 62–82. Reproduced by permission of Blackwell Publishing.

Part I

Setting the Scene

Part I sets the scene. It dismisses the simplistic view that participating in the global economy automatically solves problems of poverty and inequality. Part II sketches a positive scenario in which globalization provides the opportunity for reducing poverty and income inequality, but argues that grasping this opportunity requires a clear strategic focus and the effective management of innovation. Part III, by contrast, is more pessimistic. It suggests that, while some may gain from globalization, the very nature of global production and trading systems may act to enhance poverty and make income distribution more unequal for others. The final chapter considers the implications of the more pessimistic outcome outlined in part III both for poverty-focused policies and for the sustainability of globalization itself.

The opening chapter focuses on the dynamics of globalization. It describes the primary character of the contemporary phase of globalization, and contrasts this with the pattern of globalization during the nineteenth century. Chapter 2 summarizes the literature on global poverty and contrasts two perspectives on globalization, poverty and inequality. The first is a residual explanation, favoured by the World Bank and other proponents of globalization. It argues that the bulk of global poverty is a result of the failure of producers to engage with globalization. If they participate in the global economy, it is believed, poverty levels will be reduced. The second perspective argues that poverty and inequality are relational to globalization. Instead of resolving global poverty, the workings of the global economy deepen the problem for many producers who are unable to compete effectively in a world of growing surplus production capacity.

Part I

Setting the Scene

1

Global Dynamics

1.1 What's the problem?

In July 1969, I left South Africa as a political refugee. It was a blustery winter day and, as the boat sailed out of Cape Town harbour into the 'Cape of Storms', I looked up at Table Mountain. It had risen to the occasion to mark my departure with a fabled table-cloth covering. And I remember thinking: 'I will never return to my homeland. The forces of racial and class domination which have subjected the majority of the population to poverty and political repression (and forced me into exile) are too well entrenched. It will change, but not in my lifetime.' I shed copious tears as these thoughts swirled around my head.

For the next fifteen years I revelled in my identity as an 'oppositionist'. I had participated in the struggle against apartheid, and had steeped myself in the Marxian culture of the times. I easily transferred this world-view and identity to broader pastures and, with many others at that time, engaged in debates and researched the 'flaws in the system'. Poverty and repression were endemic; low-income countries were caught in a trap of dependency, and would not progress without fundamental structural change.

But things changed. I got tired of working *against*, rather than *for*, and wanted to feel that I was constructing rather than destroying. Moreover, not only were the socialist economies of Eastern Europe floundering, but my eyes were opened to historical reality by a paper comparing labour conditions in South Africa's mines with those in Stalinist Russia; by comparison, South Africa seemed like a holiday camp. And then a series of professional opportunities opened up to combine my academic life with policy advice. Over a seven-year period (why do phases always last seven years?), together with colleagues,

I provided policy support to a range of countries, including Cyprus, the Dominican Republic, Jamaica, Kenya and, in later years, Armenia, Kazakhstan and Russia. Yes, the world was filled with positive and negative energy, and it was uncertain. But the glass was half full – on balance there were enough positives in the system to make progress possible.

Then, in the late 1980s, the impossible seemed to happen. South African politics became unstuck. Suddenly, new students arrived on the scene, not just having experienced the all-too-familiar torture and solitary confinement, but expectant of returning home, and into government, after their studies. And then my political exile was lifted and I, too, was allowed back. Old contacts were renewed, and, in combination with comrades in the African National Congress and the Confederation of South African Trade Unions, I embarked on a thirty-month multisector investigation of the determinants of competitiveness with a view to constructing an industrial policy for the new South Africa.[1] It was a world of new opportunities, growth and optimism about what could be achieved in a new democratic political dispensation.

At about the same time, I and my colleagues at the Institute of Development Studies at the University of Sussex were developing a programme which reinforced this optimism. Our view was that it was not a matter of *whether* to participate actively in the global economy. That was a given, both because of the opportunities it offered, and because international political pressures made it difficult for low-income economies to withdraw from the global economy. Rather, the challenge was *how* to join in the global economy in a manner which provided for sustainable income growth. Similarly, with my colleagues at the Centre for Research in Innovation Management at the University of Brighton, I came to be concerned less with policy design than with policy implementation (the hard part of the story). This led to an extended collaboration with friends and colleagues at the University of Natal in South Africa. We focused on researching the determinants of successful innovation management, and on actively assisting groups of firms in the auto, clothing and furniture industries to become globally competitive. We also worked closely with the sectoral groups of the Department for Trade and Industry, which was responsible for industrial policy. The glass was still half full, the possibilities were numerous.

But there was a nagging worry. I thought back to the firms I had worked with in so many low-income economies over the previous decade, and how much less dynamic they were than their South African counterparts. How were they managing to cope with the pressures of globalization? And then one day, when I was working in a furniture factory in Port Shepstone in South Africa, the penny dropped. The firm reported that it had gained little from currency devaluation – the gains had all been appropriated by buyers. For example, the price it received for bunk beds fell from £74 in 1996 to £48 in 2000. Thinking that this might have been an aberration, I interviewed a second firm; its records were less up to date, but it reported that the sterling price it received for bunk beds also fell, from £69 in 1996 to £52 in 1999. So, what about other products? At that time, we were working with a group of three wooden-door exporters, and their story was similar. The largest exporter had seen the sterling price of its major export item (accounting for 40 per cent of sales) fall by 22 per cent between 1996 and 2000. Like the other furniture firms, it managed to stay in business only because of devaluation. In none of these cases was productivity change anything like this rate of price decline.

Well, perhaps this was a phenomenon unique to Natal-based manufacturers, or to the exporters of bunk beds and doors? What story did the aggregate data tell for other South African furniture exporters? Figure 1.1 recounts their experience. Between 1988 and 2000, South African furniture exports had grown tenfold in local prices, reaching $82 million in 2000. But they had done so on the back of falling unit export prices, made possible by currency devaluation. Perhaps this was a story unique to South Africa? What had happened to the price of global furniture exports? Figure 1.1 reports the evidence, using EU imports as a surrogate for world prices, and evening out year-to-year fluctuations by using three-year moving average prices. It tells a similar story – sustained falling unit prices.

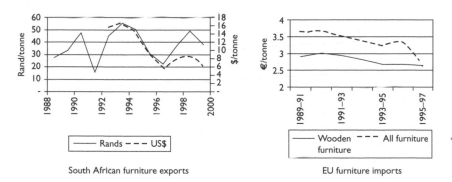

South African furniture exports   EU furniture imports

Figure 1.1   Unit price performance of South African furniture exports and EU furniture imports, 1988–2000

Source: South African data was drawn from Industrial Development Corporation database; EU data from the European Commission's Eurostat Statistical Office's database on external trade

My perspective had shifted. The glass was no longer half full, it was half empty. If South African firms found it difficult to manage the pressure of global competition, how much more difficult would it be for firms in other low-income countries in which I had worked, all of whom had much less sophisticated manufacturing capabilities than did their South African counterparts. Did it still make sense to believe that all could gain from globalization, if only they followed our prescriptions for upgrading their capabilities? Perhaps, instead of placing their faith in books on innovation management, firms and governments would profit from work of an earlier commentator (box 1.1),

---

Box 1.1   What did Lewis Carroll have to say about globalization?

'Nearly there!' the Queen repeated. 'Why, we passed it ten minutes ago! Faster!' And they ran on for a time in silence, with the wind whistling in Alice's ears, and almost blowing her hair off, she fancied. *[For this, read a country opening up to global competition.]*

'Now! Now!' cried the Queen. 'Faster! Faster!' And they went so fast that at last they seemed to skim through the air, hardly touching the ground with their feet, till suddenly, just as Alice was getting quite exhausted, they stopped, and she found herself sitting on the ground, breathless and giddy. The Queen propped her up against a tree, and said kindly, 'You may rest a little now.' *[Unused to competition, firms begin to innovate – a new process, it's tiring.]*

Alice looked around her in great surprise. 'Why, I do believe we have been under this tree the whole time! Everything's just as it was!' *[Despite this innovation, the firm is making little competitive progress – it wants to know why.]*

'Of course it is', said the Queen. 'What would you have it?'

'Well, in *our* country' *[the days of import substitution, before opening out to imports]*, said Alice, still panting a little, 'you'd generally get to somewhere else – if you ran very fast for a long time, as we've been doing' *[that is, learning how to innovate after years of relative stagnation]*.

'A slow sort of country!' said the Queen. 'Now, *here*, you see, it takes all the running *you* can do, to keep in the same place. If you want to get somewhere else, you must run at least twice as fast as that!' *[The pressures of global competition are insuperable for some.]*

Source: Through the Looking Glass (Carroll 1916)

who had inadvertently provided a window into the challenges of globalization in the late twentieth century? In the case of Alice, it didn't matter how fast she ran, the frontier still seemed an insuperable distance away.

This book looks at the impact of globalizing production and trade systems on poor countries and poor people. After the pervasiveness of global poverty and inequality is documented in chapter 2, part II examines the case for a win–win outcome to globalization – a half-full glass in a world of uncertainty. Chapter 3 provides a theoretical perspective for generating sustainable incomes, and chapter 4 summarizes the practical steps of innovation management that are required to translate this theoretical agenda into practice and examines the role played by global buyers in connecting producers to customers. In chapter 5 we see evidence of the successful global spread of production capabilities in three key sectors – textiles and clothing, furniture, and autos and components.

By contrast, part III looks at a win–lose outcome to globalization – the glass as half empty; the very success of some in the global economy is a cause of the poverty of others. In chapter 6 this is evidenced by an examination of the performance of the global price trends of approximately 4,000 products over the period 1988–2002, and the different price behaviour of low-income economy exports and imports over a similar period. In chapter 7 we explore ways in which this price outcome to globalization may lead to either a win–win or a win–lose outcome, and conclude that, for many, the latter is more probable. Much of the discussion in these two chapters focuses around the nature of the global labour market and the existence of a reserve army of increasingly educated labour. The recent experience of China and its impact on the global economy is a central part of this story. Given this outcome, the final chapter examines the implications this holds for policy, particularly in those countries in Africa and Latin America which have failed to gain substantively from the global integration of production and trade. It also explores the sustainability of globalization in the context of the growing inequality arising from its extension.

Of course this is not the first book to examine the impact of growing exports from low-income economies on employment and inequality. During the 1990s there was a vibrant debate on this issue, but it was confined almost entirely to the high-income economies.[2] What is relatively new in this study is that it focuses on the mechanisms through which this export surge from low-income economies has affected employment and inequality in other low-income economies. In covering this agenda, our analysis harks back to discussion in the early 1950s on the determinants of declining terms of trade of low-income economies.

In the remaining sections of this chapter we set the context by considering the specific element of globalization being addressed in this book – the globalization of production and trade (section 1.2). Then, in section 1.3 we chart the extension of the global economy in the latter parts of the twentieth century. Finally, section 1.4 briefly reviews the historical specificity of this era of globalization, since this is not the first time that we have witnessed an outward extension of global production and trade. This sets the scene for the final chapter in which we will consider, among other things, the sustainability of this outward breath of the global economy.

1.2   The manifold dimensions of globalization

Summary: Different perspectives on globalization

Globalization is a complex and multidimensional process. It can be viewed through a variety of lenses. The first characterizes it as a process in which the barriers to cross-border flows are being reduced, not just for economic flows, but also for the global extension of knowledge, information, belief systems, ideas and values. But this perspective lacks agency, so globalization can also be seen in relation to the ambitions and actions of key global actors, including firms and groups seeking political and religious hegemony. Further, globalization is an outcome of technological advances, and of the natural curiosity of the human species, fuelled by increasingly cheap and sophisticated communications systems.

In organization development practice there is a technique called Metaplan which I use each year in a course I teach on globalization to a group of multidisciplinary students drawn from an astonishing variety of countries. I give each of them three or four Post-it stickers, and ask them to write on each one a single definition or dimension of globalization. After a suitable pause for reflection and writing, each person reads out their individual contributions. Then, we stick each one of these Post-its on a large board, grouping them if possible in terms of subject matter. They represent a form of 'voting', each Post-it providing support for a particular dimension of globalization.

I am always taken aback by the results of this exercise. For one thing, my own lens – that of an economist – is clearly blinkered. I begin by thinking of globalization as an expansion of the geography of trade, capital and labour flows; my audience invariably sees it as an extension of Western 'values' (the multinational cohort of students is usually highly critical of 'Coca-Colarization'), and the domination of third world governments by imperial powers and global financial institutions. For another thing, I am repeatedly struck by the multiple dimensions of globalization which the audience provides. The list is never the same, and it usually encompasses more than twenty dimensions; no doubt if I gave the exercise more time, the list would grow even longer.

How do we make sense of this multidimensional agenda of globalization? Is there a single definition which allows us to capture the complexity of what Dicken calls 'the Global Shift'?[3] We can begin with what might be termed a 'boundary definition', that is, one which focuses on the reduction of obstacles to mobility. Thus,

> *globalization is characterized by the systematic reduction in the barriers to the cross-border flow of factors (labour, capital), products, technology, knowledge, information, belief systems, ideas and values.*

The advantage of this boundary definition is that it reflects a change in the parameters which govern global flows. It also is wide enough to capture a range of globalizing phenomena, which includes both primarily economic flows and those which are more social in nature. Under the first category, for example, we might think of the lower barriers to the migration of people as components of a labour force, of physical equipment and technology, and of finance. But there is also a decline in the barriers to broader, more social flows across borders, including values, ideas, and people searching to learn more about other cultures.

The weakness of this boundary definition is that it lacks *agency*. It fails to focus on the actors who drive the global flow of factors, products, technology, knowledge, information, belief systems, ideas and values. A more '*agent-oriented*' definition of globalization might thus go as follows:

> *globalization is the purposeful pursuit of objectives – be they personal, economic, social or political – which leads individuals, institutions and nations to widen their activities across national boundaries.*

Typically, 'we' (that is, the economists and political scientists who make a living by analysing and documenting these globalizing processes) concentrate on entrepreneurship and the corporate sector. In the quest for enhanced profit, these investors expand across national borders in the search for larger markets and new and improved inputs. In the modern era, the key institution driving this global expansion is the transnational corporation (TNC). These TNCs produce in a range of countries for both the local and the global market. But, increasingly, the global shift arises not only from direct foreign production by TNCs, but also as a result of their purchases from suppliers in other countries. More recently, as we shall see in chapter 4, the global extension of production networks has also been driven by specialized large-scale buyers. They serve global markets, often with globally branded products, by sourcing merchandise from a large variety of geographically dispersed producers, including nationally owned firms.

Often, in a crude and reductionist step, we then make the leap to characterize the institutions of global economic regulation – the International Monetary Fund (IMF), the World Bank and the World Trade Organization (WTO) – as the instruments which play the tune of transnational enterprises. Similarly, the political expressions of economic integration – the European Union (EU), the North American Free Trade Association (NAFTA) and the Association of South-East Asian Nations (ASEAN) – are seen as political alliances which meet the needs of global entrepreneurs, redefining national and international frameworks to facilitate the expansion of global business. This harks back to the earliest Marxian critiques of global capitalism expansion in the nineteenth century when he distinguished the 'superstructure' (institutions, values) from the 'economic base' (the drive for capital accumulation).

Unquestionably, it is the quest for profit which actively drives the shift across national boundaries, not just of goods, capital, labour and technology, but also of accompanying values and ideas. But there is a danger in ignoring the power of autonomous political processes and the search for influence and hegemony. There are powerful globalizing agents at work which reflect the desire to impose their values on people living in other countries. These hegemonic values include religions (how can we ignore this in an age of growing religious fundamentalism?) such as Christianity and Islam, but also idea systems ('basic human rights') such as those which promote ethnic and gender equality. And although there is often a correspondence between the spreading across borders of profit-oriented economic activity and the search for political hegemony, it is possible to characterize the driving force for global expansion as being primarily political in nature. That is, it arises from autonomous political imperatives which are facilitated by the spread of commerce and production, rather than being driven by the profit motive with accompanying facilitatory institutions in tow.

There is a third perspective on globalization which provides a different lens to that which reflects the weakening of barriers or the widening horizons of entrepreneurs and power-hungry political processes. This is one which focuses on technology:

globalization arises as a natural outcome of the growing complexity and reach of scientific and technological advances.

As the millennia have advanced and the human species has evolved, we have witnessed the growing sophistication of processes of knowledge enquiry. It is not that so-called primitive peoples lacked technology; on the contrary, many of these communities lived in ecosystems which required sophisticated knowledge systems. They knew how to inter-crop to avoid famines, and how to read weather patterns from leaves and shoots. To this day, the Khoisan hunters and gatherers in southern Africa are able to track animals, with wondrous knowledge of flora and fauna. However, since the advance of the industrial age in the eighteenth century, the knowledge content in production and social systems has expanded exponentially. Production is now a highly specialized task and, unlike the Khoisan communities where knowledge of tracking is largely passed down within families, contemporary production systems require an extensive social division of labour, not just in knowledge production, but also in learning systems. One of the consequences of this is that, increasingly, knowledge production depends on cross-border cooperation. As the acknowledgements to this book made clear, for example, I could not have researched and written this material without the active collaboration of colleagues in Africa, Asia, Europe and North America.

But there is an additional component to the scaling-up of technological progress. The growing cost of technological complexity has meant that it can only be accompanied by profitable utilization if sales are spread over an increasingly large market. Thus, the producers of technology are required to widen their global reach in order to sustain their profitability, nowhere more graphically displayed than in the need to sell weapons systems in order to defray the costs of their technological complexity. Here we can see the interweaving between the technological and economic and political dimensions of globalization.

Thus, technological progress leads to the advance of global processes in the production of knowledge. This might be termed the benign side of

technological globalization.\However, there is also a malign, more disruptive component to technologically induced globalization which
reflects a darker side. This is what economists call 'negative externalities' and environmentalists refer to as the 'spoilage of the global
commons'. The scale and reach of technologies are widening, such that
their spillover effects increasingly cross national borders. The Chernobyl
nuclear power station meltdown in 1986 led to adverse environmental
impacts among sheep in the western and northern borders of the United
Kingdom. Similarly, the changing weather patterns induced by excessive
use of carbon-based fuels in North America and Europe are disrupting
the ecosystems in the Antarctic.

And, finally, the intensity of the global spread also reflects the
natural curiosity of the human species:

> *as technology and communications allows a widening of personal*
> *and social horizons, globalization is a natural outcome of the*
> *curiosity of the human species.*

This has always been a factor in human existence, but has come to
have so much more global impact now that technology allows for a
speeding-up and widening of this drive to experience other places and
other cultures. The most far-reaching expression of this spread is to be
found in the rapid growth of global tourism. Between 1990 and 2001,
the number of global tourists doubled, from 325 million to 688
million, and the value of earnings from tourism rose from $256 billion
to $426 billion.⁴ Each of these tourists carried a few of their own
values and ideas across national borders and, in turn, absorbed some
from the foreign countries which they had visited.

In this book we adopt a narrow focus on globalization. The intent
is to explore whether the widening disparities in income and the durability of absolute poverty reflect the very workings of the global
economy, and, if so, to assess the implications for poverty-centred
policy. Within this, our focus is narrowly on economic factors in
general, and on the characteristics of systems of global production and
exchange in particular. In terms of the four perspectives on globalization outlined above, it addresses the reduction in barriers and the
global spread of factors (labour and capital), technology and products
rather than the cross-national extension of knowledge, information,
belief systems, ideas and values. Agency is also central to the discussion, since, as we will see, global production systems are increasingly
coordinated. Much is of course left out in this narrowing of the
agenda. We will not focus in any detail on the technological or 'human
curiosity' drivers of globalization. Even in the economic sphere we

ignore significant processes at work which have a major bearing on the incidence of global poverty. For example, the functioning of global financial markets leads to large surges of hot money which periodically sweep across the global economy, with devastating social impact, as reflected in the Asian financial crisis of 1997 or the financial crises which have repeatedly beset many Latin American economies such as Argentina and Mexico.[5]

There is no alternative to this narrowing of the agenda if anything useful is to be said. Indeed, some might even say that the attempt to explain the determinants of global poverty and inequality through an examination of global production systems *and* trade in the *whole of* manufacturing is in itself unmanageably ambitious. But the line has to be drawn somewhere, inevitably to some extent arbitrarily.

1.3 The extension of the global economy in the latter twentieth century

Summary: Globalization in the late twentieth century

Globalization in the latter half of the twentieth century was characterized by the very rapid expansion of global trade in manufactures, fuelled by the systematic reduction in the barriers to trade. Increasingly, this trade was in semi-processed manufactures, produced in coordinated global production networks.

Many of these global production networks involved extensive foreign direct investment. But, as productive capabilities grew in many parts of the world, production was increasingly undertaken by locally owned firms, benefiting from the global mobility of finance.

Although the dynamism of globalized production and trade speeded up in the 1980s and 1990s, the seeds to this outward surge in the global economy were planted in 1944 at a meeting in Bretton Woods in the USA. The Bretton Woods conference involved representatives from the USA and the UK and anticipated the end of the Second World War a year later. It was explicitly tasked with establishing a stable and appropriate institutional architecture to back global economic progress. This resulted, *inter alia*, in a system of controls over capital flows, the establishment of stable exchange rates between currencies, and the creation of global financial institutions such as the

IMF, the World Bank and the General Agreement on Tariffs and Trade (GATT).

During the course of the second half of the twentieth century, the GATT and its successor, the World Trade Organization (WTO), orchestrated a concerted programme of trade liberalization. This led to the elimination of most of the quantitative controls which had governed much of global trade. It also reduced many of the tariffs on cross-border trade. Many formerly protected low-income countries were dragged to this policy table unwillingly and, in the context of growing external debt, were subject to great pressure from the global financial institutions and aid-giving governments to liberalize their trade regimes. But, as the twentieth century wore on, much of this resistance crumbled, and the idea that trade should not be restricted is now widely accepted in policy circles.

Figure 1.2 evidences the extent and significance of this pervasive trend towards tariff reduction; bear in mind, though, that perhaps even more important than tariff reduction was the abolition of quantitative controls in most countries and in many sectors. By the turn of the millennium, although South Asia in particular and many other regions maintained tariffs over imports, the level of this protection had declined significantly from the early 1980s. The revival of post-Cancun WTO trade talks is designed to sustain this momentum of tariff reduction in the twenty-first century and to provide a framework for the continued globalization of production and trade.

The consequence of this generalized reform of trade policy was a very significant expansion of global trade during the latter half of the

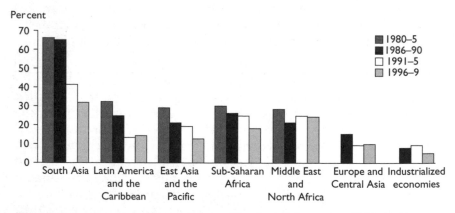

Figure 1.2   Average reduction in unweighted tariffs by region, 1980–1998

Source: World Bank (2002)

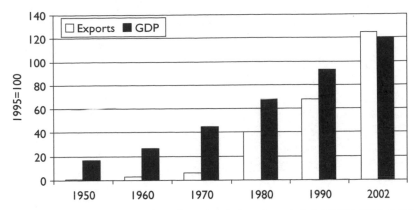

Figure 1.3 The growth in the value of global trade and global GDP, 1950–2002

Source: Calculated from WTO, *International Trade Statistics* (2003)

twentieth century. By 2002, while the value of global exports had grown by 125 times when compared to 1950, that of overall economic output (gross domestic product, GDP) rose by only a factor of seven (figure 1.3). In the first three post-war decades, the primary impetus to trade growth was the minerals sector, but in the last two decades the driving force for the expansion of global trade lay in manufacturing. The value of manufactured exports in 2002 was more than four times that of 1980, whereas the value of agricultural exports was only 20 per cent higher and that of mineral exports 40 per cent higher. By contrast, when comparing 1980 to 1950, it was the minerals sector which saw particularly rapid trade expansion – in this earlier period, the growth in its value was roughly twice that of manufactures and four times that of agricultural products.

The overall result of this rapid growth in trade was a developing openness of almost all economies, reflected in the ratio of their trade to overall economic activity. Table 1.1 shows the trade–GDP ratios for a number of high- and low-income economies. With the singular exception of India, the degree of openness grew significantly over the period – by a factor of three for the global economy in aggregate, and especially rapidly in some economies such as Korea, the Netherlands and Germany. As a general rule, it is evident that low-income (and large) economies appear to be less open than high-income (and small) economies.

Driving this globalization of trade, as we have seen, was the dynamism of trade in manufactures. A key factor in this was the growing importance of footloose investment, searching for the site of most profitable production. As figure 1.4 shows, the growth in the value of

Table 1.1 Merchandise exports as a share of GDP (%), 1950 and 1998

	1950	1998
France	7.6	28.7
Germany	6.2	38.9
Japan	2.2	13.4
Netherlands	12.2	61.2
UK	11.3	25.0
USA	3.0	10.1
USSR/Russia	1.3	10.6
Argentina	2.4	7.0
Brazil	3.9	5.4
China	2.6	4.9
India	2.9	2.4
Indonesia	3.4	9.0
Korea	0.7	36.3
Mexico	3.0	10.7
Thailand	7.0	13.1
World	5.5	17.2

Source: CEPR (2002)

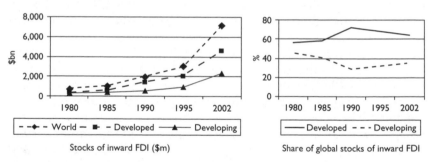

Stocks of inward FDI ($m) — Share of global stocks of inward FDI

Figure 1.4 Stocks and flows of FDI, 1980–2002

Source: Calculated from UNCTAD (2003)

foreign direct investment (FDI) was particularly rapid during the 1990s. Roughly one-third of this went to low-income economies. During the 1990s, this FDI was complemented by flows of portfolio investment into low-income and emerging-economy stock markets, allowing domestic firms to draw on external funds to finance their expansion of manufacturing production and exports.

It was not just the dynamism of manufacturing that was so significant, but also its changing character. This is reflected in the changing character of FDI during the latter part of the twentieth century. During the early post-war decades, most foreign investment was destined to increase production for domestic markets in recipient countries. This is often referred to as 'tariff-jumping FDI', attracted by the protection offered to domestically located producers and induced by the awareness that, without local plants, they would not be able to sell into these markets. As the decades rolled on, however, an increasing proportion of this FDI became outward oriented. As we will see in chapters 4 and 5, TNCs began to use low-cost overseas production sites to service global markets. Moreover, increasingly, much of this sourcing was not of finished products (for example, computers and clothing), but of components (printed circuit boards and integrated circuits; clothing accessories and clothing assembly).

The growth in this trade in sub-products has been very significant. It can be measured by computing the ratio between trade and value added: the greater the thinning out of production into these subcomponents of manufacturing, the larger this ratio. Table 1.2 shows the trends in a series of industrial economies, in Asia and in Latin America. What is so striking is the extent to which the Asian economies in general, and the newly industrializing economies in particular, engage in this form of disarticulated trade.[6] It is also significant how rapidly the ratio has grown in Mexico as a result of the increasingly prominent role played by its *maquiladora* export-processing zones in

Table 1.2 The growing disarticulation of trade in manufactures: ratio of merchandise trade to merchandise value added, 1980, 1990 and 2000

	1980	1990	2000
Major industrial countries	46.2	51.6	76.3
Canada	63.7	70.6	108.8
France	50.6	62.0	90.0
Germany	52.0	63.7	96.7
Italy	45.7	46.9	76.7
Japan	28.7	20.6	24.2
UK	52.0	62.4	83.5
USA	30.9	35.1	54.6
Emerging market economies			
Asia	93.8	115.6	168.5
China	12.1	23.7	32.9
India	11.3	12.4	21.6
Newly industrializing economies	216.5	259.3	365.5
Western hemisphere	37.2	42.6	58.6
Argentina	25.3	13.2	29.7
Brazil	19.4	14.6	34.1
Chile	42.8	55.8	60.9
Mexico	22.8	48.3	102.6

Source: IMF (2002)

producing for the US market. Also significant is the rapid growth in the ratio for China, albeit from a low base.

It should not be thought that all of this growth in trade in manufactures was due to the overseas production sites of TNCs, for there were other factors at work driving the globalization of sales. A critical role was played, as we will see in chapters 4 and 5, by global buying-houses. They were less concerned with who produced what they sourced abroad than with the price, the delivery reliability and the capacity of distant suppliers to deliver the volumes they required to meet the needs of their global customers. To some extent these traded products were sourced from the subsidiaries of TNCs, but, particularly in Asia, increasing use was made of locally owned or regionally coordinated production networks. Much of the investment utilized for this expanded production capability was provided by capital inflows from abroad. Following the abolition of fixed exchange rates in 1971, these capital flows were lubricated by a series of policy interventions by the Bretton Woods financial institutions designed to liberalize and force open capital markets in low-income economies. For example, in many economies, controls on foreign exchange were abolished, not just on remittances of profits and limited personal savings but also to allow for the inflow and repatriation of large tranches of capital and hot money.[7]

To summarize, therefore, the globalization of the latter half of the twentieth century was focused distinctively on the cross-border flow of products, increasingly of semi-manufactured components. This was facilitated by the globalization of capital, in the form of both foreign direct investment and portfolio funds. Underlying this was a globally coordinated architecture designed to facilitate trade growth (under the aegis of the WTO) and to promote capital flows (under the aegis of the IMF).

1.4   But not for the first time . . .

Summary: Comparing globalization in the late nineteenth and late twentieth centuries

The globalization in the latter half of the twentieth century was not unique. On a smaller scale, there have been many previous eras of expansion across boundaries, and these were not driven just by Western Europe or North America. The first truly global era was that in the latter half of the nineteenth century, when, for the first time, virtually all parts of the world were linked through economic, political and social intercourse.

Comparing nineteenth- and twentieth-century globalization, the recent period was distinctively characterized by the globalization of trade. By comparison, nineteenth-century globalization was deeper in the global spread of finance and people.

History shows that globalization has not been unstoppable. The inter-war period of 1918–1950 was one of inward orientation.

Comparative integration

The extension of the global economy in the late twentieth century has been so significant and rapid that it is easy to lose historical perspective. However, this phase of globalization is not unique. Indeed, albeit on a smaller scale, we have witnessed many previous eras of outwardly oriented economic progress, backed in each case by a dominant political and military power. Some 4,000 years ago, the outward drive in Europe was driven by Greek hegemony, widening economic intercourse between nations in the Aegean and Mediterranean. They were in turn supplanted by the Roman Empire, whose trade routes stretched right across Western Europe and led, *inter alia*, to the exploitation of forestry and iron deposits in much of Britain. Similar tales can be told of empires in Asia and in Latin America.

In each case, the political hegemony of the dominant power and its accompanying geographical extension was followed by a period of inward orientation. We will return to this theme in the final chapter. But, for now, our focus lies in the process of internationalization which was a characteristic of the second half of the nineteenth century. Although this period of history is similar in many respects to previous eras of outward expansion, its significance is that it really did begin to touch the boundaries of the globe. That is, it increasingly incorporated peoples in very distant regions – including Africa, Latin America and large parts of Asia and Australasia – in processes of economic and social interchange. Previous eras of outward expansion had been regionally based.

But globalization in the late twentieth century took a different form. For example, if we focus on trade openness, as measured by the share of exports in GDP (table 1.3), it is indeed the case that the nineteenth century was a century of growing internationalization. However, for almost all economies, the levels of this type of openness reached at the

Table 1.3   Merchandise exports as a share of GDP, 1870, 1913 and 1998 (%)

	1870	1913	1998
Australia	7.1	12.3	18.1
France	4.9	7.8	28.7
Germany	9.5	16.1	38.9
Japan	0.2	2.4	13.4
Netherlands	17.4	17.3	61.2
Spain	3.8	8.1	23.5
UK	12.2	17.5	25.0
USA	2.5	3.7	10.1
Russia	N/A	2.9	10.6
Argentina	9.4	6.8	7.0
Brazil	12.2	9.8	5.4
China	0.7	1.7	4.9
India	2.6	4.6	2.4
Indonesia	0.9	2.2	9.0
Korea	0.0	1.2	36.3
Mexico	3.9	9.1	10.7
Thailand	2.2	6.8	13.1
World	4.6	7.9	17.2

Source: Calculated from CEPR (2002)

high point of nineteenth-century internationalization were lower than those at the end of the twentieth century. For the global economy, for example, the ratio rose from 4.6 per cent in 1870 to 7.9 per cent in 1913, and then more than doubled to 17.2 in 1998. There were some exceptions, though – Argentina, Brazil and India do not show the same trends. Their twentieth-century experience of globalization was not as 'successful' by comparison with that of the earlier period as it was for the other countries in this dataset; we will return to the significance of this in the final chapter.

But there were other respects in which nineteenth-century internationalization was deeper than that of the latter twentieth century. Three types of internationalization stand out in particular. The first was the globalization of capital flows. Relative to the level of economic activity, these were higher in the nineteenth century than in the twentieth century. Figure 1.5 bears this out by focusing on the ratio of the capital account (reflecting various types of financial flows) to GDP for a number of the largest, now high-income economies.[8] With the exception of Germany and the USA, these were significantly higher in the nineteenth century era of globalization than in that of the twentieth century. These differences are ones not only of magnitude but also of nature. Capital flows in the earlier period were more long-term in

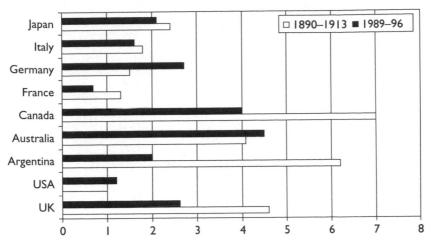

Figure 1.5 Capital account as % GDP, 1890–1996

Source: Data drawn from Baldwin and Martin (1999)

nature and were not characterized by the volatility and surges of those of the latter twentieth century which have been so damaging to many economies.

Another key difference between these two periods concerns the global mobility of people. The nineteenth century saw massive emigrations across national boundaries. Approximately 60 million Europeans emigrated to the USA between 1820 and 1914, and a similar number moved from China and India to surrounding countries. In some countries the rate of emigration was startling. For example, in the 1880s, more than 140 people in every thousand emigrated from Ireland, and almost 100 in every thousand from Norway. Between 1900 and 1910, more than 100 per thousand emigrated from Italy. At the same time, immigration rates into some countries were equally significant. In the first decade of the twentieth century, the rate of immigration was around 300 per thousand residents in Argentina, 160 per thousand in Canada, and more than 100 per thousand in the USA. There were no equivalent flows of people in the latter twentieth century. Whereas the proportion of global population living in countries in which they were not citizens was 10 per cent in 1900, in 2000 it was around only 2 per cent. Moreover, the flows in the latter period were dominated much more by skilled labour than in the nineteenth century.[9]

There is one further important difference in the patterns of globalization during these two periods. In the nineteenth century, trade was in complementary products (raw materials exchanged for manufactures), while in the late twentieth century it tended to be in similar and

	Internationalization	Globalization
Time-period	Late nineteenth and early twentieth century	Late twentieth and early twenty-first century
The flow of people	Migration of the unskilled	Migration of the skilled and the monied
The flow of capital	Long-term capital flows; foreign direct investment	Short-term capital flows; foreign direct investment
The flow of products	Trade in commodities and finished products	Trade in components and producer services
	Trade in complementary products	Trade in competitive products

Figure 1.6 Internationalization and globalization compared

highly competitive products. This is reflected in the ratio of trade to value added, as opposed to GDP. As we saw in table 1.2, the latter half of the twentieth century was characterized by a very rapid advance in the disarticulation of trade.

Figure 1.6 summarizes this brief historical overview and contrasts the main features of these two periods of global integration.

The breathing of the global economy

What happened in between these two periods of global integration, whose beginnings (roughly 1850 and 1950) are separated by one hundred years? The answer is that the global economy turned inwards. We will return to the significance of this 'inward–outward breath' in the final chapter, but here we will just note the characteristics of this process. In the earlier discussion of the outward spread of the global economy in the twentieth century we documented the important role played by tariff reduction in facilitating the growth of world trade. Figure 1.7 extends the time-period on tariff rates and shows that, indeed, tariffs did fall significantly during the latter part of the twentieth century. But they also fell (albeit at a lower rate) during the early years of the twentieth century. In between, they rose, sharply. The consequence was that the degree of openness in the decades between the two phases of globalization fell virtually throughout the global economy. Figure 1.8 illustrates this and shows the pattern of openness for four key economies – the USA, the UK, France and Germany – measured by the ratio of merchandise exports to merchandise value added. In each case, the inter-war period was one of significantly declining global integration.

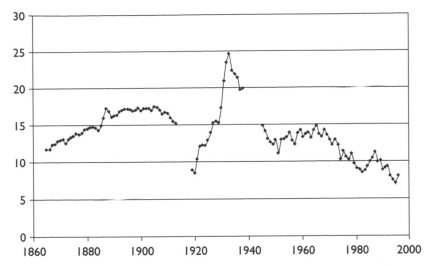

Figure 1.7   Average (unweighted) tariffs, thirty-five[a] countries, 1860–2000

[a]The thirty-five countries include most of the current OECD countries, plus a number of developing countries with prominent trading sectors during the nineteenth century (for example, Argentina, Mexico, China and India).

Source: CEPR (2002)

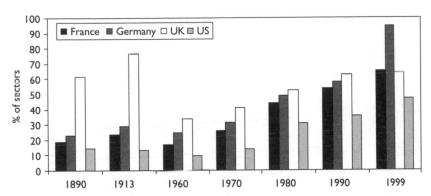

Figure 1.8   Merchandise exports as a share of merchandise value added, 1890–1999 (%)

Source: Calculated from CEPR (2002)

The same story of the 'outward–inward' breath of the global economy can be told in many different ways, and has been extensively documented elsewhere.[10] But one key element of the globalization of production and trade on which we will draw in later chapters is the flow of finance. Figure 1.9 presents a stylized representation of the

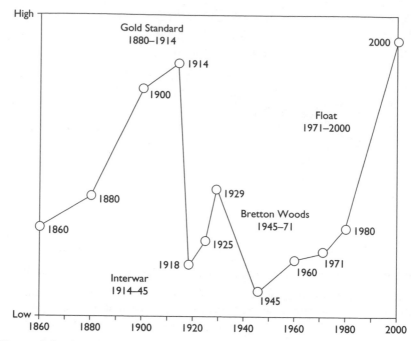

Figure 1.9 A stylized view of global capital mobility, 1860–2000

Source: Obstfeld and Taylor (2004)

globalization of capital flows over the past 150 years, spanning both nineteenth- and twentieth-century eras of internationalization. It tells a story of a massive advance in capital mobility during the nineteenth century, followed by a sudden and very sharp decline after the First World War. After the establishment of a regulatory framework at Bretton Woods in 1944, and particularly after the abolition of fixed exchange rates in the major economies during the 1970s, the global integration of finance resumed its outward drive.

1.5   Globalization, poverty and inequality

This book focuses on the mechanisms whereby globalization contributes to global poverty and inequality through the extension of global production and trading networks. As we shall see, there is widespread recognition that globalization may induce greater inequality. But the idea that it might cause greater poverty runs against much of current conventional wisdom. This, as we shall see, argues that inequality and poverty are caused not so much by the workings of the global economy as by the failure to engage positively with globalization.

We begin the analysis in chapter 2 by documenting the changing incidence of global inequality as a prelude to the analysis of win–win outcomes to globalization in part II (chapters 3–5) and of win–lose outcomes in part III (chapters 6 and 7). In the final chapter we will return to two themes which we have addressed in this opening chapter. First, there is currently a sense of triumphalism that globalization is unstoppable. The same view was widespread during the latter stages of the nineteenth century and the early twentieth century. Yet it was followed by a period of inward orientation. May history be about to repeat itself? And, second, if it is true that global production and trading systems may be the cause of poverty and inequality for many, what are the policy implications for these victims?

2

Globalization and Poverty

Rewind to my privileged white childhood in South Africa during the 1950s. The world was my oyster, my horizons were unlimited. But it was not a world free of troubles. For one thing, there was the continuous fear of an uprising of the poor ('the blacks') – the hordes of the unemployed who trod the streets, often begging at our door for jobs or food ('make sure you lock the door when strangers approach'). Self-interest and the preservation of our opportunity-filled life depended either on keeping these masses at bay or on ensuring that their basic needs would be met. But it was not just self-interest that focused our minds on the needs of the poor. Some – in fact a small and vocal minority – were also drawn to their plight as fellow human beings, even though this meant wading our way through layers of prejudice ('wash your hands after handling money – you never know who has touched it before you'). Often this prejudice was dressed up in racial stereotypes ('blacks worship their ancestors and are obsessed with the past, so it is obvious that they cannot invest in education for their future'), whereas in reality it helped to have an unlimited supply of cheap labour.

For those of us with a modicum of human compassion or a rational interest in self-preservation, a concern with distribution was a central driver of our growing consciousness. It is not surprising therefore that so many politicized and privileged South Africans have subsequently found themselves working in areas of public interest. Although postwar South Africa was a particular mould in the development of social awareness, it was of course by no means unique. Many others drawn from privileged elites in other countries have developed a similar awareness of the need to address the central problem of distribution. It hardly bears mentioning that, for those coming from an unprivileged background, a concern with poverty and distribution is obvious.

But clearly it is not that obvious. Most of the individuals making decisions about the allocation of resources which drive globalization and economic growth fail to recognize the importance of poverty and distribution. Their focal point is the accumulation of personal and aggregate social wealth. This distributional myopia is not just morally reprehensible. It is also short-sighted. For poverty and inequality – particularly if they are expanding – threaten the sustainability of growth more generally, and globalization more specifically. These distributional outcomes and their consequences are the central concerns of this book and a topic which we will consider in more detail in the concluding chapter.

In this chapter we focus on distribution and review the patterns of poverty which have emerged in the most recent era of globalization. These, as we shall see, are complex and open to much debate. They encompass both absolute poverty (section 2.2) and relative distribution (section 2.3). Some of this discussion is technical, exploring ambiguities in measurement, and readers may wish to skip the detail and focus on the summary text boxes. But it is an important discussion since there is persuasive evidence of the stickiness of absolute poverty and the growing incidence of inequality in the recent era of globalization. But are globalization, poverty and inequality causally linked (section 2.4), and, if so, how might this affect the sustainability, or indeed the desirability, of globalization during the early twenty-first century?

2.1 What do we mean by 'poverty'?

Summary: The meaning of poverty

The concept of poverty has two central meanings. The first is the absolute standard of living, reflected in satisfying the minimum basic needs required for survival. The second is relative poverty, that is, the gap in incomes between the rich and the poor.

There are many problems which arise in the measurement of poverty. The 'basic needs for survival' cannot be easily divorced from the general standard of living. That is, even measures of absolute poverty need to be situated in a relative context. The use of a monetary measure of income runs up against the differential purchasing power of money in different countries. To solve this latter problem, economists have generated an artificial form of currency called 'purchasing power parity dollars'.

To most people poverty means the inability to sustain livelihoods – inadequate shelter, too little food to stay alive and active, helplessness to withstand the elements, and the prevalence of ill-health. The pioneering study of poverty by Seebohm Rowntree in York, England, at the turn of the twentieth century, for example, defined it as occurring in families where 'total earnings are insufficient to obtain the minimum necessaries for the maintenance of merely physical efficiency.'[1] Yet what do we mean by 'necessities'? As Adam Smith pointed out in 1776, '[b]y necessaries I understand not only the commodities which are indispensably necessary for the support of life, but whatever the custom of the country renders it indecent for creditable people, even of the lowest order, to be without.'[2]

So, the definition of an absolute standard of living is not without its problems, notably with respect to the contextual definition of necessities. This difficulty is compounded when we compare living standards between people or groups of people. What *numeraire* (that is, what unit of measurement) should we use? Physical parameters can provide a means of comparison. But they are not always homogeneous – for example, a calorie obtained from eating complex carbohydrates provides for longer-lived streams of energy than that produced by simple carbohydrates; and how would we define an 'active life', or one 'free from ailments'? This heterogeneity of physical measures is dwarfed by the difficulties which arise when the numeraire is money. Here the problem is that not all consumers pay the same prices for the same products or services. This is true within a country – for example, characteristically it is said that 'poverty is expensive', that is, the poor tend to pay more than do the rich even when they purchase the same good. But it is even more the case when monetary values are used to compare incomes across countries – a dollar in Geneva buys considerably less than a dollar in New Delhi.

For many years, it was customary to estimate living standards by adding up the total value of goods and services produced in a country (the gross domestic product), estimated in local prices. So, the UK would have its GDP measured in terms of pounds sterling, the USA in dollars, Germany in the Deutschmark and India in the rupee. For each country this total figure of national production can be translated into per capita standards of living by dividing it by the population. The same data can also be used to measure income shares – the proportion of the country's GDP going to different groups of people (for example, the richest 10 per cent of the population; wage- and profit-earners; rural and urban dwellers; men and women; etc.). By using the exchange rate between currencies (rupees to the dollar; sterling to the dollar, etc.) it is then possible to compare living standards across countries, and, similarly, to estimate global income distribution (for example, the share of global GDP going to different countries or in relation to their share of the world's population).

The problem with this methodology is that it assumes that a dollar will buy the same amount of goods or services in each country. This is patently not the case, since living standards differ substantially between countries. Moreover, in a world of flexible and volatile exchange rates between countries (which was not the case before 1971, when currencies were fixed for many years), these international comparisons became very misleading. One response to this was to develop artificial indicators of cross-national purchasing power – the 'McDonald's index' or the 'Mars Bar index' (how much the same burger or chocolate bar cost in different countries) – and to use these to adjust international currencies. But this was a crude and unscientific way of adjusting purchasing power, and for this reason a new, artificial, numeraire has been created. This takes account of differential purchasing power by using a number of different products (not just a specific burger or chocolate bar) and is called purchasing power parity, usually measured in terms of US$ – hence PPP$. This forms the basis for the recalibration of earnings and living standards and is used in comparing real incomes over time and between countries.

PPP$s have been widely used to measure levels of absolute poverty. The most common measure defines absolute poverty in terms of what a single dollar would have bought in the USA in 1985, which was considered to reflect 'absolute necessities' in the USA in that year. This was then translated into local currencies – for example, the same goods (or a very similar bundle) could have been bought for much less than a dollar in India in the same year. The numbers – local currencies converted into PPP$ – were then used to calculate the numbers living in absolute poverty in each country of the world. These were defined at two levels: those living at below PPP$1 per day (in 1985 PPP$) and those living below PPP$2 per day. (In recent years the World Bank has recalibrated this PPP$1 to 1993 prices to take account of changes in relative prices.) Incidentally the same procedure can be used for comparing national income across countries, and it is now customary even in newspapers to see country comparisons being expressed in PPP$ terms.

As we shall see below, the PPP conversion rates are not without their problems, but they do play a prominent role in estimations both of the absolute numbers living in poverty and in relation to the inter-country comparison of living standards and income distribution. One of the most significant uses of this measure is in relation to the definition of what have come to be called the Millennium Development

Goals, that is, a series of targets agreed to by the global community in an attempt to reduce global poverty. Although there are a number of targets (relating to education, health, water supplies and so on), the primary Millennium Development Goal is, between 2000 and 2015, to halve the percentage of people living in absolute poverty (that is, below PPP$1 per day) to 15 per cent of the global population.

The comparison of absolute standards of living across countries using PPP dollars hints at a second meaning to the concept of poverty. In the early 1970s Townsend produced a seminal study of poverty in the UK. He concluded that, although absolute poverty was of major concern, it was too limited and needed to be complemented by a focus on relative living standards: 'Poverty can be defined objectively and applied consistently *only in terms of the concept of relative deprivation.*'[3] This distributional perspective on poverty has diffused widely over the past two decades and, for example, forms the basis for the estimations of poverty in the EU – defined as those living on less than half the average wage level in each country. It is notable, however, that distribution does not surface in any of the Millennium Development Goals, all of which are focused on the elimination of levels of absolute poverty.

Let us now turn to these estimations of global poverty – both absolute and relative – in the recent era of globalization.

2.2   Patterns of absolute poverty

Summary: Trends in absolute poverty

The primary Millennium Development Goal set by the global community for alleviating poverty is to halve the proportion of people living in absolute poverty by the year 2015.

The World Bank calculates that between 1990 and 2000 an additional 850 million people were living above the PPP$1 per day poverty line. Nevertheless, although the absolute number of people living below the PPP$1 per day level has fallen somewhat, it continues to exceed 1.1 billion people.

Most of the progress was achieved in China and other parts of Asia. The number of people living below the poverty line rose in Africa, Latin America, Eastern Europe and Central Asia.

There is considerable dispute about these numbers. Some studies suggest that they are massively overstated, others that they are similarly understated. On balance, it would appear that the World Bank numbers are unlikely to exaggerate the extent of absolute poverty and may indeed understate it.

In the 160 years between 1820 and 1980, the number of people living in absolute poverty increased consistently (figure 2.1). This reflected a combination of slow economic growth and rapid population growth in most of the developing world. However, during the last two decades of the twentieth century there was a reversal in trend, and the number living below the $1 per day line decreased, despite an increase in the rate of population growth.

Table 2.1, based on the World Bank's estimates of global poverty, throws more light on this change in trajectory. It focuses on the decade of the 1990s, and uses the PPP$1 per day and PPP$2 per day estimates of absolute poverty (uprated to $1.08 and $2.15 respectively to reflect inflation between 1985, when the poverty level was first defined, and 1993). The salient conclusions which emerge from this are as follows:

- There were 864 million more people on the planet who were living above the $1 per day line in 2000 than in 1990.
- The number of people living below the $1 per day level fell between 1990 and 2001 from 1,219 million to 1,101 million people; those living below $2 per day rose from 2,689 million to 2,733 million (in part reflecting the 'graduation' of people from the poorest category).

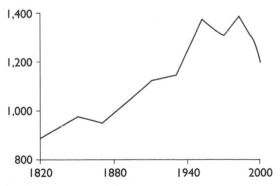

Figure 2.1 People living on less than $1 per day (millions), 1820–2000

Source: World Bank (2002)

Table 2.1   World Bank estimates of absolute poverty, 1990 and 2001

| | Poverty rate (% below . . .) | | | | Number of poor (1,000,000) | | | |
| | $1.08/day | | $2.15/day | | $1.08/day | | $2.15/day | |
	1990	2001	1990	2001	1990	2001	1990	2001
East Asia (incl. China)	29.6	15.6	69.9	47.64	472	284	1,116	868
China	33.0	16.6	72.6	46.7	377	212	830	596
East Europe & Central Asia	0.5	3.7	12.3	19.7	2	18	58	94
Latin America	11.3	9.5	28.4	24.5	49	50	125	128
Middle East & North Africa	1.6	2.4	21.4	23.2	6	7	51	70
South Asia	40.1	31.1	85.4	76.9	462	428	958	1,059
Sub-Saharan Africa	44.6	46.5	75.0	76.3	227	314	382	514
Total	27.9	21.3	61.6	52.8	1,219	1,101	2,689	2,733

Source: <http://www.developmentgoals.org/Poverty.htm#povertylevel>

- Because the world's population grew in the same period (from 4.4 billion in 1990 to 5.1 billion in 2000), the proportion of global population living below the poverty line fell from 27.9 per cent to 21.3 per cent at the $1 per day level, and from 61.6 per cent to 52.8 per cent at the $2 per day level.
- The improvement in the absolute numbers living above the poverty line arose almost entirely from the good economic growth performance of East Asia in general, and China in particular; if these countries are excluded from the total then the proportion of the world's population living below the $1 per day line was stable and the absolute number living below $1 per day rose.
- This reflects the fact that the number of people living below the $1 per day level rose sharply in most parts of the world other than Asia.
- These trends are more starkly evident when the proportion and numbers living below the $2 per day line are considered.

Naturally, these estimates of levels of global poverty are not free from controversy. For one thing, many of the data widely used to measure the incidence of poverty are incredible, literally unbelievable. As Baulch points out:

> In a few cases, we regard the WDI [the World Bank's World *Development Indicators*] 2003 estimates of $1/day poverty as implausible. For example, the WDI 2003 estimate for the $1/day poverty in Uganda was 82% compared to 37% in the WDI of the previous year. In contrast, Pakistan's international 'poverty rate' fell from 31% to just 13%. Finally, Nicaragua, one of the more successful middle-income economies in Central America, has no $1/day poverty numbers in the WDI of 2002 while an incredible 82% is listed in WDI 2003.[4]

But the year-to-year reliability of poverty data is only one problem. There is also controversy over the World Bank's estimates. Some believe that the World Bank figures overestimate the numbers living in absolute poverty, others that they underestimate the incidence of poverty.

'The World Bank overestimates global poverty numbers'

Each country produces its national accounts, calculating the total value of the goods and services produced each year (and taking account of imports and exports), measured in local currency. Using PPP calculations it is then possible to convert these currencies into internationally comparable PPP dollars (as described in the previous section). There also exists information on the distribution of income in most countries, calculating the share of GDP going to each quintile (20 per cent) of the population – the richest 20 per cent through to the poorest 20 per cent. Given information on the number of people in each country, it is thus possible to calculate roughly the number of people living below PPP$1 per day and PPP$2 per day.

Sala-i-Martin undertook this exercise for 125 countries, with a population of 5.23 billion (comprising 88 per cent of the global population), for the period up to 1998. He uses 1996 PPP dollars (which, because of inflation since the 1985 baseline was set, confusingly gives a cut-off point of $1.46 in 1996 prices for the lower-level measure, and $2.93 for the upper-level measure). His calculations provide strikingly different estimations of global poverty levels, and of the progress in reducing poverty, to those of the World Bank. (Figure 2.2 provides a graphical picture of his results. The horizontal axis (log income) is a measure of real living standards and the vertical axis a measure of the number of people.) As can be seen, using these numbers there is little doubt that, in aggregate, there was a significant reduction in those living in absolute poverty, and that average global living standards rose consistently over the past three decades – the lines shift out to the right as time moves on and globalization deepens.

There is a significant difference between the poverty estimates of Sala-i-Martin and the World Bank (table 2.2). The World Bank numbers are above the 1.2 billion mark and, despite progress made between 1993 and 1998, still comprised around one-quarter of the global population at the millennium. By contrast, the estimates by Sala-i-Martin are much

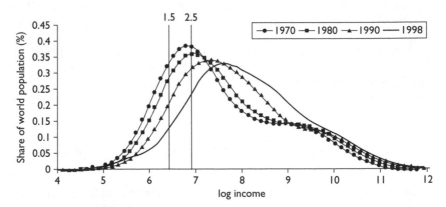

Figure 2.2 A falling number of people live in absolute poverty, 1970–1998

Source: Sala-i-Martin (2002)

Table 2.2   Contrasting estimates of global poverty, 1987–1998

	1987	1990	1993	1998
World Bank				
Number living below $1/day (million)	1,197	1,293	1,321	1,214
% of global population	29.7	29.3	28.5	24.3
Sala-i-Martin				
Number living below $1/day (million)	390	400	371	353
% of global population	8.8	8.6	7.6	6.7
Pogge and Reddy				
Number living below $1/day (million)				1,640
% of global population				32.2

Source: <http://www.worldbank.org/research/povmonitor/>; Sala-i-Martin (2002); calculations from Pogge and Reddy (2002)

lower, falling from 400 million in 1990 to 353 million in 1998. He calculates that the proportion of global population living below PPP$1 per day was much lower, falling below 7 per cent in 1998.

'The World Bank underestimates global poverty numbers'

If Sala-i-Martin provides an estimate of global poverty which is far lower than that given by the World Bank, then the analysis by Pogge and Reddy provides a radical counterbalance. Making the required adjustments (see below), they suggest that global poverty numbers are between 30 and 40 per cent higher than those produced by the World Bank. Applying this factor (at a median rate of 35 per cent), they estimate the proportion of the global population living in poverty as 32 per cent compared to the 24.3 per cent of the World Bank and the 6.7 per cent of Sala-i-Martin. Moreover, they believe that the problems of under-recording have become exaggerated since the baseline poverty measure was defined in 1985.

Making sense of the confusing numbers on absolute poverty?

How can these three different sets of estimations of levels of absolute global poverty produce such overwhelmingly different numbers, ranging from 353 million (and a mere 6.7 per cent of the global population) to 1,640 million (32.2 per cent of the population) for the same year? Let us begin with Sala-i-Martin's low-range estimate. One of the architects behind the World Bank's analysis of global poverty numbers provides a convincing critique of the use of national income accounts. Bear in mind that Sala-i-Martin applies figures of income distribution (in quintiles) to the national accounts. Ravallion's argument is that the data on income distribution severely under-report the incomes of the rich.

> For example, one study found that the mean income of the 10 highest income households in each of 18 surveys for countries in Latin America was generally no more than the average salary of the manager of a medium to large sized firm. Clearly there is massive under-reporting by the rich. Careful data work for India has found that for categories of consumption accounting for over 75% of the consumption of the poor, the divergence between the national accounts and the national household surveys is small.[5]

By contrast, the World Bank poverty estimates are based on a series of household surveys – more than 300 in over ninety countries since the 1980s. They take great care to define representative samples, and to calculate effectively the monetary value of agricultural production which is not sold on the market (another area where the national accounts data are inaccurate). Their estimates are also based on consumption rather than incomes. That is, they include remittance incomes from migrant labour and government income support. It is for this combination of reasons, argues Ravallion, that the poverty estimates by Sala-i-Martin (and Bhalla) are inaccurate and produce unbelievably low numbers.[6] As we shall see below in the discussion of global inequality, there are a number of other reasons why Sala-i-Martin's optimistic estimates are questionable.

Does that mean that the World Bank has got it right on the numbers living in absolute poverty? Pogge and Reddy don't think so. Their criticism goes back to the basket of goods which the World Bank uses – the 'necessities' – in its calculations of PPP prices. This comprises a mix of goods which are internationally traded (transport technologies, electronic consumer goods) and those which are not (predominantly foodstuffs, but also services). They argue that there is much more of a 'world price' for these traded products than for the non-traded ones, and that it is the poor who tend to consume relatively more non-traded products:

> Existing data about the prices of foodstuffs and, more specifically, of staple bread and cereals, show that these items (a large part of the consumption requirements of the poor) cost far more in poor countries than is suggested by general-consumption PPPs. The same is true for many basic necessities other than food. It is very likely that the World Bank, were it to use PPPs more closely

linked to the needs of the poor, would translate its $1/day standard into substantially higher national poverty lines for most poor countries.[7]

An added problem is that there is abundant evidence that in the same country the poor tend to pay more for the same commodity than do the rich. This, argue Pogge and Reddy, is especially the case for purchased basic foodstuffs.

Whom to believe? The critique of Sala-i-Martin is compelling, and his low estimates of global poverty fly in the face of casual empiricism. It is true that many people around the globe have experienced rising incomes; but it is not credible that the numbers of the absolutely poor have fallen so sharply, or indeed that they comprise less than 7 per cent of the global population. Moreover, Ravallion's explanation of the reasons why these low-level estimates based on national accounts are wrong is convincing. But does this mean that the World Bank has got it approximately right, or indeed that we should gravitate towards the midpoint of two extreme estimates (Sala-i-Martin and Pogge and Reddy)? Here we have to make a judgement call. Some of Pogge and Reddy's critique has considerable merit (although, as Ravallion points out, in other cases they misrepresent and/or misunderstand the World Bank's revisions of their data). They are not able to provide any detailed estimates of the numbers of absolute poor since they lack the resources of the World Bank to marshal household surveys. For good reasons, they also question the veracity of the data provided by international databases such as the World Bank's *World Development Indicators* (which are based on national income accounts, adjusted for PPP currency conversions) – we noted above Baulch's observation of unbelievable year-on-year variations in poverty levels. Nevertheless, their central conclusion, that the World Bank's numbers of those living in global poverty is an underestimate, is credible. But it is unlikely to be an underestimate of more than 30 per cent.

2.3   Patterns of relative poverty

Summary: Trends in relative poverty

There are a large number of potential measures of relative poverty; the evidence which is summarized focuses on the distribution of income within countries and the global distribution of income between countries.

Considering intra-country income distribution, the evidence is overwhelming that, in the majority of countries for which data exist, income inequality has worsened.

With respect to the global distribution of income, the conclusion depends on whether account is taken of the population size of individual countries (that is, if it is population-weighted). Ignoring this, there has been a slight deterioration and global inequality has increased. Taking account of population size, it would appear that global income distribution has become more equal as globalization has advanced.

However, there is a very important caveat. This improvement in the global distribution of income arises as a result of the very rapid economic growth in China (and to a lesser extent in India). Given their population size, this has a major impact on global distributional patterns. Paradoxically, this positive impact on global income distribution has occurred despite the significant worsening of income distribution within China (and India).

There are a large number of dimensions which can be used to judge the nature and trend of global poverty as reflected in patterns of income distribution. Figure 2.3 lists a selection – sixteen in fact – and gives examples of what types of measures can be generated for each of these categories. The categories include individuals, classes, genders, age groups, regions, countries and time.

Clearly there is no practical way that we can measure, analyse and summarize all of these dimensions of relative poverty. One important organizing principle in choosing which are important is 'fit for purpose', that is, the dimension which most clearly illuminates the central line of enquiry. Another is practicality – do the data and methods exist to make these measures of inequality feasible? Given these considerations (and the focus of this book on global incomes), the discussion below concentrates on two dimensions of inequality: the distribution of income within countries and the global distribution of income.

These two categories reflect only a single dimension of livelihoods – income per year – and take no account of other components of welfare. For example, they exclude a consideration of volatility in incomes. In many parts of the world, particularly where incomes are determined by environmental factors (for example, the weather) or by fluctuating world prices (for example, that of coffee), a major element of poverty is its periodic and repeated nature. Another excluded factor is the comparison of environmental conditions, with many poor people and poor countries experiencing a low-quality and rapidly

Dimension of inequality	Who is involved – some examples
Interpersonal	Comparison between *all* individuals
Inter-class	Labour and capital; farmers and landless labour
Intra-class	Financial capital and industrial capital; large farmers and small farmers
Inter-sectoral	Agriculture and industry
Intra-sectoral	Within agriculture and industry
Inter-generational	Adults and children; working adults and the retired
Inter-gender	Males and females
Intra-gender	Within gender groupings
Inter-temporal	Over time
Intra-temporal	Within time-periods
Inter-regional, intra-national	Town and countryside; between cities; between provinces and districts
Intra-regional, intra-national	Between towns within a region
Inter-regional, international	Between continents; between country types
Intra-regional, international	Within continents; within country types
Between countries – unweighted	Comparing country averages and ignoring population size
Between countries – weighted	Comparing country averages taking account of population size

Figure 2.3 The many dimensions of relative poverty

deteriorating environment. The data also do not take account of what is termed 'the social wage', that is, services provided by the government to its people. Moreover, the two chosen dimensions of intra-national and international distribution also focus at the national level, and exclude sub-national regions, gender differences and other categories of income recipients.

The distribution of income within countries

There is a tremendous variety in country experience with regard to income distribution. Using PPP national accounts statistics, Sala-i-Martin compares the profile of income distribution over four time-periods – 1970, 1980, 1990 and 1998 – for a large number of countries. This shows a variety of experience, with no consistent pattern emerging. For example:

• India has experienced rapid growth in per capita incomes with some degree of inequality growth.

- The USA shows only slow per capita income growth, with some increase in inequality, reflecting the relatively slow growth of income among the poor and a more rapid growth among the richest segment of the population.
- Japan has experienced rapid growth, with a tightening of distributional patterns; inequality has been reduced because there has been a process of catch-up by the poorest members of society.
- China's economy has grown very rapidly and shows widening income disparities, particularly (as in the Indian case) as a result of income growth among the next-to-richest groups in society.
- Brazil shows virtually no growth in incomes (except among the poorest segments of society), substantial inequality and, in general, widening inequality, with income being increasingly concentrated in two groups – those in the middle and those towards the upper levels of income.
- Nigeria displays a picture of falling per capita incomes over time and of rising inequality.

A second feature of intra-income distribution over time which emerges from Sala-i-Martin's data is the growth of what has come to be called the 'twin-peaks' phenomenon.[8] This describes a world in which incomes cluster around two points, leaving something of a gulf in between, and suggests enduring patterns of relative affluence and relative poverty. A trend towards twin peaks is widespread, and particularly significant in the case of Brazil (figure 2.4) and Nigeria, but its emergence can also be observed in China, India and the USA. It is a striking result of both intra-country income distribution and inter-country distribution that these twin peaks have become more evident over time.

This picture of intra-country income distribution provided by Sala-i-Martin, denying the existence of any common trend, suffers from the same criticism as that levelled against his analysis of absolute poverty levels. It results from a series of questionable methodological leaps in which a limited number of data observations in a single country are extended backwards and forwards to *assume* the very patterns of distribution which Sala-i-Martin is trying to evidence.[9] So, what patterns emerge when we use household incomes to measure the distribution of intra-country income and consumption? Using household income data, Ravallion reports a complex picture and also concludes that no consistent pattern emerges. Income distribution improves in some cases and deteriorates in others. But, as Milanovic points out, Ravallion's calculations suffer from many of the problems experienced by Sala-i-Martin – the mixing of household and

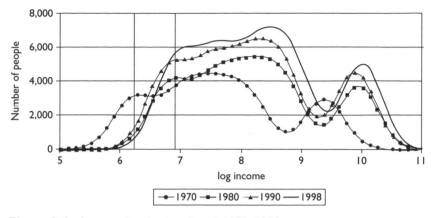

Figure 2.4   Income distribution, Brazil, 1970–1998

Source: Sala-i-Martin (2002)

individual income distribution, conflating studies providing expenditure data with those using income data, assuming empty data-points, and so on.[10]

More commonly, studies of income distribution which use different datasets to those of Sala-i-Martin and the World Bank report a tendency for intra-country distributional patterns to worsen:

- A review of the experience of seventy-three countries in the post-Second World War period covered 80 per cent of the world's population and 91 per cent of PPP-adjusted global GDP (table 2.3). It found a common pattern in which, in forty-eight countries, inequality fell in the period from 1950 to the mid-1970s and then rose sharply in the last two decades of the twentieth century; distributional patterns remained largely unchanged in sixteen countries and improved in only nine (mostly small economies).
- In high-income economies in general, income distribution tended to become more unequal during the 1980s and 1990s (particularly in the Anglo-Saxon economies),[11] and then to stabilize.[12] It is striking that, while in Europe the distribution of incomes became more unequal, the distribution of consumption was less adversely affected because of the role played by the welfare state in providing social services to those with low incomes.[13]
- In the Netherlands real wages fell between 1979 and 1997.[14]
- In the USA, real wages were lower in the mid-1990s than they were in the late 1960s, and family incomes held up only as a

Table 2.3 Changes in income inequality in seventy-three countries from the 1960s to the 1990s

Inequality	Developed countries	Developing countries	Transitional countries	Total
Rising	12: Australia, Canada, Denmark, Finland, Italy, Japan, Netherlands, New Zealand, Spain, Sweden, UK, USA	15: Argentina, Chile, China, Colombia, Costa Rica, Guatemala, Hong Kong, Mexico, Pakistan, Panama, South Africa, Sri Lanka, Taiwan, Thailand, Venezuela	21: Armenia, Azerbaijan, Bulgaria, Croatia, Czech Republic, Estonia, Georgia, Hungary, Kazakhstan, Kyrgyzstan, Latvia, Lithuania, Macedonia, Moldova, Poland, Romania, Russia, Slovakia, Slovenia, Ukraine, Yugoslavia	48
Constant	3: Austria, Belgium, Germany	12: Bangladesh, Brazil,[a] Côte d'Ivoire, Dominican Republic, El Salvador, India,[a] Indonesia,[a] Puerto Rico, Senegal, Singapore, Tanzania,[a] Turkey	1: Belarus	16
Declining	2: France, Norway	7: Bahamas, Honduras, Jamaica, South Korea,[a] Malaysia, Philippines,[a] Tunisia	0	9
All	17	34	22	73

[a]Countries may have experienced rising inequality between 1998 and 2000.
Source: Cornia and Court (2001)

consequence of longer working hours and more working members in the family.[15] Between 1970 and 1992, the proportion of national income received by the bottom quintile was broadly stable (in fact it fell from 5 to 4 per cent), while that of the top quartile rose from 41 to 45 per cent (and that of the top 5 per cent rose from 16 to 18 per cent).[16]

- In Chile, often thought to be the paradigmatic gainer from globalization, the gini coefficient increased from 0.46 in 1971 to 0.58 in 1989.[17] (The gini coefficient calculates the proportion of cumulative income going to the proportion of cumulative population – the higher the gini, the greater the income inequality).[18]

- Inequality has grown markedly in the transition economies. The gini coefficients in most of these during the late 1980s were in the region of 0.20 to 0.25. Within a very short period of six years after transition, they rose sharply, reaching 0.37 in Lithuania, 0.47 in Ukraine and 0.48 in Russia.[19]

- Inequality between skilled and unskilled wage-earners tended to increase in the industrially advanced countries and in Latin America during the 1990s.[20]

- It is in China that the changing pattern of internal income distribution has been most marked and, as we shall see below, has had the greatest impact on global income distribution. In the context of a very rapid pace of economic growth and integration into the global economy – the export–GDP ratio rose from 10.5 per cent in 1985 to 21.3 per cent in 1995 – there was a sharp rise in inequality. This was between urban and rural areas, between coastal and interior provinces, and within urban and rural areas; the only indicator which did not worsen was that between rural areas (figure 2.5).[21] So great has this income inequality become that, in 2003, despite achieving a growth rate of 9 per cent, for the first time in many years the number of people living in absolute poverty in China rose, by 800,000.[22]

The global distribution of income between countries

What about the distribution of world income? How has it fared as globalization has deepened? One way of analysing these trends is to look at the evolution of per capita incomes in different countries over time. In other words, the per capita income is compared between countries, PPP-adjusted. Figure 2.6 displays the gini coefficient of 144 countries between 1950 and 1998. Each country is

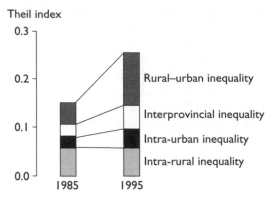

Figure 2.5 Changing patterns of income distribution in China, 1985 and 1995

Note: The higher the Theil index, the greater the inequality
Source: World Bank (2002)

considered as a separate data-point of equal weight, irrespective of size, per capita income or population. It can be seen from this that, after a period of considerable stability between 1950 and 1980, global inter-country income distribution became markedly more unequal in the last two decades of the twentieth century. This reflected the fact that, in this era of particularly rapid globalization, countries experienced very different growth paths, with Asia growing rapidly and Africa and Latin America growing slowly or not at all. This contrasted with the similarity of growth experiences in the post-war years.

This observation of rising inter-country inequality is widely acknowledged to be accurate. But it suffers from one serious flaw in that it gives the same weight to the per capita income of China, India, Dominica and the Cayman Islands, despite the fact that they have very varying populations (1.3 billion, 1.05 billion, 72,000, and 63,000 respectively in 1999). But if we are truly to reflect global income distribution patterns – that is, the distribution of income between the people of the world rather than the countries of the world – then we obviously need to take account of country size and to weight these incomes by each country's share of global population.

Milanovic shows the impact of population-weighting global comparisons (figure 2.7). Merely comparing per capita incomes by country (irrespective of population) shows a clear tendency towards greater inequality. But if population is taken into account, the picture changes radically and the world becomes more equal. This, however, is entirely due to the growth performance of China; if China is removed from the

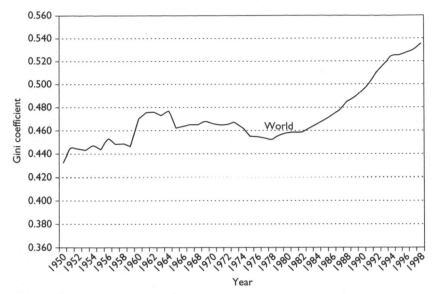

Figure 2.6 Gini coefficient of global inter-country income distribution (not weighted by population size), 1950–1999

Source: Milanovic (2003)

equation, the gini of global population-weighted inequality has risen since the mid-1980s.

After all this methodological confusion, is there any basis for making any judgement on the pattern of population-weighted global income distribution? The answer is that, in balance, the distribution of global income among individuals in the world has probably either been static or become marginally better over the past two decades. There is, however, a clear explanation for this result – China. China's economy, as we have seen, has grown at a phenomenal rate in recent decades, at an annual rate of 10 per cent during the 1980s and the 1990s. Yet China accounts for almost 20 per cent of the global population. So it is almost an arithmetic certainty that this will show up as an improvement in global income distribution, despite the paradoxical fact that, at the same time, China's internal income distribution became considerably more unequal; indeed, in 2003 there was an increase in the numbers living in absolute poverty. Taking China out of the equation, measured by the distribution of income among the global population of individuals and households, there can be little doubt that the world has indeed become a more unequal place over the past two decades.

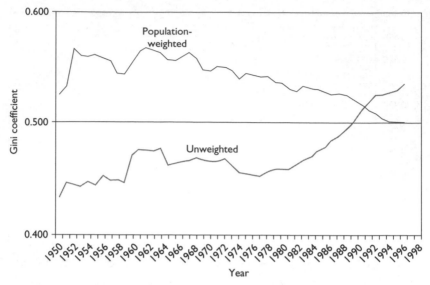

Figure 2.7 Weighted and unweighted income distribution (gini coefficients), 1950–1999

Source: Milanovic (2002)

A summary perspective on poverty trends

In the light of these complexities, what conclusions can we draw on the incidence of poverty in the most recent era of globalization, given that we are concentrating on incomes and consumption (and not on the environment or various indicators of physical welfare) and on countries (and not class, gender and sub-national regions)?

First, focusing on absolute levels of poverty:

- Using household survey data and a diverse bundle of 'necessities', there is strong evidence that since the early 1990s, the overall number of people living below the PPP$1 per day poverty line has remained stable, or perhaps reduced marginally; that the number of those living below the PPP$2 per day poverty line has increased; and that a significantly larger number of people live above the PPP$1 per day level. It is notable that, good though this perform- ance was, it fell below the expectations of the World Bank, which had predicted in 1990 that the numbers living below $1 per day would fall to 825 million in 1998 (rather than the actual figure of more than 1.2 billion).

- However, if a more narrowly defined food-intensive basket of 'necessities' is used, there is some dispute about these numbers, with reasons to believe that the World Bank may have underestimated the numbers of absolutely poor; an alternative view that the World Bank has overestimated the extent of global poverty is less credible.

And what of poverty considered as a relative concept? Here there is widespread agreement that:

- The distribution of global income treating each country independently of its size has worsened. Weighted by population size – in other words, the share of global population – this distribution may have either been static or improved slightly. But this is due overwhelmingly to China's (and to a lesser extent, India's) very rapid and sustained economic growth and, as a subsidiary reason, to the stagnation of large numbers of economies, particularly in Africa, the former Soviet Union, and Latin America and the Caribbean. In reality, excluding China, the world has become considerably less equal than it used to be.
- There is a disputed view on the pattern of intra-country income distribution. Some observers believe that no patterns have emerged – income inequality has improved in as many countries as it has deteriorated – and that there are no common characteristics of this differential country performance. However, on balance it is probably more accurate to conclude that intra-country income distribution has indeed worsened in the majority of cases, particularly since the 1980s. In those countries where it stabilized or narrowed (particularly Europe) this was often due to social expenditure by governments.

2.4 Globalization, poverty and inequality: relational or residual?

Summary: The effect of globalization on poverty

The last quarter of the twentieth century saw an increase in globalization, a reduction in the proportion of the world's population living in absolute poverty and a growth in inequality. Were these developments related in any causal way?

Biblical
warning!

One view, firmly pushed by the World Bank, is that the poverty in the globalizing economy is *residual*. The poor is made up of those who have held back from participating in the global economy. As they change their attitudes, and as globalization deepens, so the poor will be mopped up. And, far from income inequality being caused by globalization, the expansion of labour-intensive exports leads to greater equality. A contrasting view is one which sees poverty as being *relational* to globalization. It is in the very nature of globalization that poverty is sustained and distribution worsened.

On the basis of these alternative perspectives, it is possible to identify three major policy challenges. The first is that the losers in the global economy have been those who have been excluded from globalization, in which case the appropriate policy response is for all producers to deepen their global presence as quickly as possible. The second is that globalization has caused poverty and inequality, in which case the losers should reduce their participation in the global economy. Thirdly and finally, it is not globalization *per se* which has had an adverse poverty impact, but the particular way in which countries have inserted themselves in the global economy. In this case the primary challenge is to refashion a country's insertion into the global economy.

As we have seen, during the latter twentieth century poverty was persistent and inequality increased. At the same time, globalization deepened. This begs the obvious question – are the two sets of developments causally related?

The first possibility is that there is no causal link. Many correlations are spurious and hence misinterpreted. For example, most traffic accidents in the UK occur with cars that are coloured silver. We might conclude from this that silver *causes* accidents, perhaps because it is such an attractive colour that it distracts or makes envious the drivers of non-silver-coloured cars. The policy response is obvious in this case – do not allow manufacturers to produce silver-coloured cars, and the death rate on UK roads will plummet. But, in reality, the reason why most accidents occur in silver-coloured cars is that in recent years this has become a fashionable colour and more than 50 per cent of all new cars sold in the UK are silver. In this case, banning the colour silver will do little to reduce the accident rate.

Similarly, it can be argued that, for autonomous reasons, recent decades have seen both a deepening of globalization and an increase in income inequality. However, this distributional outcome may have little to do with globalization *per se*, but may instead be due to exogenous factors such as technological change. For example, new information and communication technologies represent epochal changes in technological regime, with a wide range of impacts on competitiveness, social organization and individual behaviour.[23] The diffusion of this technology simultaneously induces deeper globalization and speeds up growth among adopters (but not among non-adopters, who fall further behind). At the same time, because the new technology is capital- and skill-intensive, its adoption leads to a more unequal pattern of income distribution. In these circumstances, the causal link between globalization, growth and poverty is spurious.

A second and different line of argument is that participating in the global economy has drawn hundred of millions of people out of poverty, reflected in the picture shown in figure 2.1 above. This is a perspective which sees poverty as a *residual* phenomenon – the global poor consists of people who have failed to engage productively with globalization. The 2 billion people living in absolute poverty reside in countries reluctant to deepen their participation in the global economy. If globalization deepens further, the argument goes, then eventually all (or nearly all) of the world's poor will be lifted out of absolute destitution. This interpretation of events is reflected in the World Bank's 2002 report entitled *Globalization, Growth and Poverty: Building an Inclusive World*.[24] It argues the case both for further globalization (notably through rapid growth in developing-country exports of manufactures) and for a programme of policy reform which pushes marketization and deregulation, as embodied in what Williamson has called the Washington Consensus.[25] In this view, globalization 'has generally supported poverty reduction' and 'would not have been feasible without a wide range of domestic reforms covering governance, the investment climate and social service provision.' Although the World Bank recognizes that there is some dispute about these issues, it pulls few punches: 'the doubts that one can retain about each individual study threaten to block our view of the overall forest of evidence. Even though no one study has established that openness to trade has unambiguously helped the representative Third World economy, the preponderance of evidence supports this conclusion.' Consequently, '[i]n sum, global economic integration has supported poverty reduction and should not be reversed.'

Related to this is an ancillary argument that globalization has not just leveraged people out of destitution, but has had a favourable distributional impact and has reduced relative poverty. The argument for this position is that globalization has led many low-income economies to specialize in labour-intensive products, a sharp contrast with the capital- and technology-intensive sectors favoured in the previous era of import-substituting industrialization. This had resulted in a relative decline in the incomes of the owners of capital, and an enhancement of the incomes of the previously unemployed, most of whom were relatively unskilled. (The reality of widening inequality is either ignored in this textbook view of the global economy, or is ascribed to other factors such as autonomous technological progress.[26])

This view that poverty is largely residual presents a rosy picture of globalization. In a world in which the losers from globalization comprise those who have failed to participate actively in the global economy, the message is clear – *join in*. But what happens if the losers include individuals, groups of people, firms and countries who have participated more deeply in global processes, but who nevertheless find themselves worse off, either in absolute or in relative terms? This is a world in which poverty is seen as a *relational* rather than a residual phenomenon, arising from the very process of globalization itself.[27]

If the link between globalization, poverty and inequality is relational rather than residual, the policy challenges are much more daunting. One possibility is that producers must temper their participation in the global economy. Instead of rushing at this in an unguided manner by allowing market forces free play in determining their global role, they should systematically shape their insertion into the global economy with a series of policies designed actively to influence the nature of this participation. In this third case, the policy response is not *whether* to participate in the global economy, but *how* to do so in a manner which provides for sustainable income growth. The logic of this position is strengthened by the fact that few countries have the capacity to resist the pressures to globalize – or perhaps we should say that few *developing* countries have this capacity, since both Europe and the USA continue to protect and to subsidize their agricultural sectors and to impose punitive tariffs in the face of WTO objections. But what if, despite their best efforts, producers are unable to participate in the global economy effectively? Should they reduce their exposure to globalization, in what ways and how might this be done?

These policy challenges are addressed in the final chapter of this book. But before we get to this outcome, we need first to determine whether poverty and inequality are indeed residual or relational to the unfolding of globalization processes. Chapter 3 provides a theoretical explanation for the relational perspective and explains how producers can be made worse off by participating in the global economy. This is followed in chapter 4 by a review of the steps which producers need to take to provide the capability to gain from participating in the global economy. This addresses the policy challenge that the issue is not whether to participate in the global economy, but how to do so. Chapter 5 presents three sectoral case studies which show that at least some low-income economies appear to be making a good fist of this challenge, at least in some sectors.

But the success of *some* countries in *some* sectors does not add up to a conclusion that *most* low-income economies will succeed in *most* sectors. The general is not necessarily a summation of the particular. How this outcome results, and the role which China plays in shaping the negative outcomes experienced by producers in other countries, is the subject matter of part III. If it is indeed the outcome of globalization, might the appropriate policy response for many countries be to dampen their participation in the global economy?

Part II

Gaining from Globalization

The argument that poverty in the global economy is largely residual rests on a developed theoretical tradition of specialization and comparative advantage, and we will consider this body of theory later, in chapter 7. If we are to produce a convincing explanation that poverty is a relational outcome of globalization, it too needs to be backed by a theoretical explanation. Part of this intellectual framework will be discussed in chapters 6 and 7 when we show how, in a global economy made up of many producers and consumers, there may be a disjuncture between aggregate production and consumption. But before we get to this, we need to begin the analysis at a micro-level, and to explain how producers may be worse off even though they expand their production and participate more deeply in the global economy.

Chapter 3 provides an analytical framework for this micro-level analysis. It draws on the *theory of rent*, that is, that it is scarcity which provides the basis for high and sustainable incomes. Given the capacity of producers to provide goods and services which customers want, incomes can be high and sustainable if producers are able to protect themselves from competition by constructing, and/or taking advantage of, *barriers to entry*. Conversely, producers unable to hide behind barriers to entry are subject to intense competition and eroding incomes. Although these barriers include heightened process efficiency and product development, there is a wider terrain of rent-providing entry barriers.

This analysis provides a framework to guide the effective positioning of firms in the global economy. It is based on the premise that there are gains to be had from deepening globalization, but that this depends on the way in which producers position themselves in global markets. To achieve this end requires an understanding of how producers translate *comparative advantage* (that is, the bundle of resources with which they are relatively well endowed) into *competitive advantage* (that is, competing effectively on a global stage).

But how can this analytical framework be used to turn comparative advantage into competitive advantage? One of the key lessons we have learnt in recent decades is that the invention part of the innovation cycle is often relatively easy. The hard part of the journey is to turn good ideas into practice. Thus it is in *innovation management* that the major challenge lies, particularly for producers in lower-income economies who are not at the frontier of global technology. Together with understanding the manner in which producers connect to distant final markets, this is the subject matter of chapter 4.

To what extent have producers in lower-income economies managed this challenge? Chapter 5 looks at the results of *innovation management in three key globally traded sectors* – clothing and textiles, furniture, and automobiles. Together they cover a range of technological complexity, offer the prospect of using a variety of different production techniques, and are not rooted in any location for climatic reasons. In each case we can observe the significant advance of key low-income producing countries. The generalization of this sectoral experience suggests that globalization offers rewards to many producers in poor countries; globalization can thus provide the means to overcome global poverty.

3

Getting it Right: Generating and Appropriating Rents

During the 1970s my family spent four especially happy years living in Kenya. We deliberately chose to live outside of the capital city, Nairobi, which displayed many of the features of the unequal and violent South African cities which we had left behind. The house where we lived and the compound in which it was situated were redolent of earlier phases of globalization. The wooden bungalow, with a corrugated-iron roof, was shipped out from Britain in the dying years of the nineteenth century. The boat sank in shallow water, and the house was subsequently retrieved from the sea some two years later. It was constructed on stilts to allow for air circulation, based on the design of bungalows used by British colonials in India. The trouble was that, while India was very hot, the Kenyan highlands (more than 2,000 metres above sea level) were frequently cold. So it was not always the warmest place to be in July and August. The house was located in a missionary compound, speaking to the ideological drivers of globalization which we discussed in chapter 1.

During our stay, we witnessed the passing of an era when the last missionaries departed in 1974. The missionary doctor, who had been there since the late 1940s, had never had an indigenous Kenyan in his house other than as a servant or a builder. The departing missionary priest's wife washed her hands whenever she shook hands with a Kenyan (a frequent custom throughout colonial Africa). The church and school in the compound had inadvertently spawned the political consciousness of the leader of Kenya's struggle for independence, Jomo Kenyatta. He died just before we left Kenya and his burial ceremony took place in the former mission church at the bottom of our garden in a ceremony filled with anti-imperialist nationalist rhetoric.

One of the more fortunate experiences in our stay was meeting and getting to know closely Kinyanjui Munanga and his family. Kinyanjui began working for us as a gardener, but then 'graduated' into the position of a driver and then a research assistant. Over the course of four years we became close friends and keep in frequent contact to this day. He was married in our house and some of our children are of similar ages.

When we first met Kinyanjui he was earning 5 shillings a day as a nightwatchman, equivalent now to around 40 US cents. He was the eldest son in the family, which had been impoverished by the early death of his father. None of his siblings had more than elementary school education. By the time we left Kenya four years later, he had saved enough to purchase a plot of land in what was then a rural area and is now a fast-growing suburb of Nairobi. Kinyanjui and his wife, like all loving and responsible parents, wanted more than anything for their children to succeed and to escape from the poverty of their own childhoods. They sought our advice and we affirmed their judgement that the most durable route out of poverty was to invest in education. Over the subsequent twenty-five years, at enormous sacrifice to the parents and the family, an enormous financial commitment was made to education, proportionately far more than we are accustomed to in Europe or North America. This investment was particularly significant given the low level of disposable income which his family had.

Now, the three eldest children have left school. The first-born son is a TV repairer, the second child (a girl) is a pharmacist, and the third (also a girl) is studying nursing. From the perspective of the 1970s and 1980s when the investments in education were decided, this should have assured the family a substantial income. Yet, the reality has been depressingly different, and the family remains at a low level of income. By the time the two eldest had graduated, their professions had become relatively commonplace. There was an abundance of TV repairers, and so crowded was the labour market for pharmacists that the eldest daughter could obtain only a low-paid position in a doctor's surgery in a rural area. The girl studying nursing is unlikely to earn a substantial income (measured by Kenyan standards) unless she migrates to one of the high-income economies where nurses are relatively scarce.

So, what is the wider significance of this story? It is that the incomes which arise from work depend on the degree of competition. During the 1970s and 1980s each of these professions in Kenya was in short supply and wages were high. Two decades later, they were abundant, and earned little premium over unskilled work. Through this story of a working-class Kenyan family we can discern the determinants of relative incomes generated in global production systems.

In this chapter we turn our attention away from the individual and the family to the firm and the cluster of firms. We begin by explaining how it is that countries and firms may be worse off even though they have opened up their borders to ease the inflow of finance, technology and imports, and have devoted an increasing share of their productive resources to serve external markets (section 3.1). As we shall see, this adverse outcome arises as a consequence of the inability of firms, sectors and countries to generate and appropriate a range of 'rents'. We then briefly set out the theory of rent in section 3.2. In section 3.3, we outline a variety of rents which are directly generated by firms, acting either on their own or in concert with other firms. This is followed in section 3.4 by a discussion of a selection of rents which affect the relative competitiveness and the incomes of producers, but which are generated by parties external to direct production. As section 3.5 shows, there are a variety of different barriers to entry protecting these rents. Some involve secret process know-how, others embody formal property rights. But a key characteristic of rents is that they are dynamic. Thus, this chapter concludes in section 3.6 by addressing the transient nature of many rents.

3.1 Getting it wrong: global presence and declining returns

Summary: Getting it wrong

Producers of commodity products have long suffered from 'declining terms of trade'; that is, the global prices of their exported products have declined in comparison with the global prices of their imports of manufactures. The experience of coffee growers is an excellent example of the difficulties facing commodity producers. For this reason, many poor countries have focused their development strategies on industrialization and an increase in manufactured exports.

But in recent years many exporters of manufactures have also begun to experience falling product prices, and this has resulted in a severe squeeze on their incomes. Thus, merely producing for the global market does not in itself provide for sustainable incomes. It depends what is produced and how it is produced.

In the early 1950s, Singer and Prebisch first highlighted the problems experienced by producers of primary products such as agricultural commodities (tea, coffee, cocoa, etc.) and basic metals and other mineral products (iron ore, copper, coal, etc.). They observed a trend in which the prices of exported primary mineral and agricultural products systematically fell in relation to those of imported manufactures.[1] These differential trends resulted from a number of factors. The prices of primary products fell because an increasing number of producers expanded the supply of these goods; the demand for primary products grew more slowly than that for manufactures; and synthetic substitutes were introduced for natural materials, as in the case of rubber. By contrast, the price of manufactures rose because of the power of organized labour in the industrialized countries. This resulted in cost-plus pricing for these products, whose prices rose as incomes in these economies grew. Moreover, the demand for most manufactures is relatively 'income elastic' – consumption grows as incomes rise.

The ratio of the price of exports to the price of imports is called the 'barter terms of trade'. This means that, to obtain the same quantity of manufactured imports, producers would have to export an increasing quantity of primary exports. If the demand for these primary products is not very responsive to a reduction in their price, this may also lead to a case of falling 'income terms of trade' – that is, despite growing physical exports, overall incomes may decline. But, even if the income terms of trade are positive, if technical progress is low in primary production, then growing export quantities may have a high opportunity cost in resource terms. This means that the resources devoted to the production and export of these commodities could be used more effectively in other sectors.

Take the case of coffee. As figure 3.1 shows, the price of coffee in global markets has fluctuated dramatically over the years. Consider, for example, the lucky farmers when prices catapulted upwards from 72 cents per pound in 1976 to $2.29 per pound in 1978. But this price spike – arising as a consequence of severe frosts in Brazil – was exceptional, and more commonly the price of coffee has fallen. At the same time, for much of this period the price of manufactures grew consistently (and often very rapidly), so that the purchasing power of coffee producers – their barter terms of trade – has tended to fall. Figure 3.2 breaks down these long-term terms of trade into sub-periods and shows that, despite the occasional price-hike, the barter terms of trade have consistently fallen against coffee producers. In the most recent cycle, the fall in prices has been so large that the income terms of trade have also fallen for many coffee producers in poor countries such as Ethiopia and Kenya.

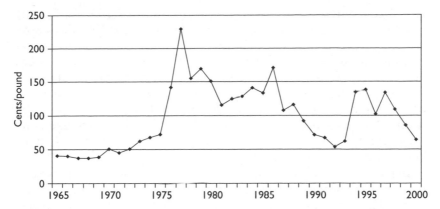

Figure 3.1   The price of coffee beans in global markets (cents/lb), 1965–2000[a]

[a] Composite coffee index

Source: Data supplied by International Coffee Organization

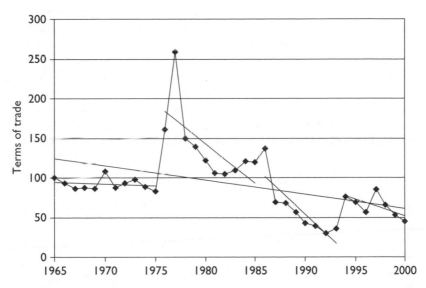

Figure 3.2   The terms of trade of coffee producers, 1965–2000 (1965=100)[a]

[a] Measured against the export price index of the industrialized economies

Source: Calculated from data supplied by International Coffee Organization and UNCTAD

It was partly as a result of these falling terms of trade of primary mineral and agricultural products such as coffee and partly because of the observed success of those economies which had concentrated on manufactures that a conventional wisdom rapidly spread through the global economy in the post-war period – industrialize. As Sutcliffe concluded in his classic text on industrialization in 1971, 'all societies are faced with the long-run desirability of industrialization as a means to higher productivity and living standards.'[2] Then, given the success during the 1970s of the Asian economies as exporters of manufactures, it rapidly became the conventional wisdom that the optimal development path lay not just in industrialization and global integration, but through the export of manufactures. Virtually all low-income countries now see industrialization and export-led manufacturing as the key to their economic growth.

But if it was only that easy. We have already witnessed, in chapter 1, the problems faced by South African exporters of bunk beds and doors. Here we consider in more detail the experience of a garment manufacturer in the Dominican Republic in the early 1990s. This was a firm which operated in an economic processing zone which gave special privileges to exporters. Such firms were exempt from taxes and import duties for all output which was exported. From the perspective of external buyers, this was an attractive source of supply, and there was a rush of American buyers into the region, where an EPZ fever had led to a rash of similar duty- and tax-free zones in other countries. As figure 3.3 indicates, the falling price of labour in the Dominican Republic – measured in US$ – was a major attraction to US clothing buyers. Between 1980 and 1990, these wages fell in US$ by 55 per cent, at a faster rate than took place in the neighbouring countries of Costa Rica (22 per cent) and Mexico (33 per cent); during the same period, the dollar value of wages in the USA rose by 15 per cent.[3] These

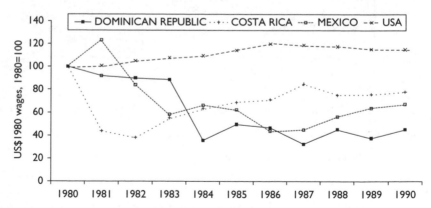

Figure 3.3   Index of wages in US$: the Dominican Republic, Costa Rica, Mexico and the USA, 1980–1990

Source: Kaplinsky (1993)

changes in relative wages were almost entirely a direct consequence of currency devaluations in the region, with neighbouring countries devaluing against the USA and each other in order to enhance their price competitiveness.

Yet, despite these falling wages, this Dominican Republic garment firm ran into trouble (table 3.1). It began making jeans under contract for a large US buyer. Its function was to sew together the denim which had been produced and cut in the USA, using other imported components such as thread, labels and buttons, and then to pack these in labelled boxes provided by its US principal. It began with a contract to assemble 9,000 pairs of jeans a week for $2.18 per pair; after nine months, the volume fell to 5,000 pairs a week, at a reduced unit price of $2.05, then three months later it fell to 3,000 pairs a week at $1.87. Thirteen months after the contract started, it was abruptly terminated. The firm's US principal had found a cheaper source in the region, a consequence of a significant currency depreciation in a neighbouring country.

What explains this corporate failure? After all, here was a firm working to modern methods of inventory control (just-in-time production) and utilizing best-practice quality-at-source procedures. It was exporting manufactures – or, rather, trying to export manufactures as the policy agenda dictated – and it was in the labour-intensive manufacturing sector where low-wage developing economies were being encouraged to specialize. And yet, thirteen months after investing $150,000, it had been forced out of business. So, as this firm found to its cost, merely producing for the global market – deepening globalization – is not a guarantee of high or sustainable incomes.

The key to understanding the problems of coffee producers and the failure of this export-oriented manufacturing firm and the wider implications of its experience lies in their inability to extract economic rents.

Table 3.1 Declining unit prices and investment instability: the case of jeans manufacturing in the Dominican Republic

	Volume (per week)	Unit price ($)
January 1990	9,000	2.18
October 1990	5,000	2.05
December 1990	3,000	1.87
February 1991	Arrangement terminated and assembly transferred to Honduras	
Total investment in equipment by Dominican Republic firm was US$150,000		

Source: Kaplinsky (1993)

3.2 The theory of rent

Summary: The theory of rent

Rent arises from scarcity. This means having something – a resource, a capability, knowledge – which others do not possess. To be enduring, rents need to be protected by barriers to entry.

Some of these rents and entry barriers are endogenous to the production chain – that is, they are constructed by producers themselves, acting either independently or in concert with other producers.

Other rents and entry barriers are exogenous to the corporate sector. They are either a gift of nature or, increasingly more likely, generated by parties external to the production chain itself, but are available to selected producers, providing a capacity for generating and sustaining incomes.

In each of these above cases – coffee production and jeans manufacturing – the ability to sustain income growth and thus to make the most of global opportunities was undermined by intense competition. Hence, the obvious policy conclusion is for firms, sectors and countries to develop growth trajectories which enable them to insulate themselves from competitive forces, in general by learning to upgrade and increase their competitiveness more rapidly than other producers. In order to explore these challenges more deeply, we need to understand the concept of rent, and the associated concept of barriers to entry.

> *Rent describes a situation where the parties who control a particular set of resources are able to gain from scarcity by insulating themselves from competition. This is achieved by taking advantage of or by creating barriers to the entry of competitors.*

The importance of rent was first identified by Ricardo: '[r]ent is that portion of the produce of the earth which is paid to the landlord for the use of the original and indestructible powers of the soil.'[4] Ricardo began with the observation that agricultural land was not homogenous, and that those who had access to the scarce, fertile plots consequently derived a rent. In a similar way, in common parlance we tend to refer to rents as being a characteristic of property. We know that, as in the case of Ricardo's agricultural rent, the better the view, the more scenic the plot, the more optimal the location, the quieter the environment, then the higher the rent which the landlord can achieve.

In each of these cases, it is a matter of degree – quiet*er* than, the bett*er* the view, and so on.

Ricardo hinted that these rents were not merely a bounty of nature, since land could be improved, for example, by investments in irrigation. But this was not a central focus in his schema. It was left to Marshall and particularly to Schumpeter to develop a framework for understanding the process whereby rents could be created. These types of rent are often referred to as 'producer', 'entrepreneurial' or 'Schumpeterian' rents.

Schumpeter provided an analytical framework to show how scarcity can be constructed. He distinguished the process of 'invention' (having an original idea, a 'new combination' in his words) from that of 'innovation' (turning a new idea to commercial advantage). Entrepreneurship is defined in the act of innovation. If this innovation proves to be difficult to copy, then the entrepreneur earns a super-profit which exceeds not only the cost of the invention and the associated innovation, but the returns to economic activity in other activities which are less well protected from competition. Over time this innovation is copied (the act of 'diffusion') or superseded by a new, superior innovation. It is this 'Schumpeterian motor', the search for producer rents, which spurs the innovation process and subsequent diffusion and which drives forward economic growth. For Schumpeter, the entrepreneurial rents were almost always dynamic.

Figure 3.4 shows the process at work. In each industry the equilibrium is defined by the 'average' rate of profit. Following the introduction of a 'new combination', the entrepreneur reaps an 'entrepreneurial surplus' which provides for abnormal high incomes. Then, as the new combination is copied and diffuses, the producer surplus is whittled away, and is transformed into a consumer surplus as prices fall and new and better quality products are made widely available. But all this does is to renew the search for 'new combinations', by either the same entrepreneur or another entrepreneur.

It is obvious from this that the link between innovation and income is to be found in barriers to entry which keep out competition. Given that the product being manufactured is something consumers want, the greater the barriers to entry, the more likely incomes will be high. So, the key questions for the producer are: How impervious are these barriers? Can the 'new combination' be easily copied? Can it be circumvented, perhaps by using a similar process, or can it be superseded by a new and even better combination? Thus it is that barriers to entry are a central component of the theory of rent, and similarly that the theory of rent provides the key to understanding the availability and sustainability of high incomes.

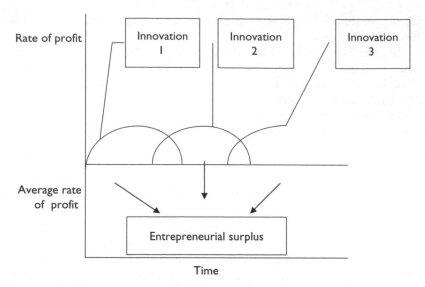

Figure 3.4 The generation and dissipation of entrepreneurial surplus

In analysing the nature of different types of rents and barriers to entry, it is possible to distinguish between two broad categories of rent. The first are those rents which arise from command over the production process, and which are largely endogenous to the firm and its partners in its value chain or the locality. They result from the purposeful actions of firms and groups of firms. The second set of rents and barriers to entry are those which are generated outside of the corporate world, or are gifts of nature. These exogenous rents may of course reflect the influence and lobbying of agents in the productive sector, but they lie in the domain of other parties, such as governments. Similarly, actors in the world outside of direct production may also be able to influence the capabilities and actions of producers who may be striving to take advantage of rents.

So far, we have discussed this concept of rent in relation to specific and abstract acts of innovation. But of course it has a direct bearing on the subject matter of this book. That is, the levels of income arising to any producer or country operating in the global economy will depend on the extent of rents which they command. The lower the barriers to entry and the easier it is to copy a particular activity, the lower the associated rents and incomes which are provided. For example, within the decade of the 1990s, Vietnam grew from a virtual non-producer to become the world's second largest exporter of coffee, accounting for 11 per cent of all exports in 2002. This new supply swamped the global coffee market, and bid down the incomes of coffee producers almost everywhere. Similarly, the Dominican Republic garment producer was undermined by the fact that its core activity – sewing together material – was easily copied in other firms and other countries, and hence its returns were bid away. In neither of these cases were the producers able to insulate themselves from competition, and the consequence has been widespread poverty.

3.3 Rents which are largely endogenous to the value chain

Summary: Endogenous rents

There is a category of rent which reflects the ability of firms to generate and appropriate rents by constructing or taking advantage of barriers to entry.

Some of these rents are generated within individual firms – new technologies (processes and products), specific and productive skills, new forms of organization, and design and marketing. Each of these rents may be protected by unwritten process know-how or by formal entry barriers such as trademarks, copyrights and patents.

But some rents which are endogenous to the productive sector are best created in concert with other firms. An ability to foster and operate networks to facilitate logistics, quality, design and marketing may provide individual firms, or groups of firms, with significant competitive advantage.

It was only in the mid-nineteenth century that formal processes of research and development (R&D) began as a specialized activity, and this was largely the result of the development of a science-based chemical sector.[5] Until then, improvements in technology, in machinery and in products had arisen largely out of the production process itself. Thereafter, as other industries became increasingly science based and knowledge intensive, more and more firms in more and more sectors set aside specific resources for technological development. Today, in some cases such as GlaxoSmithKline and Microsoft, annual firm-specific investments in R&D run into many billions of dollars.

This technological complexity meant that firms had to specialize, and that innovation could therefore no longer be a firm-specific agenda. Increasingly it involved other parties in the local and national arena (the 'regional' and 'national system of innovation'), including neighbouring firms, research and technology organizations (RTOs), educational establishments, service providers, business associations and government.[6] Moreover, with growing technological complexity and firm specialization, production chains became more complex and extended across national boundaries. Thus the locus of innovation also extended from the firm to the group of firms linked in global value chains or cooperating in project-specific research consortia. Another feature in the evolution of innovation is that knowledge intensity became more pervasive. Thus innovation could not be effectively pursued merely by investing in 'high science' (white-coated PhDs in laboratories), but required the systematic application of knowledge in all areas of production, including assembly.

With this evolution of innovation in mind, it is possible to distinguish five major types of Schumpeterian rents which are largely endogenous to the chain – technology rents, human resource rents, organizational rents, marketing and design rents, and relational rents. Let us consider each of these categories briefly in turn, bearing in mind that the central component of rent is its scarcity, which arises from barriers to the entry of competitors.

Technology rents

Technological rents arise when producers command scarce capabilities with regard to processes or products. A classic example of a process technology providing high rents was the discovery during the 1960s of the float glass process by the British firm Pilkington. It began in the kitchen when the inspiration behind the float glass process was doing the washing-up. He noticed that the fats floated to a film on the surface of the water, and wondered whether the same idea could not be applied to glass manufacture. By investing considerable resources in the science of this flotation, Pilkington invented a process whereby molten glass was cooled on the surface of a bed of molten tin. In doing this, Pilkington was able both to produce a superior product and to remove the costs of grinding which had previously been used to produce flat glass. This float glass process was heavily protected by patents as a barrier to entry. And while these patents lasted Pilkington was one of the most profitable UK companies, with prestigious headquarters and generous expense accounts for staff. But once the patents expired in the early 1990s, its profitability collapsed, and the headquarters had to be sold off. Pilkington has since languished as a relatively unprofitable company, vulnerable to takeover by competitors who had mastered the float technology and improved it even further.[7]

A similar story can be constructed in regard to a number of product technologies. In some cases, product technology rents are protected by property laws, such as those governing branded pharmaceuticals. When these patents expire, competitors produce generic substitutes and the innovation rents are eroded. The story of the modern pharmaceuticals sector is the continual search for new products, with even the most successful companies (those investing more than $1 billion per annum on R&D) happy if they are able to produce one or two new products a year. In other cases, product technology rents are eroded by superior products. For example, for many years the computer operating system developed by Apple was a superior product to those of its competitors, and the Apple Computer Corporation was highly profitable. But when the PC-based operating systems produced software of equivalent or superior quality, Apple's high profitability collapsed.[8] The new commander of software – Microsoft – is currently benefiting from barriers to entry in its product capabilities, although there are signs that competing products such as Linux may erode these product rents in the future.

Human resource rents

As process and product technologies become more complex, so the skill and training content in production has become increasingly demanding. From the producer's perspective, this makes demands on both generic and specific skills. In most cases, generic skills are provided by public educational systems, and this includes basic numeracy and literacy. Other generic skills are sector-specific, and are often the province of industry training boards. In many low-income countries targeting the export of garments, for example, this is reflected in training schools focusing on sewing skills. Skills which are specific to a particular firm – for example, determining the accuracy of production or speed of machine changeover – tend to be the responsibility of the firm itself.

As we shall see below and in chapter 4, recent decades have seen a revolution in manufacturing philosophy, from serial mass production to what has come to be called World Class Manufacturing. A key characteristic of this new production system is that it has altered the approach towards knowledge generation in the firm. The dominant 'Fordist' and 'Taylorist' forms of work organization which preceded

World Class Manufacturing were developed in the early twentieth century and named after Henry Ford, the architect of mass production, and Frederick Winslow Taylor, the parent of 'scientific management'. They explicitly excluded participation by shop-floor workers in technological change. One of the primary contributions of the new production paradigm developed in Japan during the 1960s and 1970s which was the forerunner of World Class Manufacturing was that it placed the detailed worker at the centre of the innovation process. As one British manager put it, 'the beauty of it is that with every pair of hands you get a free brain.' It is in this application of knowledge throughout the production chain, and at all levels of activity, that modern competitive advantage is forged.

Invariably, the higher the level of skills and training in the labour force the higher the productivity with which resources are converted into final products. But this is not the same as saying that the higher the level of skills and training, the higher the level of incomes which are sustained. This is because, if all producers utilize similarly skilled labour forces to the same effect, although productivity may be higher, there will be no human resource rents, and incomes will be bid down. These rents arise only when a producer has a *relatively* more skilled labour force than its competitors. Hence, two or three decades ago it was believed that countries and firms with a literate labour force were at an intrinsic advantage and could expect to benefit from higher living standards. Then as more and more countries invested in primary education it was believed that secondary education was the key asset. Now that countries such as China and India – with vast numbers of secondary school graduates and significant investments in industrial training programmes – have entered global production networks, it is increasingly believed that firms with tertiary-level skills will triumph. But the process of ratcheting-up continues. Human resources rents, like all rents, are intrinsically dynamic.

Organizational rents

The transition from mass production to World Class Manufacturing began in the global automobile industry. During the late 1960s and early 1970s, Japanese automobile producers accounted for a growing share of the US market. At that time the auto industry was the world's second largest economic sector, and this market penetration was of growing concern to US policy-makers and individual firms alike. The response of the US industry was to focus on technological innovation, which they saw as the key to the growing process and product competitiveness of their Japanese rivals. Between 1976 and 1985, General Motors alone invested more than $75 billion in advanced electronics-based automation technologies. At the beginning of this investment surge its market share was 44 per cent; one decade later it had fallen to 33 per cent (and it is currently less than 28 per cent).

The reason why General Motors got it wrong is because the company misread the basis of Japanese industrial strength. Although process and product technology played an important role (more for Nissan than Toyota), the key to the success of the Japanese firms lay in their development and adoption of a new form of production organization.[9] The ability which this new production system provided to slim inventories, to produce high-quality products at a low cost and with growing flexibility in product innovation and design, and to shrink time-to-market of new products laid the basis for sustained income growth. Conversely, it eroded the incomes which General Motors and other auto firms had obtained from their innovation in previous decades of mass production organization. As the US (and belatedly the European) auto firms learnt to copy this new form of production organization, so the Japanese firms were forced to ratchet up their organizational competences and to deepen the rents derived from product technologies. Those auto firms which pioneered the development of new forms of production organization (such as the satellite plant built by Ford at Camacari in the north-east of Brazil in 2003) have been able to raise profitability and will continue to benefit from this until their rivals catch up.

This change in organizational paradigm spread rapidly from the automobile industry to other sectors. New approaches to quality management made a particularly important contribution in the electronics sector, where quality was especially critical. They allowed workers to monitor their own quality during production rather than requiring specialized quality managers to inspect and rectify defects after production. The same quality procedures are now widely used across the full range of industries. Similarly, for example, just-in-time inventory control in logistics has spread to the supermarket sector, and has become the basis of the growing global competitive advantage of the UK retailer Tesco.[10] Rapid response, reflecting the transition in production control from make-to-forecast to make-to-order, dominates large parts of the garment sector, and has been the source of Dell's rush to prominence in personal computers. Cellular production, just-in-time flow control and team-based organization have even been extended to the hospital sector.[11] And the use of targets to drive continuous improvement has formed the core plank of the UK government's approach towards the delivery of a range of government services.

Thus, command over organization and logistics has become one of the most critical determinants of competitiveness across a range of sectors, and not just in manufacturing. In many respects it is the core competence required to convert comparative advantage into competitive advantage, and even where embodied complex technologies are important, such as in flexible manufacturing systems, they can be effectively utilized only in the context of the prior implementation of new organizational routines.[12] Most firms in economies subject to competition have begun to engage with this agenda of organizational change. But, because it involves changes in established patterns of personal and social behaviour, progress is both difficult and slow. Thus, considerable rents are to be found in the gap between slow and shallow and rapid and deep adopters of new organizational behaviour.

Marketing and design rents

In recent decades, design rents have become increasingly prominent. There are two major reasons for this. First, the combination of growing incomes and income inequalities has led to the increasingly prominent role of 'positional goods' in consumption baskets. (Positional goods define status as well as performing a function. For example, a Gucci belt does more than hold up a pair of trousers!) Customers want something individual and unusual, or a product which 'signifies' status, taste and exclusivity. No longer will customers accept a 'Model T Ford in any colour as long as it is black' – they now want a BMW which is built to meet a specific order, and one which will not be driven by everyone else. A second reason why design rents have become important has to do with the nature of the property rights and barriers to entry which are involved (figure 3.5 below). The patents which protect many technologies have a limited lifespan, generally between fifteen and twenty years. By contrast, copyright lasts for the lifetime of the creator plus fifty to seventy-five years (depending on the country of jurisdiction).

The durability of these product attributes does not guarantee high incomes. They require continual investment in advertising and brand support, and even these are not always successful, at least in all markets. For example, in 2002, Levi's 501 jeans were seen in the USA, as a 'commodity', selling for $26.99 at Macy's, $34.99 at JCPenney Online and $30 at a single-outlet store in Manhattan. In the UK, where 501s retain something of a premium 'positional' status, they sold at between £45 and £49.99, nearly double the US price.[13] Consequently, design rents are increasingly allied to marketing rents and investments in brand support. This is given additional impetus by the property rights which are applicable to brands – they last in perpetuity.

As we shall see below and in subsequent chapters, the relative impermeability and durability of these design and marketing rents has meant that there has been a much more significant process of globalization in production than in the indirect activities in the value chain – design, advertising, marketing.

Relational rents

'A chain is only as strong as its weakest link' is an old adage which has come to particular prominence in industrial organization in recent years. Towards the end of the 1980s, after a growing proportion of firms had begun to reorganize their internal operations and master World Class Manufacturing, there was increasing recognition that the frontier of competition lay in more effective forms of inter-firm relations. One form of inter-firm cooperation lay in horizontal networks of firms operating in the same locality. In some countries, many of these firms were relatively small and medium-sized enterprises (SMEs). Faced with the demands of growing technological complexity, but benefiting from the agility which comes with size, they began to build on local production networks, cooperating on a range of scale-intensive fronts such as marketing, purchasing and training, and drawing on specialized skills in local research and technology organizations. Such clusters of firms cooperating on a local basis were particularly prominent in Italy and Taiwan. But, on detailed investigation, they were 'discovered' in a wide range of countries, including the USA (the Hollywood film cluster and the Massachusetts and Silicon Valley electronics clusters) and Brazil (the footwear industry).[14]

A second area in which relational rents – that is, the rents which arise in *relatively* unusual synergies between firms – are found is in the vertical value chains in which firms operate. Increasingly, as technologies became more complex and firms specialized more and more, often across national boundaries, they came to realize that it was of little value to be an island of efficiency in a sea of inefficiency. If, for example, Toyota slimmed down its inventories of incoming materials to reduce working-capital costs and to promote flexibility, any gains would be eroded if its supplier made a complementary and equivalent investment in its inventory of finished goods. There would be no savings in inventories, but merely a relocation within the chain. Hence the same factors which drove organizational change within firms (see above) have increasingly come to be applied to firms with linked production in global chains. Just-in-time, total-quality-control and concurrent engineering procedures have been pushed through the whole chain, both within each link in the chain and in the relationship between the links in the chain.

In both the horizontal and vertical clusters, the competitive advantage of individual firms is relatively unimportant. The key unit of competition is the cluster or chain of firms. Here there are no formal barriers to entry to protect relational rents. These rents are constructed over time and, as we shall see in chapter 4, rely heavily on relationships of trust and governance. They are fragile and can easily be eroded. But when they do function effectively – as in the Hollywood film cluster, in Toyota's supply chain or in the production of ham in Parma in Italy – they can be the source of high and durable incomes.

3.4 Rents which are largely exogenous to the chain

Summary: Exogenous rents

A second category of rent is that which is determined outside of the corporate sector. One example of an external rent is scarce natural resources, although this is of diminishing significance in a world of increasingly synthetic and knowledge-based inputs. Effective policy design and implementation is a second example of externally generated rent, often reflected in trade policy privileges accorded to key suppliers. It is also reflected in the efficiency and cost of the infrastructure which greases production networks and of the system financing investment and production. There are, of course, other forms of rents generated outside of the corporate sector itself, including relative peace and security, effective property rights and an effective educational system.

In all of these cases, the link between the rents and sustainable income growth is to be found in relative performance. How good are natural resources compared to those of competitors? How significant is preferential market access and effective industrial policy? How does the quality and the pricing of infrastructural inputs compare with those in other countries? And how well, relatively speaking, does the financial system operate?

The rents described in the previous section are largely those which are under the control of the firm, either in its internal operations or in its relationships with other firms and the local science and technology system. Although the firms may be assisted by other parties in the pursuit of these rents, and in the construction of barriers to entry, they are essentially operating in an environment where they, or cooperating or competing firms, make the key decisions. However, there is a second category of rents in which other parties external to the firm or its competitors play the leading role. Although some of these may also be partially 'constructed' by the firm (which may exercise pressure on policy-makers, or engage in collusive activity), they cannot be classified as innovation or Schumpeterian rents in the same way as those which are endogenous to chain participants.

We discuss a number of these exogenous rents, but these are only illustrative. Others, such as relatively effective property laws, relative peace and security, and a relatively efficient educational system, reflect the same principles of differential access to scarce resources which are generally created by the purposeful actions of those outside of the corporate sector.

Resource rents

Leaving aside technological rents which reduce the costs of extraction (and where the capabilities are unevenly spread through the world), resource rents in both agricultural and commodity industries are defined by the bounty of nature. Gold, tin, copper and all other minerals are to be found at different levels, in different topographies and with differential purity. Thus countries and corporations with otherwise low-productivity production structures have been able to achieve relatively high incomes through their access to low-cost deposits. This is especially true of the Middle East hydrocarbon deposits, where the costs of uplift are much lower than those of marginal producers in other parts of the world such as the North Sea. It is the high extraction cost of the marginal producer which sets the world price for oil. The difference between these extraction costs accrues as a resource rent, split to varying degrees between host countries and oil companies.

But constraints on resource availability are not always a bounty of nature – that is, absolute constraints on supply. They can also be artificially induced by a cartel of producers. Although this has often been the case in oil, because of its longevity, the most striking case of this resource rent is the diamond-selling cartel, in which the De Beers Corporation organized a central selling office for diamonds for many years. This limited the quantity of diamonds put on the market, and allowed not just South Africa to sustain a relatively high level of income, but also other cartel-member countries such as Botswana and Russia. Indeed, Botswana was one of the most rapidly growing economies in the world between the 1970s and 2000, despite having virtually no industry and particularly poor agricultural land. This was almost entirely due to its deposits of low-cost, high-quality diamonds and the workings of the diamond cartel.

Despite their fragility (see below), resource rents have been an important determinant of the global distribution of income. The most notable examples are oil-dependent exporters in the Gulf. But many other countries gain from the exploitation of scarce natural resources, including 'industrialized' economies such as those of the USA, Canada and Australia. Where the industrialized countries differ is that they have been able to augment natural resource rents through Schumpeterian innovation rents, and to extend their operations along the value chain to undertake downstream processing activities. For example, the development of hybrid maize in the USA during the 1930s transformed the productivity of the Midwest land resource. Similarly, while the Gulf States extract oil, high-productivity extracting economies such as the USA and the UK have more developed hydrocarbon-based processing activities; India and South Africa are large producers of aluminium (where the primary 'resource' is in fact energy rather than bauxite), but Canada and the USA complement their aluminium production more effectively with the production of aluminium products; Brazil and South Africa produce pulp, but Finland and Sweden not only export pulp, but also manufacture paper-making machinery.

Policy rents

Policy rents arise from differential access resulting from government policies. By creating barriers to entry, these rents may affect the distribution of income within countries (with particular groups gaining disproportionately from the policy regime) or between countries (with producers in different countries benefiting from privileged access to efficient policy regimes).

It is currently not fashionable to acknowledge the competitive advantages which arise from policy rents, particularly in low-income economies. This is because, during the 1950s, 1960s and 1970s, many low-income economies promoted industrialization through the regulation and licensing of industry. In some cases, these policies led to a variety of inefficiencies and inequities, and to corruption. Consequently, they were subjected to both an intellectual onslaught (the literature on 'rent seeking' behaviour)[15] and what might be termed a 'policy onslaught' by the international financial institutions such as the World Bank, the IMF and the WTO. However, there is persuasive evidence that governments have indeed played a key role in the rapid externally oriented growth achieved in Japan, Korea, Taiwan, Singapore and Malaysia, and South Africa.[16] They have done this through a combination of measures which have promoted technological development and education and skills, provided effective infrastructure, facilitated 'national champions' and aided the external expansion of industry. The amazing success of the Chinese economy over the past decade has reflected a range of policy-induced rents, arising not just from national-level policies, but also from province- and district-level government. Efficient government – that is, *relatively* efficient government – offers much to aid the competitive advantage of producers.

In the international arena, trade policy rents are probably the most significant form of policy rent affecting the global distribution of income. For many countries, trade policy substituted for industrial policy, particularly as deregulation and liberalization were pushed through the developing world during the 1980s and 1990s. But, as we saw in chapter 1, this form of policy rent has come under pressure, and there has been a general trend towards lowering international tariffs. Nevertheless, many low-income countries continue to gain from preferential access to external markets. In some sectors, as we will see in chapter 5, this has played, and continues to play, an important role in the incidence of global poverty.

The experience of those countries that have taken greatest advantage of these various forms of trade policy rents to generate sustainable income growth has been that this ability is fostered by having a flexible productive system, capable not only of upgrading the unit value of exports within individual sectors, but of redefining product specifications as trade preferences reach their limit or change their nature. Yoffie gives a number of examples of the flexibility of East Asian producers in taking advantage of changing trade policy rents during the early period of export-oriented growth.[17] For example, in the 1970s, Hong Kong producers had exceeded their import quota limits into the USA on coats, but not on vests or apparel components. A fashion was thus deliberately created of jackets that had zipped sleeves and collars. This allowed the Hong Kong producers to continue to ship 'vests' and 'components' (sleeves and collars), and to assemble these rapidly in the USA prior to sale. Another form of corporate response to trade policy rents, of increasing importance in those sectors still governed by quota access in major markets (such as apparel), was what Gereffi has termed 'triangular manufacturing'. Agile producers in countries which had exhausted available quotas for their exports to the USA and Europe acted as entrepreneurs and intermediaries to global buyers by nurturing and expanding production in countries whose quotas had not been taken up.[18]

Infrastructural rents

The reaping of competitive advantage by individual firms or by groups of firms is significantly affected by the availability of suitable infrastructure. With the onset of the industrial revolution, transport became a primary infrastructural input. Adam Smith observed that the division of labour (which provided scope for substantial productivity improvements) was limited by the extent of the market. Producers who had the ability to penetrate distant markets therefore found themselves at an increasing competitive advantage. So, from the onset of the industrial revolution, there has been a strong link between corporate growth and profitability and the physical infrastructure that has provided access to markets.

The importance of access is not limited to product markets, but also applies to factor and input markets, reflecting the ability of producers to bring suitable inputs (raw materials, components and also labour) to the site of production at low cost and with reliability. In earlier generations of the industrial revolution, a key infrastructural driver of globalization was the reduction in shipping costs. More recently, in the post-1945 global economy, low-cost air travel has had a significant impact in lowering the costs of transporting not just physical materials, but also the skilled professionals who coordinate global production networks and buyers who scour the world for new sources of supply. A key component in this evolving transport infrastructure has been the role played by energy – initially steam in the case of the nineteenth-century railroads, and then hydrocarbons to fuel the internal combustion engine in the twentieth century.

In recent decades, technology has increasingly become disembodied and located in tacit knowledge in individuals (that is, in human resource rents) and in organizational and relational rents. The ability to communicate relatively effectively and relatively cheaply has become important. This is a reflection not just of the reduced costs of air transport, but also of very significant advances in telecommunications and information-processing technologies. But energy and information-processing and switching technologies are not the only infrastructures that influence the efficiency of production systems. Clean water (important in the electronics sector) and an unpolluted environment are also important constituents of effective production, as well as being incentives that help to keep highly skilled staff. So too are reliable and low-cost energy supplies.

Many infrastructural services are public goods, that is, access cannot be restricted and in general they are not used up in the process of consumption. For this reason, they are generally difficult to appropriate, and there is thus a reduced incentive for individual firms to invest in their production. Moreover, many infrastructural services also have significant spillovers (for example, through pollution), and this too is a further reason why there may be a divergence between private and social benefit. It is for these reasons that governments have historically come to play an important role in the provision of infrastructure.[19] It is also one reason why countries display different endowments of infrastructure, as is reflected by the indicators of infrastructure in table 3.2. Thus the ability of a firm, or a group of firms, to compete in global markets is to a significant extent enhanced by the quality of national infrastructure. Since this infrastructure is unevenly spread through the global economy, it provides a form of rent to those firms operating in infrastructure-rich environments. It is significant that the disparities in national availability are higher for those forms of infrastructure that are particularly important in the latter part of the twentieth century (the Internet) than for those that were important in the earlier decades of the century (energy) (table 3.2).

Financial rents

There is a large body of evidence that suggests that access to finance has been a significant component of economic success in many parts of

Table 3.2   Some indicators of the per capita global distribution of infrastructure (in ascending order of per capita incomes), 2000

Ranking of per capita income (lowest to highest)	Commercial energy use (kg of oil equivalent per capita) (2000)	Internet users per thousand (2002)
Argentina	57,601	112
Brazil	185,083	82
Chile	23,801	238
Costa Rica	3,481	193
India	531,453	16
Kenya	15,377	13
Malaysia	51,608	320
Nigeria	95,444	3
South Africa	107,738	68
Zimbabwe	9,882	43
France	265,570	314
Italy	171,998	352
United Kingdom	235,158	423
United States	2,281,414	551

Source: World Bank (2004)

the global economy. This is partly a reflection of the quantum of finance available to spur innovation. Analyses of the experience of the East Asian newly industrialized countries suggest that a key part of their competitive performance has been their high savings and invest-ment ratios. In fact, some observers believe that it is these high savings rather than the increase in productivity that explain their rapid growth.[20] But the key to their success lies not just in their relatively high savings rate and hence the quantum of finance available for investment, but also in the terms on which that finance is made available to the pro-ductive sector. There is a strong correlation between indicators of effective financial intermediation and economic growth.[21]

A number of factors are important here. The first is the quality of the system of financial intermediation. An efficient financial services sector reduces the cost of providing funds to borrowers. The second is the terms on which finance is made available. This is a function both of the costs of the loan and of the conditions on which it is provided. For example, in areas of new technology such as biotechnology and electronics, financial intermediation needs to have a venture capital facility. For, although stock markets have an important role to play in providing finance, as the experience of the UK shows, the short-termism and risk-aversion of much of this finance militates against the reaping of technological and other forms of rent that have relatively long gestation periods. Another important feature of the banking system is the extent to which it provides development finance to rescue ailing firms and innovators rather than to liquidate them in times of difficulty. Here, historically at any rate, the Japanese and German banking systems seem to have played a different role to those in the Anglo-Saxon economies.[22] Finally, effective financial systems need to be insulated against volatility. In many countries in recent years growth has been plagued by sudden and significant outflows of funds.[23]

Thus, innovators who obtain access to relatively low-cost funds, to funds that have a relatively long maturity period, to funds with undemanding security requirements and to stable funds are clearly advantaged. As in the case of all other areas of rent, it is the relative rather than the absolute performance of the financial system which promotes sustainable income growth. How well does the financial system perform compared to those in competitor countries?

3.5 Barriers to entry in endogenous rents

Summary: Barriers to entry

Various types of barriers to entry exist to enable innovators to protect themselves from competition and to sustain their incomes. Most of these apply to the endogenous category of rents. While some of these entry barriers are informal – that is, they are not registered – most are formal and exist as forms of intellectual property rights.

These property rights include patents, copyrights, design registration, trademarks, brand names and geographical indicators. They have varying lives, ranging from ten years in the case of some trademarks to perpetuity in the case of brand names.

As we have seen, both the existence of rents and the ability to appropriate rents arise from the existence of barriers to entry. There are a variety of different forms of barriers to entry, almost all of which are constructed through purposeful action. The exception here are the barriers to entry which result from natural resource scarcity, although, as we have seen, these are seldom absolute and are generally of diminishing significance. Most of these barriers to entry protect the endogenous categories of rents, since those created as acts of public policy (policy rents, infrastructure, financial intermediation and so on) are not really subject to protection.

There are essentially two forms of socially created barriers (figure 3.5). The first of these are those which are not legally codified, that is, trade secrets. This applies to much process technology, where the act of registering a patent would provide potential competitors with the knowledge required to replicate the invention. But it applies not only to processes of manufacture. For example, the formulations of a number of drinks (such as Coca-Cola and Drambuie) and perfumes are locked away in a safe to which only a limited number of people have access. The extent and degree of this non-registered process and product technology vary between sectors and over time. But in general it is a minor form of entry barrier and one which, from the perspective of the innovator, is sub-optimal.

The other category of property rights are those which are subject to formal registration and hence to legal protection. The main types of intellectual property rights are as follows. *Patents* apply to production processes and to products. They are usually granted for twenty years, providing a temporary monopoly to an inventor. In some cases, where there is a significant public interest or where a patent remains unexploited, the property rights can be overriden and access can be

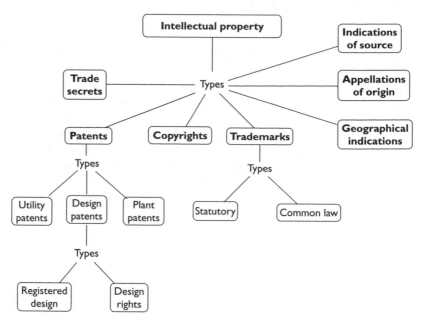

Figure 3.5 Differential forms of property rights

Source: Adapted from Ulrich and Eppinger (2003), Tidd et al. (2001) and Bugliarello (1999) by Santiago Acosta-Maya

granted to competitors. But this is an unusual event. More durable are *copyrights*, which protect the expression of ideas but not the ideas themselves, and in which the holder must have used their own skills and effort to create the work. The length of copyright varies. For literary, dramatic, musical and artistic works a copyright is normally valid for seventy years after the death of the author (fifty years in the USA), and for recordings, film and broadcast and cable programmes it generally lasts for fifty years from the creation of the work. *Design registration* is an amalgam between copyrights and patents, covering the visual and aesthetic appearance of an artefact, and lasts for twenty-five years. *Trademarks* distinguish one supplier's products from those of another and tend to have a limited life, whereas *brand names* exist in perpetuity as long as registration is maintained. Finally, a form of intellectual property of relatively recent significance are the various forms of *geographical indicators* which have been introduced. These protect the locational and cultural identity of a product and have been increasingly widely used to protect various types of agricultural products such as champagne (only from the Champagne Valley in France; for everyone else it is 'sparkling wine') and port (from Portugal; for everyone else it is 'fortified wine').

A further entry barrier is one of scale. The minimum resources required to enter a new product line or to produce a new product may be so substantial that, *de facto*, new entrants are excluded. An example of this would be the millions of lines of code in state-of-the-art microprocessors or application software. This is a reflection of both absolute scale and cumulative investments. Even if a new entrant had the resources to compete with Intel or Microsoft, it would require a number of generations of trial and error before the potential competitors could reach the technological frontier. It is not surprising that incomes in these sectors are high and have been sustained over a substantial period of time. They are very difficult, but not impossible, to erode, as IBM found to its discomfort at an earlier point in the personal computer's evolution.

3.6 Rents are cumulative and dynamic

Summary: Rents are cumulative and dynamic

Although rents provide a source of sustainable incomes, they are not easily constructed. They cannot be plucked from a textbook manual. Firms which achieve rents generally do so on the basis of lengthy and sustained investments. This means not only that rents are cumulative – investments in new technology build on past investments – but also that they have trajectories. Firms are thus oriented in particular paths, and this orientation constitutes a screen which constrains the technological opportunities that the firm can grasp effectively.

In addition rents are dynamic. They are invariably eroded by competition and when property rights such as patents expire.

The associated concepts of rent and barriers to entry are thus important analytical tools in understanding the determinants of income distribution in production. Their importance arises not just in terms of 'positive' analysis (that is, explaining *why* things are as they are), but also when applied as 'normative' tools (that is, *how* can the existing order be changed?). In this latter regard there are two features to rent which are particularly important – rents are cumulative, and rents are dynamic.

Consider, first, the cumulative nature of rents. At the beginning of the 1980s, the total global market for computer-aided design (CAD) equipment was $100 million. It was widely (and correctly) believed then that this market would grow to more than $4 billion by the end of the decade. The largest CAD firm at that time was Computervision, with a turnover of $70 million. Its CEO was asked whether, in the light of this major market opportunity, he was worried that firms such as General Electric, with a post-tax profit figure of more than $1 billion, would see this market opportunity and seize it. His response was, 'You can't make a baby in one month with nine women.'[24] As it turned out, although he was too sanguine about Computervision's ability to ride out competition (as its technological rents were eroded), his judgement about the cumulative and sequential nature of innovation rents was correct, and the new winners came from closely related sectors. Thus, a primary characteristic of many barriers to entry – particularly in innovation rents, but also in infrastructural and finance rents – is the trajectory and path-dependency of individual firms and of groups of firms. This is true whether they operate as part of a local cluster or are imbedded in a particular global value chain.

The second important feature of rents and barriers to entry is their dynamic nature. As we saw above, the transitory nature of rents was an explicit component of Schumpeter's innovation model. Table 3.3 gives examples of how primary areas of rent have shifted in each of

Table 3.3 Examples of shifting rents

Type of rent	Previous areas of rent	New and emerging areas of rent
	Endogenous rents	
Technology	Copy lathes	Computer-aided design, electronic data interchange and flexible manufacturing systems
	Internal combustion engines	Fuel cells
Human resources	Toolmaking artisans	Software engineers
Organizational	Mass production, quality inspectors	Single-unit flow, quality-at-source
Marketing/design	Levi Strauss	Diesel, Earle, The Gap
Relational	Short-term arms-length suppliers	Long-term suppliers, obligational relationships, supply-chain development
	Exogenous rents	
Resources	High-grade copper deposits	High-grade platinum deposits
Policy	Support for plant efficiency	Promotion of value chain efficiency and industrial clusters
	Import protection	Export marketing support
Infrastructure	Roads and railways	Telecommunications
Finance	Low interest rates	Venture capital

the domains discussed in the previous section. Each of these areas of rent is dynamic, both within categories (as in table 3.2) and between categories. In this latter regard, we are witnessing an important shift – the barriers to entry in some categories are increasingly falling and competitive pressures are growing. For example, those rents which are based upon natural endowments are being eroded by technological progress. This is partly because new deposits are generally found for most materials (stimulated by high resource rents) and partly as a result of the development of synthetic substitutes. One of the most striking examples of the development of new sources has been the maturation of technologies to make it feasible to mine small deposits of gold productively. This has opened up gold exploitation in Asia and in Latin America to the cost of the large-scale South African producers. Synthetic substitution has eroded resource rents in a large number of products, most notably in the case of rubber, where the synthetic product displaced production of the natural, climate-specific product. A further source of instability in resource rents arises from the fragility of sellers' cartels. The diamond cartel is a somewhat unusual case of enduring cooperation. But it is counterposed by the declining success of OPEC and the International Coffee Organization (ICO) and the rapid death of CIPEC (the copper producers' attempt at cartelization).

A second type of rent which is being eroded is policy rents. Global political pressures are growing against industrial policies designed to promote the development of Schumpeterian rents in the private sector. Governments are no longer permitted to provide a range of subsidies and other forms of support which facilitated industrial growth in previous eras.[25] Similarly, despite the setback experienced at Cancun in 2003, the remaining quota and tariff barriers governing world trade are being reduced through multilateral negotiations promoted by the World Trade Organization. But it is a complex agenda, which simultaneously reduces trade barriers and changes the incidence of preferential agreements. For example, the USA has drawn Mexico, Canada and an increasing number of Latin American economies into preferential agreements. It has also established a preferential system favouring the import of manufactured products from Africa through the African Growth and Opportunities Act (AGOA). The European Union has not only widened its membership, but has been systematically engaged in bilateral free-trade agreements with individual countries in Africa and elsewhere, as well as providing preferential market access to a group of low-income economies (the Cotonou Agreement). These various agreements have not only lowered the extent of trade policy rents, but have also changed the distribution of potential beneficiaries. As we shall see in chapter 4, there is increasing evidence that a new form of trade barrier – certification – is flourishing, for example, in the form of ISO9000 quality standards, ISO14000 environmental standards and labour standards. But, unlike the trade barriers of the previous generation, these are erected not by public bodies (such as governments), but by firms in the private sector as an integral part of their global operations.

At the same time, new forms of rent are becoming pervasive. In all product groups the importance of intangible activities and elements in value chains is increasing. This is represented by a shift of costs and rents from the transformation of tangible goods. Thus, just as barriers to entry in manufacturing are falling, so barriers to entry in brand names and marketing are increasing. Similarly, while the capability physically to transform materials into outputs is diffusing (for example, sewing of clothes or manufacture of furniture), the increasingly sophisticated optimization of inventories and logistics is providing greater power to systems integrators (such as The Gap and IKEA).

3.7   Towards the effective management of innovation

We have seen, therefore, that merely participating in the global economy is replete with dangers – it can easily result in diminishing incomes and be a source of poverty and inequality. It is also clear in principle what needs to be achieved if producers are to participate in global markets in a way that provides for sustainable income growth. In brief, they are required to escape the pressures of competition by adopting a number of overlapping but related strategies: identifying pockets of activity which benefit from barriers to entry; learning how to leap over the barriers constructed by rivals; generating new barriers to entry (notably through innovation); and doing so on a dynamic basis. Although these entry barriers may be 'gifts of nature', more often they are 'constructed', either within the production chain itself or by actors external to the chain (notably governments providing a range of public goods designed to assist the productive sector).

To some extent this involves the development of what Schumpeter called 'new combinations', the introduction of new products or new processes which confer a competitive advantage over rivals. This is an agenda which faces those firms operating at the frontier of technology, ranging from the Microsofts of the world to innovative engineering firms in Japan and Germany. How can they protect their historic competitive advantage in the face of capability growth by new entrants? But, for other firms in the global economy engaged in catch-up, the challenge is not so much to push the innovative frontier forward as successfully to copy the performance of the existing leaders.

Both types of firms are involved in innovation – the former in the sense of introducing fundamentally new processes and products, the latter in the sense of introducing processes and products which are new to them. Either way the agenda is similar. But the real challenge is to translate these objectives into practice, to develop effective processes of innovation management. How to accomplish this is the subject matter of chapter 4. But so, too, is the associated issue of how, once they have developed the capacity to manage their innovative processes effectively, producers connect to distant final markets.

4

Managing Innovation and Connecting to Final Markets

My father was born soon after the turn of the twentieth century in a small town in what was then Poland. During the 1914–18 war, the town was overrun first by the Germans and then by the Russians. In each case his 'nationality' changed, as did his textbooks and 'mother tongue'. After 1918 the town once again became part of Poland, and after the Second World War, it was incorporated in the Soviet Union. It is now deep in Belarus!

The growth of anti-Semitism during the 1920s and 1930s led to the global exodus of many Jews from Central and Eastern Europe. Those who, unlike my father, did not migrate perished in the Holocaust. In my father's case, this meant both his parents, four of his siblings and most of his extended family. (As the first grandchild born after the war, I was given the name of my father's father and a derivative of his mother's name, a 'responsibility' which perhaps partly explains my political activism.) My father chose to migrate to South Africa. At first he earned his living as a trader and petrol-station manager. But he had a pride in manufacturing and longed to start his own business. Soon after the end of the Second World War he established his rope-making factory, continuing a family tradition, and using the same labour-intensive rope-walks which his father and grandfather had used in Poland from at least the latter half of the nineteenth century. This was a primitive technology, made viable by the fact that he could draw on the labour of young teenagers, paying them very low wages. Labour was in unlimited supply. Some years after, he began to diversify his product range and to make nets for the thriving local fishing industry. This was a new product and required new skills. This change was made possible by the availability of a pool of low-paid dextrous female workers.

The combination of this product range and labour-intensive process technologies served him well until the end of the 1950s. But by the beginning of the 1960s, there was a process of consolidation in the fishing industry. Line-based artisanal fishing could not tap deeper waters, which required trawlers and large fishing nets. This, in turn, led to a growth in ownership concentration in fishing and to more powerful and demanding buyers. These buyers began to pressure my father to change the technology which he was using, both in the manufacture of twine and in the manufacture of nets. He was forced to innovate.

In the context of modern economies these changes might not seem to involve such a big jump. However, for my father, drawing on family artisanal skills and used to the cosy life of undemanding customers, the jump was insuperable. At great cost he imported mechanized net-making technology from Finland. Unable to make it work effectively, he obtained the services of a Finnish technician for a short while. But the innovation challenge proved to be too daunting – he had to find a new way to talk to his customers, he had to introduce new products and he had to use radically new processes. And, if that were not enough, he could no longer draw on the artisanal expertise of his low-paid labour force. They, too, were incapable of meeting the requirements of this new business challenge. The business was bankrupted in the mid-1960s, two decades after it was started. One hundred people lost their jobs.

This personalized microcosm of a single business throws into perspective many of the challenges which businesses face when competing in the global economy. They are confronted with new and different buyers. They are required to introduce new products and to do so by utilizing new processing technologies. And they need to develop a new way of working, not just with their existing labour forces, but often by recruiting new and different skills. In the economic environments of low-income countries previously characterized by low levels of competition, these challenges are the more daunting.

In this chapter we review these business challenges, drawing on the experience of firms in many countries, and referencing this to the literatures on business strategy, innovation management and production engineering. The point of this discussion is to address the issues raised in the two previous chapters. In chapter 2 we rejected the simple notion that the gains from globalization were automatic. Reaping these gains, it was argued, depended on how producers inserted themselves into the global economy. In chapter 3 we showed that sustained income growth depended on developing the capability to stay ahead of the pack, to generate and/or appropriate rents. Unless this dynamic capability can be endogenized into the production system, participating in intensively competitive global markets is unlikely to provide sustainable incomes. More likely they will lead either to bankruptcy and closure (as in the case of my father) or to reduced incomes (as in the case of the Dominican Republic clothing manufacturers described in chapter 3). We focus in this chapter on the innovation challenge characterized by what we termed 'endogenous rents', that is, those largely within the grasp of the private sector itself.

In pursuit of this objective, we will consider two main issues. The first can be grouped broadly under the heading of innovation management, beginning in section 4.1 with the sets of activities which individual firms have to accomplish if they are to appropriate the endogenous rents described in chapter 3. However, as we saw in chapter 3, the innovation frontier has moved from the firm to the network of firms. Thus section 4.2 addresses the management of innovation in horizontal local clusters and section 4.3 the management of innovation in vertical value chains. Arising from the value chain perspective is a framework for the management of strategic positioning – referred to as the challenge of upgrading – and this is discussed in section 4.4.

The second main issue which helps to explain how global production networks feed into an understanding of global poverty patterns is the role played by global buyers (section 4.5). Not only do they link producers to distant markets, but they actively search out new sources of supply and play an important role in fostering, shaping and limiting innovation management in producing countries.

4.1   Managing innovation in the firm

Summary: Managing innovation in the firm

Managing innovation requires attention to eight interrelated components of firm-level activity. These are:

- understanding the need to change
- 'hearing' the specific needs of markets and market segments
- appropriately assessing core competences
- developing a business strategy which links competences to market opportunities

- deciding and implementing a product strategy
- deciding and implementing a manufacturing strategy
- deciding and implementing a human resource strategy
- developing the capacity to implement change rapidly and effectively.

Generating and appropriating the endogenous rents described in the previous chapter requires that the firm should begin by setting its own house in order before it moves to take advantage of relational rents through collaboration with other firms and institutions in the regional, national and global systems of innovation. The firm needs to understand the markets in which it operates, and then to determine what it has that is special and that protects it from competition. Figure 4.1 provides a framework for this strategic focus on the determinants of firm-level competitiveness. This schema is drawn from the experience of many firms making the transition from mass production to World Class Manufacturing (sometimes referred to as lean production, post-Fordism, flexible specialization or mass customization).[1]

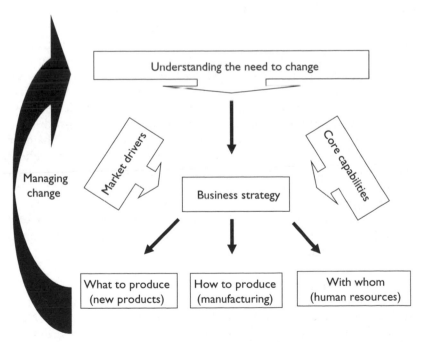

Figure 4.1   A framework for achieving competitive advantage at the firm level

As can be seen from figure 4.1, achieving firm-level competitiveness requires the firm to engage in eight key strategic activities.

1) Understanding the need to change

It may not sound believable, but many firms do not understand the need for change and innovation. In some cases this may be a function of limited capabilities, that the entrepreneur (or collective management) lacks the intellectual and professional capacity to recognize the underlying dynamic determinants of competitiveness. Such firms are unlikely to survive. In other cases, where a firm possesses a durable and absolute advantage over competitors, there may be no need for change. But, as we saw in the preceding chapter, this is true for only a small minority of firms. More typical are those cases where the firm does not adequately recognize either the need to innovate or the particular reasons which guide innovation in appropriate directions.

This latter weakness can be evidenced very widely through the world economy. Kodak, for example, recognized only belatedly that the future of photography lay in digital imagery and has been a relatively late participant in this new technological segment; Polaroid, before it, missed the boat completely and no longer survives. Similarly, historically the dominant clothing retailer in the UK was Marks and Spencer. It failed to foresee the growing importance of small-batch fashion goods and positional consumption, and has witnessed a rapid erosion of its once-dominant position. But it is in developing countries that the inability to scan the environment has been most damaging to corporate survival. Many firms in these economies had long been accustomed to a cosy protected environment characterized by shortages. The opening-up of their markets to international suppliers, producing higher quality and more differentiated products at lower prices, left many of these producers unprotected, and the mortality rate of firms has been high. They were able to comprehend neither the drivers of change (global pressure on national governments) nor the nature of the new competition (World Class Manufacturers).

Hence the route to successful innovation management begins with the ability to scan the external environment, to foresee disruptive forces, and to understand their nature.

2) Understanding the market

Once the need for change has been recognized, the challenge is for the firm to understand its market and meet the minimum needs of customers – for example, minimum prices and quality levels, delivery schedules and so on. These are referred to as the 'order-qualifying' characteristics. But the extra features that sustain high incomes are those which persuade customers to pay that little bit extra to buy the product (the 'order-winning characteristics'). In meeting this agenda, firms are required to recognize that modern markets are characterized by two key features. The first is that they consist of an increasing number of segments. Few products sell well, or at a premium, if they aim to satisfy everyone's needs. Secondly, contemporary global markets are increasingly volatile.

The interaction between market segmentation and market volatility means that firms have to cope with a rapidly moving agenda in their final markets. In each of these segments, customers have particular preferences ('critical success factors'). For example, purchasers of Gucci clothes require not only high quality but also exclusivity – ideally they would not want to be seen in the same city, let alone the same room, as someone else wearing the same clothes! By comparison, Walmart's customers require low prices, and are less concerned with exclusivity. But these critical success factors are themselves volatile, and change over time. What was order-winning (for example, quality) becomes order-qualifying, and new order-winning critical success factors emerge (for example, variety, or the rapid introduction of new products).[2]

Understanding and meeting these market needs is essential for profitable production. The problem for producers in poor countries, particularly those which have been insulated from competition for some time, is that they have only a poor capacity to 'hear' these market needs, and often lack the discerning customers domestically who could educate them about the needs of consumers in external global markets. Buyers, as we shall see, therefore become a major conduit for producers to understand the needs of their final customers.

3) Identifying core competences

If all firms have the same capabilities, there are no rents to be earned and incomes will be bid down, or the firm will go out of business. This was the lesson of the analytical framework presented in the previous chapter. It is only when a firm has developed distinctive competences that it is able to escape from these competitive pressures. Three features of core competences allow rents to be appropriated.[3] The first is that they must be distinctive, something which is unique to the firm or a small number of firms. Second, the competences must be of value to the customer – this sounds obvious, but it is a lesson which many firms manage to forget, investing significant resources in developing a capability which earns little premium in the market. And, thirdly, they must be difficult to copy. Without some forms of barrier to entry – which may, as we saw in chapter 3, be legally defined (copy-rights, patents) or processes or skills that are difficult to copy – competitors will be able to take advantage of the new market opportunities which have been identified.

As with an understanding of the market, competences need to be fluid and the emphasis must be placed on dynamic capabilities.[4] What was unique becomes more common with the passage of time; what was attractive to the customer becomes less appealing as new order-winning features are introduced by customers. At the same time as some existing competences are being strengthened and new competences are being built, there is the need for firms to jettison what have become 'core-rigidities', historic competences which stand in the way of dynamic competitive advantage.[5]

4) Defining an appropriate business strategy

It is no use identifying profitable market opportunities if the firm is unable to serve these because it lacks the necessary competences; conversely, what is the use of distinctive competences that are difficult to copy if they do not meet a profitable market need? Hence a basic task for any firm is to be systematic about its capacity to absorb the determinants of change, to 'hear' the critical success factors in its increasingly external markets, and to have a realistic inventory of its distinctive core competences. Business strategy arises in this interface between the determinants of change, market needs and firm competences. And it is the resulting business strategy which allows the firm to decide *what* to produce, *how* to produce it, and with which *human resources*.

5) Defining a product strategy

The dynamic nature of most final markets requires a firm's capability to upgrade product offerings. In some cases this may mean producing wholly new products, but more often it involves frequent changes to an existing product family and/or offering many product varieties.

Effective product development arises from a combination of hardware (for example, computer-aided design) and new and appropriate forms of organization. However, it is the new forms of organization that have had a major effect in facilitating product development. Moreover, because of the difficulty in managing these product development processes, they have become significant barriers to the entry of competitors. These include developing cross-functional teams which cover the range of a business's functions (for example, marketing, production, logistics, procurement) rather than confining product development to specialized teams of designers. Such cross-functional teams may be 'lightweight' and subject to decisions made by senior management, or 'heavyweight' with a large measure of autonomy. The appropriateness of these different types of team will depend on the nature of the product development process in question: *derivative projects* involve small changes to existing products or systems; *breakthrough projects* create new markets or products and require significant resources and a strategic view; *platform projects* target significant incremental improvements but are still linked to some basic platform; *R&D projects* are future-oriented, and speculative, but explore where the company might be in five years or more; and complex products require *alliances* with subsidiaries and often even with other companies.[6]

6) Defining a manufacturing strategy

As we have seen in preceding discussion, the past three decades have witnessed a revolution in thinking about optimal manufacturing strategy. From the onset of the twentieth century until the early 1980s there was a single and dominant perspective on what constituted 'best practice'. This was a focus on mass production, involving the standardization of the final product, the development of special purpose, scale-intensive machinery, and the use of a hierarchical and specialized labour force. As this system was implemented, it provided for significant cost-reducing economies of scale and fuelled the development of industrialization, not just in the historically industrialized countries of Europe and North America, but in Eastern Europe and the developing world as well.[7]

But mass production ran out of steam. On the one hand, increasingly discerning customers no longer wanted standardized products; they wanted the variety, the quality and the product innovation which we have described above. On the other hand, the production process itself became overwhelmed by its inventories, poor quality, and bad work relations. So, mass production has come to be superseded by a new form of industrial best practice – World Class Manufacturing.

World Class Manufacturing is characterized by a number of central organizational principles, predominantly affecting products manufactured as individual units, such as automobiles, garments, shoes, toys and computers. (Products resulting from process-oriented technologies such as chemicals and beverages also benefit from these principles of World Class Manufacturing, but to a different degree and in different ways.) Foremost, the new system strives to produce to customer orders, rather than to forecasts of customer orders. Bearing in mind the fragmentation and volatility of markets, this requires the capacity to produce with flexibility. In turn this demands that inventories be kept low – just-in-time rather than just-in-case – and this can be achieved only through high levels of component quality. High quality is achieved by making all workers responsible for quality at source, generally requiring the introduction of quality teams. But the pervasiveness of teams is also related to the objective of speeding up change through the introduction of continuous improvement programmes, involving all of the workforce in a programme of incremental improvements to process and product. Structural changes are also required in plant layout and production flow. Instead of shipping large batches of semi-finished products between functionally specialized divisions on the shop floor, work in progress flows as single units (or in small batches) between newly laid-out production cells, each of which incorporates a variety of different types of equipment.[8]

Once these changes have been introduced – but only after they have been established – it will make sense to introduce sophisticated electronics-based automation technologies. Although these have the potential to enable manufacturing of great precision and flexibility, their effective use depends on prior changes in manufacturing organization.

7) Defining a human resource strategy

The transition from mass production to World Class Manufacturing has been associated with a major transition in the way human resources are developed and integrated into the production process. The demand for flexibility of output requires a change in the division of labour. This can be achieved only if workers perform a number of different tasks, that is, if they become multi-taskers. In turn, this requires that workers need to absorb a number of different capabilities, that they become multi-skilled. Teams become more important and (as we saw in the case of product development) are increasingly cross-functional, drawn from a variety of divisions of the firm. But teams are also an important component of continuous improvement programmes, so workers are required to develop a combination of analytical and communication skills (including, for example, making presentations to groups of fellow workers and management). All of this increasingly requires not just a basic level of numeracy and literacy, but often also a depth of education. In most firms producing for global markets, therefore, even in low-income countries such as China and India, new recruits to the labour force are required to have some years of secondary education as a minimum requirement.

But, perhaps most controversial and important, the basis of authority and hierarchy in work organization has changed. The old command-and-control structure has had to give way to a much more participative style of management. This is especially important given the need to take advantage of the potential offered by routines promoting continuous improvement in which competitive production is enhanced through the accretion of very many minor changes introduced by detailed workers.

8) Implementing change
The business world is awash with intelligent strategies – whether these be business, product, manufacturing or human resource strategies. But implementation is a different story, and this is a challenge which requires heavy investment in people, the development of trust relations, processes of continuous improvement, and changes in organizational structures. The steps required for effective change management are clear and well known: commitment from top management; the involvement of the workforce in the design and implementation of change; providing the workforce with the necessary skills; the introduction of appropriate reward systems; and the development of the security and trust which encourages the workforce to engage constructively with the process of change. But the reality is much more complex, not least because change inevitably requires the jettisoning of the core rigidities described above and what we might term an adjustment in the 'politics of production'. It would not be far wrong to conclude that the key to the reaping of firm-level rents, particularly in a dynamic world, lies in the effective management of change.

These eight challenges define the internal competitiveness of firms in the global economy. This agenda of intra-firm change emerged over the last three decades of the twentieth century, influenced in large part by the development of new production systems in Japan. From the perspective of the 'catch-up' of American and European firms, the major mileage had been covered by the early 1990s and has been extensively documented.[9] It was then that it increasingly came to be realized that a chain was only as strong as its weakest link – that is, that improvement by individual firms was a necessary but by no means sufficient step in 'making globalization pay'. Individual firms were imbedded in networks of firms, and it is in this networked interrelationship that sustainably profitable production lies. An important type of network is that which is clustered in a particular location, an agenda of innovation management which we will now consider.

4.2 Managing innovation in local clusters

Summary: Managing innovation in local clusters

In many parts of the world and in many sectors, firms achieve competitive advantage by virtue of their links with local actors. This arises from three characteristics of well-developed clusters.

- They involve spillovers between firms in a locality.
- Firms often engage in joint actions, such as in marketing, purchasing and training.
- Firms engage with other institutions in the local economy, including research and technology organizations, service providers and local governments.

Writing in the second half of the nineteenth century, the influential economist Alfred Marshall pointed to the economic significance of clusters (which he termed 'industrial districts'). He had in mind the sectorally clustered activities in the Midlands, at the heart of Britain's industrial revolution. But for the following century the importance of these clusters was largely overlooked, not just in academic discourse but also in policy analysis and formulation. It was the success of the Italian industrial districts of the 'Third Italy' (largely the Emilia Romagna region) that led to the recent revival of interest in clusters. There the agglomerations of small businesses, usually geographically co-located and sectorally specialized, had developed an edge in a series of fast-moving and design-intensive sectors. This was not just in consumer goods such as apparel and footwear, but also, among others, in machine tools and food industry equipment.

Suddenly clusters were discovered everywhere, not just in the Third Italy, but in Hollywood, on Route 128 in Boston, in Jutland in Denmark, in southern Germany, in the M4 corridor in the UK and even in developing countries. These vigorous clusters have in recent years come to be widely considered as providing the key to economic dynamism, not just in the economy at large, but also in regard to regional development (where previous attempts to promote backward regions through inward investment had generally not proved to be very successful). They also play a key role in the successful insertion of SMEs into global markets.

Effective clusters exhibit three distinct but complementary characteristics. The first is what economists call '*externalities*' – to be more precise, positive externalities. These are spillovers between firms, that is, actions by firms that have the unintended but real effect of enhancing the competitiveness of neighbouring firms, some of which may be close competitors. One example of such externalities is in regard to skill development. Training undertaken by a particular firm can benefit a rival firm in the case of labour mobility. A second major type of externality is that which arises from supplier development. Suppliers to a particular firm can become suppliers to a wider range of businesses; indeed, when a large number of users exist in a given locality, this may provide the scale for new suppliers to enter the region. Clustered firms also develop a reputation and are therefore attractive to buyers who can justify visits to a region in the expectation of meeting a number of different potential suppliers. Finally, clustered regions may also develop a reputation, enhancing their attractiveness both to new firms and to new suppliers and customers.

The second attribute of successful clusters is when participating businesses realize the existence of these unintended externalities and join together to achieve common purposes. This *joint action* is an important complement to externalities. Together, these unintended and intended aspects of co-location achieve what has come to be termed 'collective efficiency'. Examples of joint action include joint marketing under a common brand name/kitemark, joint purchasing of inputs, joint training, and lobbying government for support/concessions.

The third feature of successful clusters is their link with the *regional system of innovation*. This comprises the range of supporting institutions that are an increasingly important infrastructure as the knowledge intensity of production increases. Examples of important institutions in the regional system of innovation include local RTOs (research and technology organizations), such as universities and research institutes; vocational training institutions; and the effective backing from local government and public–private agencies that roll out government support for marketing, training, upgrading and other determinants of competitiveness.

Of course successful clusters do not necessarily exhibit all three of these characteristics, and their balance and importance may change over time. At a minimum, clusters are generally defined by the existence of externalities – if they didn't exist why would firms cluster at all, even if they may deny or be sceptical of the existence of these spillovers? However, as a general rule, the greater the degree of joint action, the more effective the local regional system of innovation, and the closer the links between the firms and these local institutions, the more competitive the cluster is likely to be.

There is considerable evidence of successful clustering and the impact which this has had on allowing firms – particularly SMEs – to participate in global markets. Indeed, exporting SMEs are particularly empowered when they participate in effective clusters, since they lack the scale required to identify market demands, to achieve economies of scale in marketing, and to meet the volumes required by global buyers. These clusters have played a prominent role in many developing countries, for example, with regard to promoting shoe exports from Brazil and surgical instruments from Pakistan (box 4.1).

Box 4.1   Clusters in low-income economies

The Sinos Valley Shoe Cluster

Between 1970 and 1990, a cluster of almost 2,000 firms in the Sinos Valley in Brazil raised its share of world leather footwear exports from 3 per cent to 12 per cent, specializing in women's shoes. By 1991 they exported nearly 100 million pairs of shoes annually, worth almost $900 million. These firms covered a range of links in the footwear chain, and created more than 15,000 jobs.

Sub-sector	No. of firms	Direct jobs
Footwear manufacture	480	70,000
Shoe components	223	28,000
Tanning	135	22,000
Service industries/workshops	710	18,000
Leather articles	52	4,900
Others	106	4,900
Leather and footwear machines	45	3,600
Export and forwarding agents	70	2,000
Total	1,821	153,400

Source: IDS (1997)

Surgical Instrument Manufacture in Sialkot, Pakistan

The surgical instrument cluster in Sialkot produces scissors, forceps and other precision instruments, using stainless steel. It involves over 300 manufacturers, subcontracting work to more than 1,500 SMEs and acquiring inputs from 200 local suppliers and more than 800 service providers.

> Over 90 per cent of output is exported, and this cluster accounts for more than 20 per cent of global trade, making Pakistan the second largest producer after Germany.
>
> *Source*: Nadvi (1999)

But these industrial districts are dynamic. Not only do they often grow from SME-based clusters into districts of large firms (for example, as in Hollywood), but the degree of joint action in which they engage may also vary over time. For example, Sinos Valley shoe exporters in Brazil cooperated effectively in the early stages of the district's growth, but when new competition arose from China they proved less successful in promoting upgrading activities.[10] An important element in this story – to which we will return below – is that the external buyers established an alliance with leading large-scale firms (which grew out of SMEs) and deliberately inhibited cluster-wide cooperation.

But what happens when these clusters are confronted by crises? The answer is that when they engage in joint action they are often able to overcome such threats to their existence. This is evident from the performance of four industrial districts in Brazil, India, Mexico and Pakistan. The first three specialized in leather footwear and related industries, and the Pakistan cluster in surgical instruments (tables 4.1 and 4.2). In each case, the cluster faced a major challenge in its external environment. The greater the degree of cooperation in

Table 4.1   Number of firms and workers in four clusters

	Footwear and related industries		Surgical instruments	
	Guadalajara, Mexico	Sinos Valley, Brazil	Agra, India	Sialkot, Pakistan
Manufacturers of end product				
• number of firms	315	391	4,500	300
• number of workers	15–20,000	83,800	48,000	10,000
Suppliers of inputs				
• number of firms	160	260	75	260
• number of workers	N/A	55,000	?	2–3,000
Subcontractors				
• number of firms	N/A	760	225	1,500
• number of workers	N/A	23,400	2,000	9,000

Source: Schmitz (1999)

Table 4.2   Correlation of cooperation and performance

Cooperation	Mexico	Brazil	India	Pakistan
		Horitzontal		
Horizontal bilateral	Positive, significant at 10%	Positive, insignificant	Positive, insignificant	None
Horizontal multilateral	Positive, significant at 1%	Positive, significant at 1%	Positive, significant at 1%	Positive, insignificant
		Vertical		
With suppliers	Positive, significant at 5%	Positive, significant at 5%	Positive, insignificant	Positive, significant at 10%
With sub-contractors	None	Positive, insignificant	Positive, insignificant	Positive, significant at 1%

Note: In the cases of India, Pakistan and Brazil the correlations are between *changes* and in the Mexican case between *levels* of cooperation and performance.
Source: Adapted from Schmitz (1999)

its responses, the better was each cluster's performance. Cooperation was much deeper when more than two firms cooperated, and when firms cooperated in a vertical value chain rather than with firms undertaking the same activities.

4.3   Managing innovation in global value chains

Summary: Managing innovation in global value chains

Increasingly, especially for firms which sell into global markets, competitive advantage depends on relationships with other firms in the value chain.

Value chains take various forms. At one extreme they are characterized by loose and impersonal relationships between firms. At the other extreme, all of the operations are internalized within a single transnational corporation. But, more typically and more commonly, chains are 'governed' by key parties who coordinate production between independent firms, often with long-lived relationships that involve a degree of trust between known parties in the chain.

There are basically two types of chains – those 'governed' by key producers and those 'governed' by key buyers. Low-income country producers generally export into buyer-drive chains.

While cooperation with neighbouring firms and institutions is an important emerging determinant of competitive advantage, so too is the degree and nature of cooperation with other firms in the vertical value chain. In understanding the nature and role of these vertical networks it is helpful to start at a high level of abstraction and begin with the description of a schematic value chain.

The value chain describes the full range of activities that are required to bring a product or service from conception, through the different phases of production (involving a combination of physical transformation and the input of various producer services), delivery to final consumers, and disposal after use.

Considered in its most elementary form, it takes the shape as described in figure 4.2. As can be seen from this, production *per se* is only one of a number of value-added links. Moreover, there are ranges of activities within each link of the chain (only those for production are detailed in the figure).

In the real world, as we will see in the following chapter, value chains are much more complex than this. For one thing, there tend to be many more links in the chain. Take, for example, the case of the furniture industry. This involves the provision of seed inputs, chemicals, equipment and water for the forestry sector. Cut logs pass to the sawmill sector, which gets its primary inputs from the machinery sector. From there, sawn timber moves to the furniture manufacturers, who, in turn, obtain inputs from the machinery, adhesives and paint industries and also draw on design and branding skills from the service sector. Depending on which market is served, the furniture then passes through various intermediary stages until it

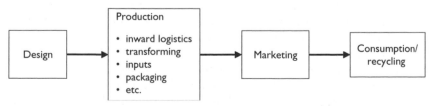

Figure 4.2   A simple value chain

reaches the final customer, who, after use, consigns the furniture for recycling.

In addition to the manifold links in a value chain, typically intermediary producers in a particular value chain may feed into a number of different value chains. In some cases, these alternative value chains may absorb only a small share of their output; in other cases, there may be an equal spread of customers. But the share of sales at a particular point in time may not capture the full story. The dynamics of a particular market or technology may mean that a relatively small (or large) customer/supplier may become a relatively large (or small) customer/supplier in the future. Increasingly, these chains span national boundaries.

Within these chains, firms can connect with customers through different forms of market and non-market relations (box 4.2). Probably the most widely perceived form of connection is that embodied in the economist's model of perfect competition. Here many independent producers sell their products into an impersonal market-place in which there is total anonymity between producer and customer, and where no individual producer or buyer has enough power to influence the price or conditions under which the exchange takes place.[11] These perfect markets exist at the juncture of each link in the chain, and there is no formal or informal connection between links at the apex and the base of the chain, or between any intervening links in the chain. At the opposite extreme from the perfectly competitive market-based chains are those which exclude all market relations and involve full 'internalization'. That is, the operations of a chain of production occur entirely within the boundaries of a firm. When chains involve production across national boundaries – for example, General Motors making cars with components drawn from a number of subsidiaries in different countries rather than entirely from its affiliates in the USA – this involves foreign direct investment. There are two dominant theoretical explanations for this process of internalization. The first concerns transaction costs: obtaining inputs from independent buyers leads to unnecessary and unproductive communication and bargaining. The second is what is termed 'moral hazard': working with suppliers can often be very risky. So, when transactions are frequent, involve extensive risk and require investments in specific machinery or extensive management in supplier relations, firms will prefer to internalize production.[12]

As described so far, these value chains involve either arms-length or fully internalized chains. In each case, production includes many links, and may be globally dispersed. But, increasingly, global value chains encompass a third form of organization. It is one which is largely free

---

Box 4.2   Governance structures in value chains

There are three major ways in which the different producers in the value chain can be linked.

1 *Arms-length chains*   Buyers and sellers operate in anonymity; they neither know nor care about the specific identity of others in their chains. The products in these chains tend to be undifferentiated and commoditized. Relationships between different links in the chain are transitory, and switching customers and sellers is both relatively easy and costless.
2 *Relational value chains*   In these chains, buyers and sellers tend to know each other's identity and, most often, relationships are enduring. This involves a degree of trust between the parties in the chain, which is important because the products they manufacture tend to be differentiated and visible (perhaps through brand names, or because they involve certification concerning environmental impact, quality, labour standards and safety). Each of the parties in these relational chains tends to have specific skills and areas of expertise.
3 *Internalized chains*   These reflect a world in which the various stages in the value chain are undertaken by different affiliates of the same firm. They are internalized because the costs of procuring them externally are too high – possibly because of the difficulty of ensuring quality and reliability, possibly because other suppliers lack the technological capacity to produce them effectively, and possibly because outside suppliers cannot produce them as cheaply.

---

from ownership links, but at the same time lacks the impersonality of the arms-length perfect markets of economic theory. There is a 'stickiness' between the different links in the chain – long-term, durable, repeated and sometimes intimate (in the sense of sharing sensitive data) relationships between links display many of the features of internalized chains. In the more advanced value chains there may be 'openbook costing' (sharing sensitive data on costs) and key firms in the chain may actively help their suppliers or customers to upgrade their operations.

The reasons why these 'sticky' intra-chain relationships have developed is because of the failings of the two alternative models. Armslength and impersonal links were favoured in the era of mass production. This was a competitive environment in which final markets were stable, innovation was relatively slow, and quality and environmental standards were either non-existent or of little competitive significance. But markets became increasingly volatile and demanding of specific attributes – quality, 'organic', low-pesticide residues, 'fair labour standards', and so on. Moreover, product innovation became increasingly important, and time-to-market provided a competitive edge. In these circumstances, the antagonistic, sequential and uncooperative relations in the arms-length model became dysfunctional. At the same time, internalization lost its attractions in many circumstances, since it tied the core firms to particular operating environments, many of which were politically risky. It also often meant that they missed out on the creative energy of new and unlinked suppliers. Thus, whereas for the arms-length producers the chains were not sticky enough, for the internalizing transnationalized firms the links were too sticky. Hence the increasing prominence of a new form of global production organization – involving a spectrum of stickiness between the impersonality of arms-length links and the suffocation of fully governed internalization.

The central characteristic of these 'sticky' relational global value chains is that they are 'governed'. That is, in each chain there are key firms which act as the ringmasters of these global production networks, despite the fact that they have little or no equity in their partners in the chain. They will define, for example, who joins the chain, allocating specific roles to individual parties. They will also determine the conditions for joining the chain. These might involve the commitment to deliver in small batches on time, and being prepared to alter delivery and production schedules rapidly and without complaining; or they might specify the quality of components passed down the chain, or the requirements of suppliers to achieve certain environmental or labour standards in their production. In some cases, the governors may directly assist suppliers to meet these demands, or orchestrate a process whereby their suppliers are upgraded appropriately.

Gereffi (who first drew attention to the importance of governance in these chains) distinguishes two main types of governance.[13] The first are those chains where the key governors are firms which hold core technologies – for example, Toyota (autos), Intel (electronics), GlaxoSmithKline (pharmaceuticals). These are often global value chains in which ownership links are important and in which there is some measure of internalization. As it were, they push qualifications and standards through the chain from below, working with subsidiaries, linked suppliers and customers. The second type of chains are those governed by buyers – for example, Walmart, Nike and Tesco.

Their control is exercised from the apex of the chain, with governance requirements cascading down the tiers of production. These chains seldom involve direct equity links between the buyers and the producers. As figure 4.3 shows, each of these chains has different characteristics with respect to the core competences of the chain governors, the barriers to entry involved, the sectors in which they participate, and the importance of ownership. Crucially, producers in poor countries participate in buyer-driven chains.

Since the mid- to late 1990s, there have been three developments in global value chains which bear on our concerns with the distributional implications of globalization. The first has been the development of what Gereffi terms 'triangular production networks'.[14] These describe production networks in which the governing buyer in the key importing country contracts the services of an intermediary governor whose task it is to organize the logistics of production and to deliver the products to the agreed schedules and to the agreed prices of the major buyer. The origins of these triangular chains were in the role played by Hong Kong and Taiwanese firms in the clothing sector. Because their quotas limiting the number of garments which they could sell in the USA and Europe were full, and because their labour costs were beginning to rise, these entrepreneurs established production networks in China, Mauritius, the Caribbean and elsewhere. These countries had a combination of unused quotas and lower labour costs. From these

	Producer-driven commodity chains	Buyer-driven commodity chains
Drivers of global commodity chains	Industrial capital	Commercial capital
Core competencies	R&D; production	Design; marketing
Barriers to entry	Economies of scale	Economies of scope
Economic sectors	Consumer durables; intermediate goods; capital goods	Consumer non-durables
Typical industries	Automobiles; computers; aircraft	Apparel; footwear; toys
Ownership of manufacturing firms	Transnational firms	Local firms, predominantly in developing countries
Typical producing economy	High-income or upper-middle-income economies	Low-wage and low-income economies

Figure 4.3 Producer-driven and buyer-driven global value chains

Source: Adapted from Gereffi (1999)

origins in the clothing industry, triangular networks have spread to other sectors, including personal computers, electronic consumer goods, footwear and toys.

Second, the relational value chains which have become so dominant in recent years require the chain governor to ensure that its standards are being met at all points in the chain. This can be very demanding. For example, in the wood furniture sector, the accreditation of the Forestry Stewardship Council (FSC) requires a 'chain of custody' as the product passes along the chain. This sets standards in logging – no cutting for a number of days after it has rained; not undermining bio-diversity; respecting the needs and culture of local peoples. But it also requires specific environmental standards in manufacture and in transport. In the auto sector and in the electronics sector, buyers set basic standards concerning defective parts (measured in parts per million, and increasingly being targeted at zero parts per million) and delivery, as well as prices. In a world of weak suppliers, particularly where some of these are in low-income countries, it has become cus-tomary for the governing agents either to assist capability growth in their supply chains directly – supply-chain management – or to ensure that some other party does so. The problem with this is that it is a costly exercise, and, given the choice, it is one which the chain gover-nors would like to avoid. Hence, in some leading sectors, the growth of producer capability has enabled key chain governors to set basic standards and then to allow qualifying suppliers to manage their own affairs. It permits the chain governors to play suppliers off against each other, and is a form of reversion to arms-length chain gover-nance. This is referred to as the 'modular' or 'turn-key' chain.[15] It has been made possible by the growing manufacturing competences in Asia. But of course it holds great dangers for the less accomplished suppliers in Africa and Latin America who have increasingly gained from, and targeted, process-enhancing supply-chain upgrading by the governors of relational value chains.

A third key element of change has been a pervasive tendency for global value chains to become increasingly driven by key buyers rather than by key producers.[16] As we shall see in section 4.5 below, buyers have come to play an important role not just in connecting producers to retailers and final consumers, but also in aiding their attempts to upgrade. But, before we discuss these developments, there is one further feature of the value chain framework which both links to the discussion of rents in chapter 3 and builds towards our focus on the consequence of producers orienting themselves to serve external markets. This concerns the paths for strategic upgrading in the search for sustainable income growth.

4.4 Managing innovation and strategic positioning: upgrading in global value chains

Summary: Managing innovation and strategic positioning: upgrading in global value chains

As firms specialize in their areas of core competence, the growing pressures of international competition and the search for rents have placed strategic attention on value chain positioning. This identifies four strategic types of upgrading:

- process upgrading – improving efficiency, within individual firms or in concert with other firms
- product upgrading – enhancing product innovation, within individual firms or in concert with other firms
- functional upgrading – changing the mix of activities undertaken within the firm, or moving into other links in the value chain
- chain upgrading – moving into new chains.

Many successful East Asian firms have followed this sequential path, moving from assembly to contract production of other firms' designs, introducing their own designs, developing their own brands and in some cases moving into new sectors.

The focus on firm-specific efficiency outlined in section 4.1 above showed the importance of core competences. These are defined as competences which are valued by customers, are unique and are difficult to copy. To be sustained, core competences require firms to develop the necessary dynamic capabilities. But this perspective on upgrading is limited to the individual plant and firm. What forms of upgrading are indicated when, as we have seen, efficiency is determined not by the individual firm, but by the network of firms operating in a value chain?

Essentially four paths of upgrading can be distinguished. These are:

- *Process upgrading*: increasing the efficiency of internal processes such that these are significantly better than those of rivals, both within individual links in the chain (for example, reducing inventories, lower scrap) and between the links in the chain (for example, more frequent, smaller and on-time deliveries)

- *Product upgrading*: introducing new products or improving old products faster than rivals; this involves changing new product development processes both within individual links in the value chain and in the relationship between different chain links
- *Functional upgrading*: increasing value added by changing the mix of activities conducted within the firm (for example, taking responsibility for, or outsourcing, accounting, logistics and quality functions) or by moving the locus of activities to different links in the value chain (for example, from manufacturing to design)
- *Chain upgrading*: moving to a new value chain (for example, Taiwanese firms moved from the manufacture of transistor radios to calculators, to TVs, to computer monitors, to laptops and now to WAP phones).

Figure 4.4 shows the different types of practices which can be engaged in to achieve these various dimensions of upgrading as well as the performance outcomes that result. For example, improving process efficiency might involve enhanced logistical procedures within the firm and/or increased R&D, as well as closer collaboration in logistics and product development in the relations between firms in the value chain. The outcome would be lower costs and faster time-to-market. Similarly, functional upgrading might involve either a change in the mix of activities conducted within a particular firm (for example, taking responsibility for purchasing formerly done by a buyer) or moving from production to design. The outcome would be the ability of the firm to enhance its profitability by being less subject to competition.

Why is this value chain perspective on upgrading important? To understand this requires going back to the discussion of rent in chapter 3. Figure 4.5 shows a common phenomenon occurring in the contemporary global economy. It is based on the simple value chain shown in figure 4.2 above, and reflects a world in which, in general, the barriers to entry in manufacturing are declining. As a result, profits in the physical transformation stage of the value chain tend to fall, whereas those in the knowledge-intensive services, such as design, marketing and technically specialized services, are growing. Hence the pursuit of rents and sustainable incomes is strategically informed by positioning within the value chain – both in relation to what activities are performed within each link in the chain, and with regard to the choice of link in which to operate. In the extreme case when barriers to entry are eroded in all links and all activities within links, the best option may be to vacate the chain altogether.

The East Asian countries which have successfully industrialized in the last quarter of the twentieth century, based in large part on the

Type of upgrading	Practices	Performances
Improving process efficiency		
Within the chain link	R&D; changes in logistics and quality practices; introducing new machinery	Lower costs; enhanced quality and delivery performance; shorter time-to-market; improved profitability; enhanced patenting activity
Between chain links	R&D; supply-chain management procedures; e-business capabilities; facilitating supply-chain learning	Lower final product costs; enhanced final product quality and shorter time-to-market; improved profitability throughout value chain; enhanced patenting activity
Introducing new products or improving existing products		
Within the chain link	Expansion of design and marketing departments; establishment or strengthening of new product development cross-functional teams	Percentage of sales coming from new products (e.g., products introduced in past year, past two years and past three years); percentage of sales coming from branded goods
Between chain links	Cooperating with suppliers and customers in new product development – concurrent engineering	Number of copyrighted brands; increase in relative unit product prices without sacrificing market share
Functional upgrading		
Within the chain link	New higher value-added chain-specific functions absorbed from other links in the chain and/or low value-added activities outsourced	Division of labour in the chain – who does what; key functions undertaken in individual links in the chain
Between chain links	Moving into new links in the chain and/or vacating existing links	Higher profitability; increase in skill and salary profile
Moving to a new value chain		
	Vacating production in a chain and moving to a new chain; adding activities in a new value chain	Higher profitability; proportion of sales coming from new and different product areas

Figure 4.4   Practice and performance in the upgrading challenge

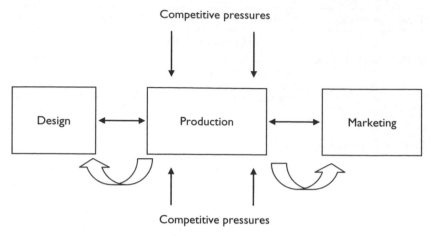

Figure 4.5 Value chain upgrading: a strategic perspective

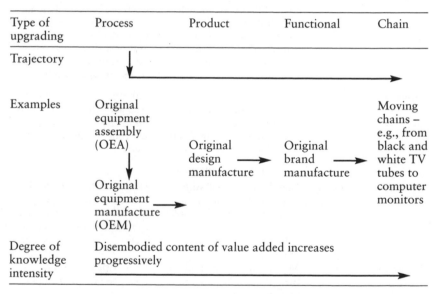

Figure 4.6 The ideal type of a successful value chain upgrading strategy

export of manufactures, have been very systematic about this strategic positioning. Figure 4.6 shows the upgrading path they have used.
It is a path which begins with the simple assembly of components
(OEA – original equipment assembly), and upgrades into the manufacture and assembly of products sold under the brand names of
other firms (OEM – original equipment manufacture). Then, when

manufacturing in these sectors becomes too competitive, they develop their own brands (OBM – own brand manufacturing), such as Daewoo and Samsung. But when even this is unable to protect their rents, they branch out into new chains. As figure 4.6 shows, this is an upgrading path in which disembodied knowledge rather than production skills alone becomes increasingly important.

4.5 Connecting producers to distant markets: the role of global buyers

Summary: Connecting producers to distant markets: the role of buyers

Although mastering innovation is the major challenge confronting producers, the latter need to get their products to final consumers. In those cases where production does not occur within a fully integrated transnational firm, this involves producers working with buyers.

There are a number of different types of buyers, who vary across and within sectors and over time. These buyers play a major role in the development and constraining of capability-building among producers, and perform a number of key functions.

- They channel producers into different market segments, which have different requirements and provide different potential for sustainable profitability.
- They signal to producers what customers want, and how this is changing.
- They help producers to identify the capabilities required to satisfy consumer demands.
- In some cases, they actively assist producers to upgrade.
- They assist in the location and in the acquisition of key inputs.

By defining the role played by individual parties in the chain, the buyers can also block the upgrading paths of producers.

Developing the competences and dynamic capabilities to earn rents in production is one side of the story. This, as we saw in previous sections of this chapter, can be achieved by enhancing a firm's efficiency, either as a stand-alone process or (increasingly commonly) in alliance with other firms. But the resultant products need to be sold to final customers. As we shall see in chapters 5 and 6, the buying function is an important factor explaining the distribution of returns in global production systems.

For producing firms incorporated in internalizing transnational firms, external buyers play only a minor role. More typically, these transnational subsidiaries feed their outputs – be they homogeneous commodities, semi-processed components or final products – into their parent's global distribution systems. For firms outside of transnational networks, external buyers play a critical role in connecting them with external markets, and in determining the distribution of returns from their incorporation in global markets.

The nature of the buyers who are involved in this connection will vary greatly, and figure 4.7, although highly simplified, shows the complexity of the links between different types of producers and buyers. The precise nature of these links will be affected particularly by whether the producer is marketing a homogeneous commodity (such as cotton), a semi-processed intermediate output (such as castings or plastic parts), machinery used by other manufacturers, or products aimed directly at final consumers. In each case there will be different types of buyers involved, reflecting the nature of each product. But even where the product being exported is relatively homogeneous, producers may feed into different types of buyer chains. For example, T-shirts may be sold either directly to a final retailer or indirectly via a wholesale importer.

In general, low-wage economies tend to export manufactures *destined for final consumption*, such as apparel, toys, footwear, processed foods and furniture. In these sectors, the following major buyers can be identified.

- Final retailers – usually giant retailers such as Walmart, Tesco or Carrefour – develop direct relationships with producers.
- Independent specialized buyers resident in the country of final consumption have come to be of growing importance. In the food industry these are termed 'category buyers', and they have competences in the global sourcing of particular products, such as apples or fruit juice, visiting many different producing countries and developing relationships to provide for assured supplies. These products are then passed on – sometimes to leading retailers (who delegate some specialized purchasing to such category buyers), but in other cases to stores with single or a limited number of outlets.
- Large international firms may source products from independent buyers and place their own brand name on them: this is referred

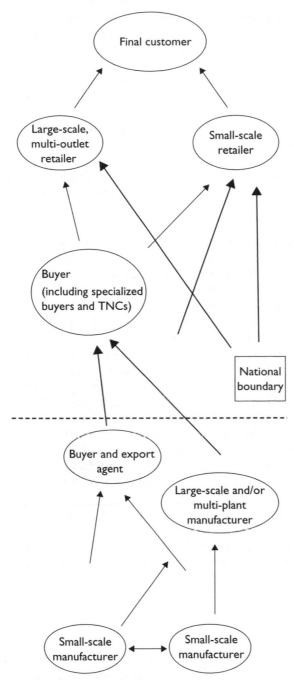

Figure 4.7   How producers connect to final markets

to in the engineering, electronic and automobile industries as original equipment manufacture. In some cases brand-name firms purchase directly from producers; in other cases they work through intermediary specialized buyers. For example, IKEA, the global furniture retailer, negotiates directly with its producers, whereas the UK do-it-yourself store B&Q more often purchases through independent and specialized buyers.

- As we saw earlier, a new form of global buyer consists of those involved in 'triangular manufacturing'. Based generally in a middle-income developing country, they both buy in other developing countries and help to coordinate manufacture in these countries. The final product is by definition consumed elsewhere, generally in high-income countries.

Where products are of *an intermediate nature and destined for further use*, it is more likely that exports are made to agents – buyers who specialize in particular forms of equipment or intermediates, such as spares and standardized components. Unlike the buyers of final consumption products such as toys and clothes, buyers in these sectors tend to be smaller, to have fewer sources of supply and to feed into national rather than international markets.

Finally there are buyers who tend to be *resident in the country of production* rather than, as in the examples given above, the consuming country. They may either scour the country to buy commodities from small-scale producers (for example, coffee and tea) or become involved in buying from larger enterprises and selling on to category buyers, brand-name firms or retailers in the countries of final consumption. These large-scale domestically based buyers have become particularly prominent in China and India in recent years, and are often linked by equity to buying houses in the final consuming countries.

Do the characteristics of these different types of buyers matter? The answer is 'yes', and significantly. This is because buyers play a major role in channelling products from producers to consumers, and thus in determining the distribution of returns as low-wage economies feed increasingly into external markets. There are five different functions which buyers perform.

1) Channelling to different market segments
Consider the case of a furniture manufacture. Its final product can be fed into a number of alternative retail outlets in external markets. Some of these stores are aimed at price-conscious consumers, perhaps buying flat-pack furniture from large discount retailers such as IKEA

or soft-wood garden furniture from garden centres. Feeding into these markets requires enormous and ongoing attention to costs; the margins are paper-thin and often negative. Profitability is therefore determined by scale. At the other extreme, furniture may be sold into exclusive stores, perhaps either a single outlet or a retailer with a limited number of stores. Producer margins on these sales are very high, but attention to quality and design are critical. These two sets of outlets involve very different competences in their value chains. A similar story is replicated in every sector – components assembled into a BMW involve different margins and quality standards to those incorporated in a Korean Hyundai or a Malaysian Proton car. And denim jeans sold into a mass retailer such as Walmart provide for a different pattern of returns and production than those marketed under The Gap label.

From the perspective of the producer, therefore, the chain into which it sells reflects not just its own competences but the final markets for its product. Caught in a price-conscious market, the producer will be locked into a trajectory of cost focus and will need to develop the appropriate dynamic capabilities. Conversely, if its chain feeds into the designer end of the consumer spectrum, the opportunity for higher margins and the imperative for the development of competences will be very different.

2) Signal what customers want – over time
In his influential book published in 1990, Michael Porter identified a key component of successful industrial dynamism as having access locally to sophisticated buyers.[17] Even when such local buyers are available, many producers find it difficult to 'hear' the critical success factors which are desired by their customers, and to determine between the order-qualifying and order-winning characteristics of their markets. And, as we saw earlier in this chapter, these markets are becoming increasingly segmented and volatile. Hence, investment in understanding and, indeed, shaping final markets has become a critical factor in the success of the world's largest and most successful transnational firms.

If this is the case, how much more acute are the difficulties faced by producers who are distant from final markets, and who manufacture in a country where the 'wants' of their domestic consumers are so very different to those in the external markets into which their products are being sold? This is a major problem and has many reflections in different products. For example, one of Europe's largest and more quality conscious coffee-roasters (Illy) invests in teaching the coffee farmers in its chain what constitutes a 'good' cup of coffee. Few farmers drink coffee and, when they do, their tastes are not discriminating. Yet Illy's competitive advantage is in the quality segment of the market. Similarly, the throw-away culture of many consumer products in the high-income consuming countries is anathema to poor workers in low-wage economies; and continual changes to design and the attention to detail in production may have little meaning to workers who have low incomes and have grown up in supply-constrained 'anything-will-sell' markets.

Some producers in the more advanced developing countries met these challenges themselves by investing in understanding the critical success factors ruling their final markets. For example, when the Korean microwave industry targeted the US market, it housed key staff in American households for a number of months to learn about consumer tastes, and then used this to branch into the production of other household consumer products. But this level of sophistication and investment is out of the reach of most producers in low-income countries, and they depend critically on their buyers to transmit information about the nature of their final markets. This may consist of fashion data – what colours will be fashionable this year? – or information about quality, or forecasts of how consumer demand will change in the future. This conduit to market demands is one of the more important functions which buyers can serve in assisting low-income producers to penetrate external markets successfully.

3) Identify what capabilities are required

Knowing what the market wants is only one part of the story. It needs to be complemented by the knowledge of how this can be achieved. Here buyers play an important role in helping producers to identify what steps they need to take. This may be to point them towards particular sorts of equipment and to potential suppliers. Or it may be to alert them to the need to be more systematic about their inventory control, or to move from out-of-date and costly quality control at the end of production to quality at source within production, and perhaps to put them in touch with appropriate service providers who can help them to make this transition.

A particularly important component of contemporary value chains is the emphasis which they place on meeting key standards. This is often a basic entry barrier for producers, without which they cannot participate in global value chains. What sorts of standards does this involve? As figure 4.8 shows, these may be standards for manufacturing processes. For example, incorporation in the networks of major auto assemblers requires component manufactures to achieve either the ISO (International Standards Organization) accreditation on quality procedures in production or firm-specific quality schemes, such as Volkswagen's VDA6 programme. Other industries may have different requirements – in furniture it is the FSC that rules. And in the clothing and footwear industries, the key standards that have to be met are those involving child labour and labour standards.

Alternatively, these standards may involve product specifications. This is particularly important in the food industry, where standards on products such as pesticide residues have to be complemented by standards in process that enable the retailer to trace back to each stage of production where problems of excess residues may have originated. But of course product standards are not limited to the food industry. Producers feeding into complex value chains of assembly increasingly have to meet demanding product standards, which may include an acceptable level of parts-per-million defects in components delivered to the auto assemblers, or frequency and variability of delivery. In toys there are standards on the lead content of paint, and so on.

Figure 4.8 shows that standards can originate from firm-specific requirements (Volkswagen's VDA6 process) or industry-specific schemes (the FSC in furniture, hazard analysis and critical control point – HACCP – in the food industry), may be cross-industry (for example, ISO9000 standards on quality and ISO14000 standards on the environment) and may or may not be legally codified. In some cases the pressures for these standards may be internal to the chain or industry, or they may arise from external parties such as governments

Type of standard	*Product*	Food hygiene standards; lead content in toys	G3 standards for cellular phones	'Homologization' of regulations on product types (e.g., for automobiles in the EU)	Firm standards supporting brand name
	Process	Health and safety standards in work	ISO9000 (quality) SA8000 (labour)	QS9000 (quality in autos, originating in the USA), BS5750 (quality standards originating in the UK)	VDA6.1 (VW quality standard)
	Legal codification	*Internationally agreed*	*Regionally specific*	*Firm-specific*
		Type of codification			

Figure 4.8 Two sets of factors determining the standards regime, and some examples

or civil-society organizations. These civil-society inspired standards have become increasingly prevalent – for example, on labour standards – and have grown in tandem with the expanding brand power of the major transnational firms that rule the industry. They can also be very costly for producing firms. For example, one Chinese firm reported being audited by teams from forty customers in a single month, from a combination of buying firms, external audit firms and NGOs.[18]

But the role of buyers is not just a general contribution making producers aware of the requirements of individual markets and chains. More importantly, they may help producers to identify the competences which allow them to meet these standards. Buyers may often also play the role of monitoring conformance to these standards, although there are an increasing number of cases where specialized agencies play this role.

4) Assist with upgrading

One step beyond the role of alerting producers to the competences that are required is the active role which some buyers play in supply-chain upgrading. In these cases, active steps are taken to assist the producers to meet the requirements of their markets. Supply-chain upgrading was first systematically developed in the Japanese auto industry, and predominantly by Toyota,[19] but has now spread very widely, covering many industries and spanning national boundaries. The standard components of an effective supply-chain scheme involve seven, generally sequential steps.[20] The first is that the buyer has to get its own operations in order, achieving in its plant what it requires of its suppliers. For example, if it has zeroed-in on low inventories, then it must necessarily achieve these standards in-house if it is to become an effective facilitator of its suppliers' inventory controls. IKEA, for example, deliberately maintains its own furniture manufacturing plants in Sweden, since it has concluded that being an effective buyer requires it to be an effective producer.

The second stage is to rationalize its supplier base. More generally this means pruning the number of suppliers after assessing their dynamic competences, that is, the capacity to move with the buyer in developing its dynamic market position. Once this step has been taken, there must be a clear message passed down to suppliers as to what has to be achieved. This third stage is often more difficult than it seems, since many buyers 'speak with multiple voices', that is, they pass down to suppliers contradictory instructions as to what is required. Fourth, the performance of the various suppliers must be monitored, and, where appropriate, suppliers must be told how they perform relatively, and what steps they need to take to achieve the desired standards. Fifth, where first-tier suppliers are unable to meet these standards, they must be assisted in upgrading. This may involve seconding engineers, designers, logistics expertise or other relevant skills to the supplier. Or perhaps the supplier's staff may work in the buyer's plant or offices. In yet other cases, it may require identifying and sourcing the external skills which neither the buyer nor the supplier possess. The penultimate step in this programme of supply-chain upgrading is to assist the first-tier suppliers to provide the same services to its own suppliers, so that efficiency cascades systematically down the whole value chain. The seventh and final step in this process, which separates out the most advanced actors in this value chain upgrading saga, is when the buyer understands that it often has as much to learn from some of its key suppliers as it has to teach them.

As described, this framework by which buyers upgrade their suppliers seems to apply most clearly to producer-driven chains. These are chains where the key buyers are not final retailers or brand-name firms but core technology-holding firms, such as the auto assemblers, the equipment manufacturers, the assemblers of electronic consumer goods, or the manufacturers of core electronic components. Yet, in fact, this is not always the case. In many sectors final retailers very actively promote supply-chain upgrading. In the deciduous canned fruit industry, for example, the major retailers have a team of supply-chain workers who visit their core suppliers on a regular basis, actively assisting them to lower costs, improve quality and meet the relevant product and process standards.[21] Similarly, in furniture, suppliers in low-wage economies such as South Africa report that IKEA provides significant inputs into assisting them with their process efficiency.

However, as we shall see in the following chapter, it should not be thought that buyers are altruistic in assisting supply-chain upgrading. For one thing, they promote intense competition among their suppliers and simultaneously assist all of their key suppliers to upgrade. This removes the rent accruing to individual suppliers who improve their operations. Or, rather, it transfers this rent from the suppliers to the buyers (or, when competition is intense, to the customers). For another thing, buyers assist their suppliers to upgrade only in areas which do not impinge on their own rents. For example, those buyers in the furniture industry who depend for their own competitive advantage on product rents will tend to focus on the process efficiency of their suppliers, and do little to enhance their design and product-enhancing capabilities. A similar story is recounted for the shoe industry.[22] Third, and relatedly, buyers will have a dynamic approach towards upgrading – assisting their suppliers intensively to get them going and then reducing their inputs, and perhaps stopping them altogether when the suppliers have mastered production capabilities and wish to enter into the core domain of the buyers themselves, which may often include design. And, finally, few buyers actively want to assist upgrading among their suppliers. They do so because the alternative to these efforts is that suppliers will languish, diminishing the competitive strength of the chain as a whole. Their preferred option – their default position – is to be able to depend on the autonomous efforts in their supply chain. In the high-income countries, as lean production is filtering through the various layers of industry, there has if anything been a stabilization in or retreat from active supply-chain management in many sectors in recent years. But, as we saw earlier in this chapter, a similar trend is beginning to emerge globally, with the rise of turnkey contract manufacturers in many of the leading newly industrializing economies in Asia. In many value chains, lead buyers are able to set standards for their suppliers, and then with confidence to allow the suppliers to achieve these standards independently. This, as we shall see in part III, poses particular problems for suppliers in those predominantly African and Latin American economies which lack the capacity for independent upgrading.

5) Locate and source inputs
A final contribution which buyers can make to the successful insertion of producers into external global markets is to identify and help source key inputs. Often buyers operate on a global scale and can use this scale to obtain inputs at preferential prices or on beneficial terms of delivery or payment. In other cases, it is not so much the price advantages which arise for producers, but the knowledge of the characteristics of different inputs and information on where they can be acquired, that is of strategic importance to the producers. The role which buyers play in sourcing has become particularly pronounced in the case of 'triangular manufacturing'.

4.6   It's not rocket science

In chapter 3 we provided an analytic framework for determining how producers can achieve sustainable income growth as they participate in the global economy. A series of rents were identified, some of which were bounties of nature, some of which were exogenous to the production chain, and some of which were internal to the chain. However, since technological progress generally erodes natural resource rents, and since many of the exogenous rents are being eroded by global agreements on trade and policy, in this chapter we focused on the endogenous category of rents. These are rents largely under the command of the firm or a group of firms. In this chapter we have focused on how these rents can be appropriated. This requires the systematic management of the innovation in order to generate and appropriate endogenous rents. We have addressed four arenas of innovation management – within individual plants and firms; within co-located industrial clusters; within global value chains; and in managing relations with global buyers.

The management of innovation contains few conceptually difficult ideas, and is hardly rocket science. It comprises a compendium of individually simple steps which are widely known. But this does not mean they are easy – if they were, all producers would be at the technological frontier and there would be no rents in production at all. But to what extent have producers in low-income countries been able to absorb these lessons of innovation management and to translate their comparative advantage into competitive advantage? In the following chapter we will focus on three core sectors – clothing and textiles, furniture, and automobiles and components – to assess the progress of producers in low-income economies.

5

The Global Dispersion of Production – Three Key Sectors

In this chapter we examine the globalization of production in three key sectors – clothing and textiles, automobiles and auto components, and furniture. In each of these sectors, producers in low-income economies have absorbed the lessons of innovation management charted in chapter 4 and pursued the rents set out in chapter 3. They have become increasingly outward-oriented, and have deliberately pursued policies of export expansion. As we saw in the previous chapter, producers tend to sell less and less into the perfectly competitive markets of economic theory, and more and more into the global value chains which are regulated by predominantly external global firms. There is a common pattern of 'chain-governance' which spans sectors and is generally associated with structured barriers to innovation and upgrading; it is also increasingly linked to the prevalence of a variety of standards that govern the participation of producers in global value chains. Yet, as we also saw in the previous chapter, there are many forms which these value chains can take, even in the same sector. Some producers may sell on an 'original equipment' basis into the final brand names of global firms such as Nike. In other cases, and in the same sector, the same or similar products will be sold to independent wholesalers or retailers and reach the final customer as an anonymous 'own brand' product. In yet other cases, the developing-country producer may sell the product in final markets under its own brand name.

Because of this diversity, there are few standard stories that can be told about any two value chains, let alone about value chains which cross different products and regions. For this reason the three case studies which follow are presented eclectically. Each raises a different set of topics and is evidenced in different ways. The common purpose is to illustrate how production in each of these sectors has become increasingly diffused in the global economy (particularly in low-income economies), and how the roles the parties play in the chain, and their capacity to upgrade and generate and appropriate rents, is determined by their positions in their chains. In each sector we can also witness a growth in concentration in buying and coordination. However, while the specifics of each chain differ, there are common characteristics which determine the rewards from participating in global production systems.

Why clothing, furniture and automobiles? The clothing sector is chosen because of its prominent role in the development of industry. It has long been targeted as one of the basic industries to be developed at the early stages of industrial development. The barriers to entry in this chain can be low; its output is purchased by people from every different income range; and, although production is generally labour-intensive, there is an increasing knowledge content in production that provides scope for participants from a variety of different types of economy. It is also one of the largest traded-goods sectors, and has been the source of rapid export-led industrialization in a number of countries. The allied textile sector – part of the same textile and clothing chain – is much more capital-, skill- and scale-intensive and tends to flourish in relatively industrialized economies. The furniture industry is similar in many ways to the clothing sector, except that in production it has more scope for automation, and hence allows producers in middle- and high-income economies to compete. It is also resource-based, and thus raises the potential for deepened forms of value-added industrialization. Like the clothing sector, it is also a buyer-driven value chain. The third sector which we will examine is that producing automobiles and components. This is a producer-driven value chain, dominated by eleven large transnational firms. It is a sector involving much higher technology, and requires elaborate stages of assembly, as each product incorporates more than 5,000 components. Finally, it has much greater economies of scale than either clothing or furniture and is thus spread less widely around the global economy.

5.1 Globalization in the textile and clothing value chain

Summary: Globalization in the textile and clothing value chain

The textile and clothing sector is exceptionally widespread and accounts for significant employment and value added in many countries, as well as for growing manufactured exports.

This sector is subject to a series of changing forces, of which four are especially important.

- Trade policies, hitherto dominant in this sector, are in a state of flux, and quota access to major markets is being reduced.
- New forms of retailing and logistics, allied to the widespread introduction of electronics-based technologies, are providing massive benefits to coordinated global value chains.
- Volatile and demanding final markets are placing new demands on producers, further reinforcing the importance of governed global value chains.
- There is growing concentration in global buying.

In the past, many low-income countries have simultaneously been able to increase their exports at the cost of workers in the high-income importing economies. But the market penetration of imports in these economies is now high, and developing countries find themselves in increasing competition with each other. The continued growth in manufactured exports by a large group of low-income countries is thus not feasible.

China is rapidly becoming the most effective producer of a full range of products. It seems likely that it will squeeze out producers from other low-income economies unless there is a reintroduction of high levels of preferential trade incentives. Its growing presence in global markets has been associated with a significant reduction in prices.

This case study highlights a number of important themes that are common to many sectors but particularly pronounced in the textile and clothing chain. Not only has the sector become increasingly dominated by trade, but, especially since the mid-1990s, producers in many countries have become incorporated into global markets through closely coordinated value chains. A series of dynamic factors have induced the spread of these value chains. These are trade policies; the related effect of new retailing and logistic technologies and volatile and dynamic final markets; and growing concentration in buying and retailing. But impending changes in the policy regime that governs global trade are likely to lead to rapid and significant changes in the global division of labour in this sector, with important implications for the spread of global incomes, particularly for many of the poorest countries.

Figure 5.1 provides a graphical picture of the various stages in the textile and clothing value chain. The first is the production of *fibres*, which may be of either natural or synthetic origin. These fibres are then turned into *yarns*, which are used in the manufacture of *fabrics*. The resultant fabric is then *converted and assembled* into a variety of different products, not just for clothing but also for use in the home, in carpets and in other made-up goods. These products are then fed to other industrial users or into the *retail* sector, either directly or through *buying* intermediaries. The whole process has to be *coordinated*, and a range of different specialized inputs – each with their own value chains – feed into different links in this textile and clothing chain. As we observed earlier, some parts of the chain are very scale-, capital- and technology-intensive, particularly those involved in the textile end. In other cases, production has far fewer barriers to entry, particularly in apparel manufacture.

Changing trade policies

During the 1950s and the 1960s the recovering post-war Japanese economy began a process of outward expansion, reflected in rapidly growing exports of clothing. Despite the fact that Europe and North America were experiencing full employment and tight labour markets, this growth in trade led to an outcry from workers in these countries, whose livelihoods were being threatened by imports. Tariffs did not seem to be able to keep out the tidal wave of imports from Japan. Consequently, the Multifibre Agreement (MFA) was established. This led to quotas being set on the number of items which could be imported from Japan: the extent of these quotas varied between different products in the chain, but they were comprehensive. And, as the newly industrializing Asian economies began in the 1960s and 1970s to replicate this Japanese industrial strategy, a strategy that was extended in the 1980s and 1990s to even more countries, the MFA

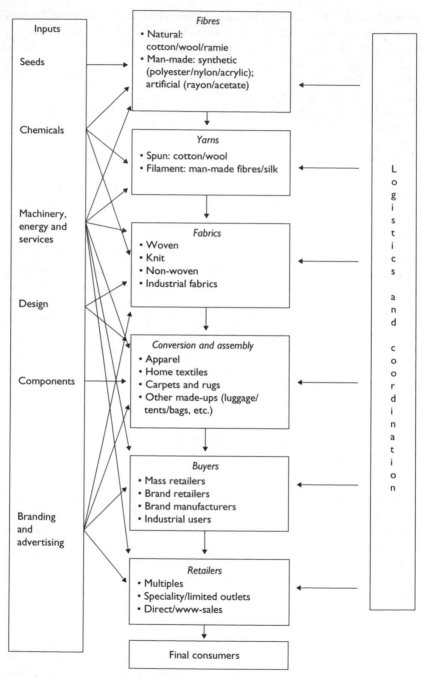

Figure 5.1 The textile and clothing value chain

grew in scope, incorporating virtually all the low-income developing countries in a web of intricately complex trade relationships governed by controls on market access. To compound matters, each of the large importing blocs reached its own bilateral arrangements with individual countries or regions. The European bloc accorded privileges – notably a reduction in tariffs – to a cluster of predominantly former colonies through the Lomé Convention, while the USA favoured its neighbouring economies in Central America, the Caribbean and Mexico, and more recently African economies (through the African Growth and Opportunities Act, AGOA). Layered on top of this were a series of complex tariff schedules which were designed to protect the more capital-intensive parts of the chain, reducing tariffs generally on only specific labour-intensive stages in the production cycle (referred to as 807 in the USA and outward-processing trade, OPT, in the EU). These allowed their home producers to take advantage of cheap labour abroad, but only for the unskilled labour-intensive part of the production cycle.

As with all complex arrangements, there were a number of unintended consequences that arose as a result of these trade policy restrictions. The first was that production spread to an ever-increasing number of countries, depending on their quota access into the major markets. Many of these entrants lacked the comparative advantages which underlay successful industrial production of textiles and clothing. For example, the small, land-locked, desperately poor and overwhelmingly rural economy of Lesotho found itself in 2001 with a textile and clothing sector which accounted for more than 90 per cent of total merchandise exports, despite neither growing cotton nor having a history of textile production. Its role in the sector arose only as a result of its preferential trade access to Europe and the USA. Secondly, and a direct driver of this global spreading of export-oriented production, key manufacturers in markets which had reached the limits of their production quotas began actively to search for under-utilized quota producers, and to organize production in these economies, often initially making use of textiles and components from their own countries. Thus, in a rapid process during the 1990s, Hong Kong garment producers opened production sites in Mauritius and elsewhere, and Korean and Taiwanese producers spread their operations to the Caribbean and to sub-Saharan Africa. Thirdly, as a direct consequence of this spread, these Asian producers began to develop the capacity to mobilize and coordinate full-package manufacture (that is, the command of all the manufacturing stages) in the textile and clothing chain. This capability was increasingly utilized by Taiwanese and Hong Kong firms to organize subcontracted production in China to take advantage of its low wages. As we saw in the previous chapter, this has led to the development of what Gereffi calls 'triangular production networks', production organized and coordinated by firms in another country, and the resulting products sold on to final buyers in a third economy. The growth of these capabilities led to the transition in production capacities in these lead Asian-based firms from original equipment assembly (OEA), to original equipment manufacture (OEM) full-package production, increasingly to original design manufacture (ODM), and in a few cases to original brand manufacture (OBM), as mapped out in figure 4.6.

However, the growing pressure towards trade policy reform placed severe strain on the MFA and other preferential trading agreements. In 1995 a decision was reached at the World Trade Organization to phase out these quotas in a decade-long process under the aegis of the Agreement on Textiles and Clothing (ATC). Quotas were reduced on 16 per cent of items in 1995, a further 17 per cent in 1998, 18 per cent in 2002 and the remaining items in January 2005.

New retailing and logistic technologies force producers into governed value chains

As we saw in the previous chapter (and as we shall see in the discussion of the auto value chain below), a new production system was forged in the Japanese auto industry during the 1960s, 1970s and 1980s. This new paradigm was developed in the search for flexibility, since during the 1950s the small size of the domestic market could not allow the scale economies then ruling in the industry to be realized. A direct consequence of this flexibility was the introduction of smaller inventories ('just-in-time production'), necessarily allied to total quality control (since there were no 'just-in-case' inventories available to buffer errors).

World Class Manufacturing depends critically on new forms of production organization involving changes in procedure, in layout, in skills and in patterns of work. As we saw in chapter 4, these changes are a necessary precursor to reducing inventories and achieving flexibility. But, to be truly efficient, the new production methods need to be allied to the introduction of sophisticated electronic equipment throughout the chain. This controls production processes and allows for higher quality and lower costs. For example, electronically controlled sewing machines are able to create intricate patterns on clothes at low cost; computer-aided design and cutting of cloth not only saves labour, but more importantly reduces material wastage from more than 12 per cent to around 5 per cent; electronically controlled dyeing processes make for more predictable colours and save energy; and so on. These electronic controls not only reduce costs but also speed up the production cycle, allowing for the rapid changeover of machinery. However, electronic controls are having a major impact not just on the production process itself. Perhaps even more importantly in a chain which is becoming increasingly more complex, with a growing variety of products and producers, electronic equipment automates the storage, analysis and transmission of data. Point-of-sale cash registers allow stores to fine-tune their product offering and to save on costs. (In the 'old' pre-electronic and mass production phase, it was estimated that 25 per cent of the cost of a typical garment was accounted for by unsold stock or missed opportunities when desired garments were unavailable and sales were lost.)

When these new forms of production organization, new electronic controls in machinery and new technologies for handling data are integrated into a coordinated chain, the competitive benefits can be overwhelming. Retailers can service their customers at much lower cost; they can put new products on their shelves – products which they know customers want – more rapidly; they can provide much more variety; and they can do so with enhanced quality. It is these systemic benefits which explain the growing incorporation of producers in developing countries into globally governed value chains and why the chain coordinators in triangular value chains play such a crucial role; they also throw light on why stand-alone garment producers in poor countries are facing increasing difficulty in serving external markets.

Volatile, demanding and dynamic final markets force producers into governed value chains

The capability that retailers have developed to serve their customers with flexibility, quality and low price has been both a response and a driver to the growing complexity and volatility of final markets in high-income countries which we described in chapter 4. Whereas the expansion of the post-war industry had been governed by a low-cost-and-pile-them-high marketing philosophy, the new order is one in which retailers have to meet multiple demands from their customers. Of course market segments continue to be important – Walmart and Versace clearly sell to different customers. But there are many cross-over points.

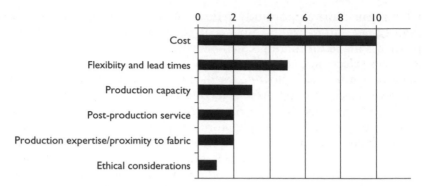

Figure 5.2 Critical success factors in UK clothing markets: the view of ten of the largest UK clothing buyers, 2001

Source: Data drawn from Gibbon (2002)

Figure 5.2 shows the demands of ten of the largest UK clothing buyers in early 2001, covering a cross-segment of the market. Clearly cost is a major concern for all of these buyers. But, at the same time, buyers also value flexibility, short lead time and production capacity, as well as (although to a lesser extent) post-production service, production expertise, proximity to fabric, and ethical labour standards. It is the nature of these critical success factors that they change, and it is likely that in the future, for example, ethical issues in production will become more important. The significance of this is that there is less scope in global production networks for the stand-alone producer. There is a greater requirement for the capacity to organize responses across the chain flexibly to meet buyer requirements for new products, quality and the systematic and persistent squeezing-out of costs from the whole chain. There is also less scope for the smaller producer, and Gibbon found, in interviews with twelve large UK buyers, that eight had actively reduced their number of suppliers (only two had increased them). Thus, without participating in these coordinated chains, developing-country producers find it increasingly difficult to meet the requirements of selling into high-income external markets.

Growing concentration in buying and retailing

We shall see in chapter 6 that there is a generic tendency for growing concentration in almost all buying markets. The degree, speed and nature of this concentration obviously varies across sectors and between countries. Nevertheless, there appears to be a series of common trends in the buying link in the textile and clothing value chain that cut across the US and EU markets.

Essentially, three main types of buyers are emerging. The first are the mass retailers such as Walmart and Kmart in the USA; Asda, Tesco, British Home Stores and Marks and Spencer in the UK; and the growing legion of Internet-based mail-order retailers. Even though they serve different market segments, the key characteristic is that they often specialize in price-sensitive lines and sell under their own label. The second category of buyers are those selling branded labels, retailing sometimes in their own stores and at other times through other outlets (including occasionally the largely own-brand stores). These labels include Liz Claiborne, Donna Karan, Ralph Lauren, Tommy Hilfiger and The Gap in the USA; Next in the UK; Decathlon and Pimkie in France; Escada in Germany; and Zara and Mango in Spain. And, finally, there are the branded manufactures such as Levi Strauss and Philips-Van Heusen who have historically manufactured their own products. But they are increasingly sourcing these from independent but highly coordinated value chains, generally triangulating the buying and coordinating function in one country, with production occurring in a third country.

The common strand running through all of these markets is the degree of concentration in the retailing sector.[1] For example:

- In the USA, between 1987 and 1991 the five largest chains increased their share of retail sales from 35 to 45 per cent; by 1995 this had increased to 68 per cent, and a further twenty-four chains controlled 30 per cent of the market. In other words, something like thirty giant retail chains supply virtually all of the US clothing market. Walmart and Kmart have become particularly dominant and, alone, account for 25 per cent (by volume) of all sales.
- In Germany in 1992, five retailers (C & A, Quelle, Metro/Kaufhof, Kardstadt and Otto) accounted for 28 per cent of the clothing market.
- In the UK, the top five retailers had 32 per cent of the market in 2000, and the top ten retailers had 42 per cent.
- In both France and Italy, independent retailers declined in importance after the mid-1980s, and specialized chains, franchise networks and hypermarkets grew rapidly.
- In Japan, the dominant role of high-fashion department stores such as Seibu and Isetan has been undermined by specialized clothing retailers competing with lower-cost imported products.

Along with the growing complexity of critical success factors in this sector, the immense buying power of these retailers has added to the pressure for producers to be incorporated in global value chains. It has also added weight to the role played by the key triangulating inter-mediaries in this sector, balancing the requirements of the buyers against the capabilities of their producer chains, and their quota access in Europe, North America and Japan.

The changing geography of production

The confluence of four factors – trade restrictions, flexible produc-tion and retailing systems, dynamic and volatile markets, and the growing concentration of buying power – overlays itself on a global production platform characterized not only by the differential capa-bilities which we have outlined above, but also by different cost structures. A key component of costs in the garment end of the textile and clothing chain is that of labour. Table 5.1 shows that, in general, the Asian producers have lower hourly compensation costs than do the Central American, Caribbean and European-periphery producers, as well as in relation to the major exporting African economies.

Table 5.1 also shows that China's labour costs are low, but not as low as those in South Asia or Indonesia. Nevertheless, labour is only one component of costs (and is of diminished importance in the scale-, capital- and technology-intensive links in the chain) and China's cost advantages extend to its infrastructure as well. As a consequence of these cost advantages – and of its complementary efficiency in meeting the critical success factors of global buyers – China's growing all-round competitiveness is beginning to show. In the textiles sector, its share of global exports doubled from 6.9 per cent in 1990 to 13.5 per cent in 2002, and in garments it more than doubled, from 8.9 to 20.6 per cent in the same period (table 5.2). Although other low-wage economies also show progress, nothing is on the scale of China's massive advance in global export markets. It is striking that some of this success has been as a result of US buyers switching their sourcing to China from Mexican maquiladora production sites. Between 2000 and 2002, Mexican exports of textiles to the USA fell by $0.89 billion while those of China rose by $0.84 billion. In clothing the respective figures were a fall of $1.11 billion and a rise of $1.41 billion.[2] Not for nothing is there talk in Mexico of 'the giant sucking sound' of jobs migrating to China.

Table 5.1   Hourly wages in the garment industry, 2002 (including fringe benefits)

	Hourly wages (US$)
China	0.68[a]–0.66
South Asia	
Bangladesh	0.39
India	0.38
Pakistan	0.41
Sri Lanka	0.48
ASEAN	
Indonesia	0.27
Malaysia	1.41
Philippines	0.76
Thailand	0.91
Mexico	2.45
Caribbean and Central America	
Costa Rica	2.70
Dominican Republic	1.65
El Salvador	1.58
Guatemala	1.49
Haiti	0.49
Honduras	1.48
Nicaragua	0.92
Africa	
Mauritius	1.25
South Africa	1.38
European periphery	
Egypt	0.77
Jordan	0.81

[a] Chinese wages outside of coastal area

Source: Drawn from USITC (2004), table 3.1

The Mexican experience appears to prefigure a trend which is likely to affect almost all other low-wage textile and garment exporters. Although dramatic, China's advance in global markets has been held back by the continued operations of the Agreement on Textiles and Clothing, in which there are a large number of import quotas. This means that, however efficient Chinese producers are, they are still constrained from selling into certain major markets. But, as the import controls are reduced, China's competitiveness is likely to grow further. For example, figure 5.3 shows the dramatic increase in China's share of the US markets in four items where quota restrictions (but not differential tariffs, which remain) were removed. In five main items of clothing subject to quota removal in 2002 (codes 239, 350/650, 349/649, 670 and 331/631), the prices of China's exports

Table 5.2   Share of global textile exports, 1980, 2000 and 2002 (%)

	1980	1990	2002
Textiles			
EU	15.0	14.5	15.2
China	4.6	6.9	13.5
USA	6.8	4.8	7.0
Korea	4.0	5.8	7.0
Taiwan	3.2	5.9	6.3
Japan	9.3	5.6	4.0
India	2.4	2.1	3.7
Garments			
EU (extra EU)	10.4	10.5	8.3
China	4.0	8.9	20.6
Turkey	0.3	3.1	4.0
Mexico	0.0	0.5	3.9
USA	3.1	2.4	3.0
India	1.7	2.3	2.8
Bangladesh	0.0	0.6	2.1

Source: WTO (2004)

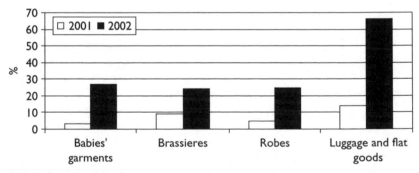

Figure 5.3 China's share of US imports following removal of MFA import quotas, 2001 and 2002

Source: USITC (2004)

to the USA fell by more than 50 per cent, more than 40 per cent, more than 15 per cent, more than 60 per cent and more than 50 per cent respectively.[3] In 2002 the USA removed quotas in twenty-nine categories of clothing. In these categories China's market share rose from 9 per cent to 65 per cent, on the back of an average price reduction of 48 per cent.[4]

In 2004, a US International Trade Commission enquiry into competitiveness in the global textiles and clothing industry provided a comprehensive overview of emerging trends and a series of country case studies conducted by industry experts. It concluded that China is 'expected to become the "supplier of choice" for most U.S. importers (the large apparel companies and retailers) because of its ability to make almost any type of textile and apparel product at any quality level at a competitive price.' Its labour costs are low on account of a combination of low wages and high productivity and its production of high-quality and low-cost inputs. As for quality, it is 'considered by industry [to be] among the best in making most garments and made-up textile articles at any quality or price level.'[5]

The surge in Chinese textile and clothing exports after the mid-1990s has taken place in a context that is structurally different from that which allowed new entrants to enter the global market in the 1980s and 1990s. In the earlier period, much of this export growth by low-income countries was at the cost of domestic producers in the high-income economies, squeezing out local production. This meant that many low-income producers could simultaneously increase their exports to the USA and Europe – this was a positive-sum game for many low-income countries. But when the domestic industry in these major consuming blocs has been eroded, then the growth of exports from one or a few low-income exporters will be at the cost of other low-income exporters – a zero-sum game for developing-country exporters.

By the turn of the millennium, the bulk of the domestic clothing industry and much of the textile sector's production had been eroded in the high-income countries. Import penetration into the EU clothing sector grew from 46.5 per cent in 1995 to 62.5 per cent in 2000. In the UK it stood at 84.6 per cent in 2002, and China's share had grown from 1.2 per cent in 1965, to 3.2 per cent in 1988 and to 12.4 per cent in 2000. In the USA, the contribution of domestically made clothing fell from 49 per cent in 1992 to 12 per cent in 1999.[6] As the ATC advances, so it can be anticipated that the evaporation of domestic production in high-income economies will continue. Hence, as the US International Trade Commission concluded, the abolition of preferential quotas for African producers, as well as for those in the Caribbean, would mean that these manufactures would be squeezed out of the US market – particularly by Chinese exports, and particularly for high-volume and low-fashion items – and that this would spell disaster for their export-oriented clothing sectors.

5.2 Globalization in the furniture products value chain

Summary: Globalization in the furniture value chain

The furniture industry is geographically widely spread and is of significant size, in terms of both global production and global trade. The availability of a range of mechanized technologies allows producers in both low- and high-income economies to survive.

Competition has grown in this sector, associated with a significant decline in prices, and low-income economies have seen an expanding share of global markets. China is now the third largest global exporter, Mexico is the sixth largest and Poland the seventh largest. Prices of final products in this sector have fallen over the past decade, and there has been a clear move towards a 'world price' in major product segments.

Global retail and buying have become increasingly concentrated. This has affected the capacities of producers to innovate and upgrade. Buyers appear willing to allow producers to improve manufacturing processes and efficiency, but not to share in design and retailing rents. Indeed, buyers have actively encouraged competition among producers, forcing down rents in production.

Like textiles and clothing, furniture is a basic industry. Furniture is one of the first commodities that consumers buy as they begin earning cash incomes, and, although at high levels of income it is an income-inelastic product (that is, it is subject to a smaller than proportionate rise in consumption as earnings rise), there are a wide range of furniture products, including those which sell at very high prices. For many middle-class families, even in high-income countries, competition in the furniture market is often not with other furniture products, but with purchases of consumer durables such as automobiles. In this sense, because of the high ticket-price of many of its products, the furniture market is much more like that of automobiles than that of clothing. In the UK, in 2000 furniture accounted for 18 per cent of all expenditures on durable goods, a significant increase in its share of expenditure over the decade since 1990.[7] Another feature of the industry which makes it attractive to producers in low-income countries is that it is resource-based. This provides the opportunity to add value and to capitalize on the natural comparative advantage of many subtropical and tropical developing countries, where trees grow much faster than in temperate climates.

Figure 5.4 briefly sketches the wooden furniture value chain. It begins with the (increasingly research-intensive) production of seeds and chemicals, and in some cases the control of water supplies to the forestry sector. From the forests, logs are transported to the sawmills. The resulting timber is combined with adhesives, components and upholstery in the manufacture of the four basic families of furniture – office furniture, kitchen furniture, bedroom furniture and dining-room furniture. This then passes to retailers through a number of buying channels – specialized buyers, wholesalers and factories controlled directly by the final retailer. At various stages of the chain,

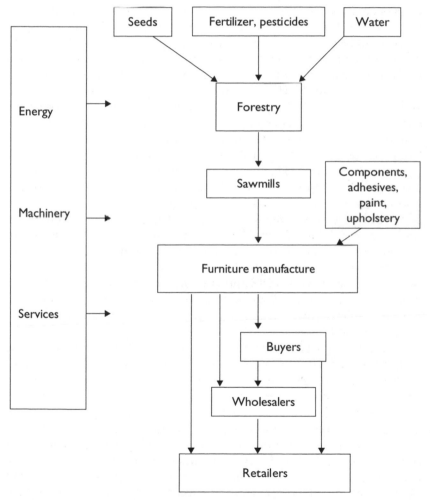

Figure 5.4   The wood furniture value chain

production is supported by machinery, energy and services provided by specialized suppliers.

Since the early 1980s, furniture has become a significantly traded product, the globalization of sales being driven by three major related developments. The first was the introduction of flat-pack products, which enabled bulky furniture to be shipped cheaply and then reassembled (increasingly by final purchasers) in the consuming countries. These flat-pack products reflected a new approach to design and the development of new composite materials such chipboard, plywood and mass density board. They provided the opportunity for mechanization, and, in Europe, wages as a proportion of industry costs fell from 50 to 28 per cent between 1960 and 1995.[8] They also provided the opportunity to source furniture from distant production sites, since transport costs could be greatly reduced. The development of flat-pack products, involving sophisticated designs and logistics, both resulted from and fed into the growing concentration of the retail sector in high-income consumer markets. In the UK, multiple-store retailers control between 35 and 40 per cent of the final market, and the four largest multiples have a market share of 21 per cent. In Germany, the majority of retailers and manufacturers are connected to the buying group Einkaufsverbände and its affiliates, which controls 60 per cent of the market.[9]

At the three-digit SITC level, in 2001 the furniture industry was the eighteenth largest exported goods sector out of 141 manufacturing product groups, with a total value of global trade of manufactures of $61.8 billion.[10] It was the second largest traditional, low-technology traded sector, falling short of the apparel sector ($153 billion), but exceeding the value of trade in the footwear industry ($36.7 billion) and the toys and sporting goods industry ($34.5 billion). The growth of world trade between 1988 and 2001 in the furniture sector (169 per cent) exceeded that for all world trade of manufactures (126 per cent), as well as that of toys and sporting goods (106 per cent) and footwear (63 per cent).

An important aspect of trade in this sector is that it involves a wide range of countries – much more so than in textiles and clothing and automobiles and auto components. This follows not only from the range of products in furniture, but from the variety of materials which can be used and the spectrum of technical choice in manufacture, which, as we saw, is much more open to mechanization in furniture than in clothing. A second significant trend in this sector is the growth of intense price competition. Table 5.3 shows both these trends. It reflects furniture imports into the EU at a high level of disaggregation (six-digit Harmonized System nomenclature) between 1988 and 2001, using two-year moving averages to iron out price volatility, and focusing on imports

Table 5.3   Unit price trends (two-year moving averages) and number of countries exceeding 1 per cent of market share of wooden furniture imports to the EU, 1988 and 2001

	Average unit price ($1,000/metric ton)		Average unit price (per cent change)	Unit price standard deviation		Total no. of country exporters		No. of low-wage country exporters	
	1988–9	2000–01	1989–2001	1988–9	2000–01	1989	2001	1989[a]	2001[b]
Kitchen furniture	3.63	2.51	−31%	4.26	1.83	15	14	2	4
Bedroom furniture	2.34	1.94	−17%	2.36	1.74	18	25	6	11
Upholstered seats with wooden frames	7.38	4.42	−40%	4.03	3.16	19	26	6	12
Seats with wooden frames	3.26	3.06	−6%	2.77	4.44	24	31	10	18
Wooden office desks	3.13	2.51	−20%	4.23	2.16	19	19	5	6
Wooden office furniture (= <80 cm ht)	4.41	2.68	−39%	3.84	2.41	19	25	3	7
Wooden office cupboards (>80 cm ht)	4.09	3.09	−24%	1.76	1.90	14	18	1	6
Wooden office furniture (>80 cm ht)	3.52	2.88	−18%	2.48	2.50	17	20	2	4
Wooden furniture (dining and living rooms)	3.26	2.07	−37%	3.32	1.99	20	35	6	18
Wooden furniture (shops)	5.31	4.73	−11%	2.51	4.64	14	23	1	7
Other wooden furniture	2.90	2.19	−25%	2.47	2.44	23	31	8	16
All wooden furniture (aggregate)	2.72	2.17	−36%			28	48	11	28

[a] Includes Warsaw Pact countries
[b] Includes Central and Eastern European countries

Source: Kaplinsky and Readman 2004, calculated from Eurostat COMEXT database

Table 5.4   The ten largest global exporters of furniture, 1980, 1990 and 2001

	1980		1990		2001
Italy	20.2	Italy	18.8	Italy	14.0
Germany	19.0	Germany	16.3	Germany	9.2
Belgium and Luxembourg	6.7	USA	6.4	China	8.2
France	6.0	France	5.9	USA	7.9
UK	5.2	Taiwan	4.8	Canada	7.7
USA	4.8	Denmark	4.7	Mexico	5.4
Sweden	4.7	Belgium and Luxembourg	4.6	Poland	4.1
Denmark	4.1	Canada	4.4	France	3.8
Netherlands	3.2	Netherlands	3.4	Denmark	3.2
Yugoslavia	2.8	UK	3.4	Belgium	2.9
Total	76.7		72.7		66.4

Source: <www.intracen.org>

from all countries which account for more than 1 per cent of EU imports in each trade category. The data display a number of trends. First, intense competition in this sector is driving down unit prices, which fell in every product category. Second, the standard deviation of prices in imports from different countries fell in seven of the eleven product categories, illustrating the move towards a common 'world price'. Third, the spread of global production capabilities is such that the number of countries with a market share of more than 1 per cent in the EU rose in all but two of the eleven product categories. And, finally, there was a generalized trend in every product category for growing participation by lower-income producers. In fact, if we turn to the share of global trade (table 5.3 is based on EU imports), only one of the ten largest exporters in the 1980s could be said to be a low-wage economy (Yugoslavia) (table 5.4). In 2001, China had grown to become the third largest exporter, and Mexico the sixth largest. Poland – a relatively low-wage producer in the European context – had become the seventh largest participant in global export trade. A further feature of interest from table 5.4 is that the share of the four largest exporters to the EU fell from 51.9 per cent in 1980, to 47.4 per cent in 1990 and to 39.3 per cent in 2001.

Who determines the capacity to upgrade in the furniture value chain?

We saw in the previous chapter that one of the contributions which value-chain analysis makes to an understanding of the distributional outcomes of globalization is that it throws new light on upgrading processes. Upgrading is an essential capability if producers are to escape from the intense pressures of global competition, and thereby generate and appropriate the rents that provide sustainable incomes. In value-chain analysis we move beyond a perspective of upgrading which focuses on the firm to that which encompasses the whole value chain. This highlights *inter*-firm procedures of process and product upgrading (to add to the traditional core-competence literature on *intra*-firm process and product upgrading). But it also identifies the importance of functional upgrading, that is, shifting activities from one link in the value chain to another – for example, from component assembly to full production, or from production to design. In general, as we shall see in later chapters, the production link in most, if not all, value chains is becoming progressively more subject to global competition, and rents are increasingly being generated in design, branding and marketing.

We also saw in chapter 4 that buyers play an important role in linking producers to final markets, and often in directly or indirectly assisting them to upgrade as well. But, since the buyers need to protect their own sources of rent, it stands to reason that the assistance they give to producers in their upgrading is unlikely to provide them with the capability to encroach on the buyers' own rents. Using the case study of the furniture value chain, we are able to chart the sourcing decisions of the major sets of buyers and the impact these have on the capacity of producers to upgrade.

Opening out the furniture value chain which we presented in figure 5.4 above, we can identify three major types of buyers in the large importing countries. The biggest and most dynamic of these are the multi-store retailers, who generally purchase on a very large scale and, except for a few minor items, tend to source directly from the producers. For these buyers, cost and volume are the major critical success factors determining their purchasing decisions. The second major type of buyers are the specialized import agents. They, too, tend to deal directly with the furniture producers, but buy in smaller volumes and sell to less price-sensitive and more design-conscious retailers. Finally, of diminishing importance are the retailers with single- or limited-retail outlets. These buyers tend to purchase in small quantities, generally from import agents or from wholesalers in producing countries, and to sell into design-conscious markets.

What sorts of activities do each of these different types of buyers outsource, and what do they monopolize for themselves? Figure 5.5 displays the sourcing decisions of these three types of buyers based in the

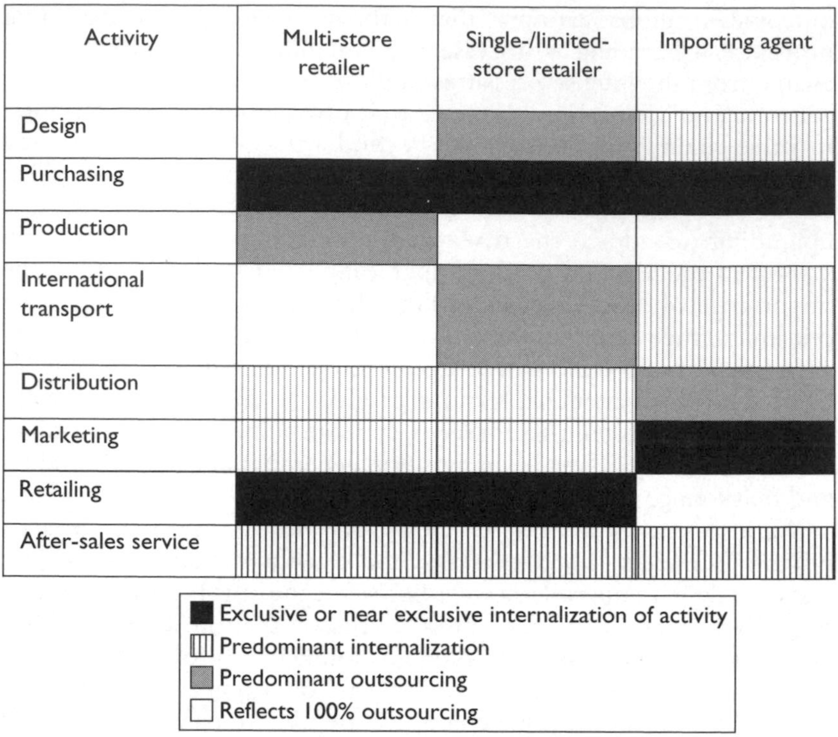

Activity	Multi-store retailer	Single-/limited-store retailer	Importing agent
Design			
Purchasing			
Production			
International transport			
Distribution			
Marketing			
Retailing			
After-sales service			

■ Exclusive or near exclusive internalization of activity
▥ Predominant internalization
▨ Predominant outsourcing
□ Reflects 100% outsourcing

Figure 5.5 The degree of outsourcing in the value chain by different types of UK buyers

Source: Based on Kaplinsky, Morris and Readman (2002)

UK. The dark areas represent complete internalization, the vertical bars show predominant internalization, light shading reflects predominant outsourcing, and no shading represents 100 per cent outsourcing. It is clear from this that the key activities are purchasing and, where the buyer has its own stores, retailing; these define the core competences of the buyers. Perhaps surprisingly, the buyers are prepared to allow a limited amount of independent activity by the producers in design and international transport, and are prepared to buy in domestic logistics, marketing and after-sales servicing. Significantly, these buyers do not regard it as being in their competence to manufacture the furniture, with one striking exception. IKEA maintains a limited number of its own factories, since it feels that it cannot be an intelligent buyer unless it fully understands the problems posed in production.

As we observed, one of the distinctive features of the furniture industry is that it involves production by both low- and high-income economies. So, given that buyers are increasingly prepared to outsource some of their activities, which of these activities are outsourced to low-income and which to high-income economies? In general, all three types of buyers are willing to outsource production to low-income economies (figure 5.6). However, only the very small retailers are prepared to allow design to occur in low-wage economies – these buyers are often 'design-takers' rather than 'design-makers'. In general, it is the single-/limited-store retailers and the import agents who are prepared to let more of their links in the chain go to low-income economies, and many of these links tend to support higher incomes (such as design, or the control of chain logistics). Yet, as we have seen, these small retailers and the import agents are being progressively squeezed out of the market as retail consolidation increases in all of the major importing countries.

Thus, functional repositioning in the furniture value chain offers very few prospects to producers in low-income economies, particularly as

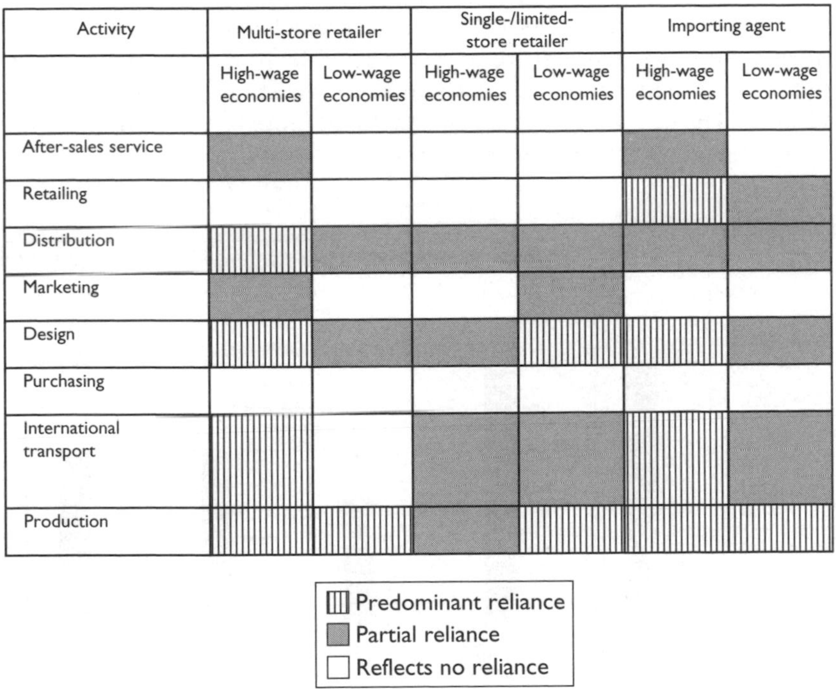

Activity	Multi-store retailer		Single-/limited-store retailer		Importing agent	
	High-wage economies	Low-wage economies	High-wage economies	Low-wage economies	High-wage economies	Low-wage economies
After-sales service	▒				▒	
Retailing					▓	▒
Distribution	▓	▒	▒			
Marketing	▒		▒			
Design	▓	▒	▒	▓	▒	
Purchasing						
International transport	▓		▒		▓	▒
Production	▓	▓	▒	▓	▓	▓

▓ Predominant reliance
▒ Partial reliance
☐ Reflects no reliance

Figure 5.6 What activities do different UK buyers outsource to different types of economies?

Source: Based on Kaplinsky, Morris and Readman (2002)

the buyer market continues to consolidate. The producers are allowed – indeed, often encouraged – to assume new tasks. But these tend to be activities which are subject to low barriers to entry, particularly production itself, where, as we have seen, there are an increasing number of participants in global trade. But what assistance do buyers provide in helping their suppliers to upgrade their processes and products? As we saw in chapter 4, buyers can impart clear signals to suppliers by setting quality, price and delivery targets and checking performance compliance; offer direct training to suppliers; provide finance to facilitate production expansion; work directly with suppliers to upgrade their performance; and assist suppliers with their own supply chain.

Figure 5.7 reports the views of major British buyers with regard to the assistance they give to producers in process upgrading. In general, the single-/limited-outlet retailers leave their producers to get on with things on their own, confining their efforts to general discussions on process capabilities. They will occasionally set process targets for their suppliers and provide inputs on solving specific problems. But they almost never offer assistance with regard to training or finance to facilitate production and export. Both the specialized large-scale import agents and the multi-store buyers provide more detailed process support to their suppliers, in some cases assisting with training and finance. The import agents are, if anything, more likely than the multistore buyers to provide close support for process upgrading.

Figure 5.7   How UK buyers perceive their role in promoting process upgrading by their suppliers

Source: Based on Kaplinsky, Morris and Readman (2002)

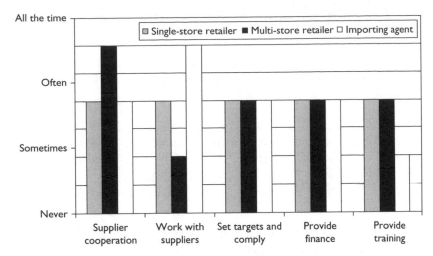

Figure 5.8   How UK buyers perceive their role in promoting product upgrading by their suppliers

Source: Based on Kaplinsky, Morris and Readman (2002)

It is clear that buyers are less prone to provide assistance with regard to product upgrading, partly because this begins to impinge on their own competences, and thus to eat into their own rents (figure 5.8). But, even where support is given for product development, this is of a minor and incremental nature. For example, suppliers to IKEA report that IKEA provides many incentives and often active support in improving process capability. However, the only changes to product design which they are allowed to make are those that facilitate process efficiency and have little impact on visual design.

A similar story can be told for the Brazilian leather footwear industry. There, major American buyers played a key role in promoting process efficiency among the producers clustered in the Sinos Valley, working to the designs provided by the buyers. Once the Brazilian suppliers had achieved the necessary scale and competences in process by the end of the 1980s, the US buyers took their shoe designs to China and actively promoted the same sorts of process efficiency there. This led to a fall in the real incomes of Brazilian producers.[11] The rents which remain in the shoe industry are concentrated in those sectors where design is important, both in leather shoes and of course in athletic shoes (which have become increasingly high-tech in design). The major beneficiaries of these product rents reside in Europe (particularly Italy) and the USA.

5.3 Globalization in the automotive products value chain

Summary: Globalization in the automobile and components value chain

With an annual global turnover of more than $500 billion, the automobile and components sector is one of the largest sectors of global value added and trade. Historically it has been dominated by producers from the USA, Europe and Japan.

A series of developments are changing this geography of production.

- Scale economies are growing, particularly in knowledge- and design-intensive activities.
- Production technologies and product design are becoming more complex.
- The sector is now dominated by eleven mega-corporations, each with an extensive global reach.
- Markets are growing most rapidly in low-income economies.
- Many low-income and emerging economies have targeted the sector for industrial promotion.

In recent years, most of the growth in production and exports has come from low-income and emerging economies, and their share of global trade is expanding very rapidly. This is based on the growth of production capabilities in this sector as formerly peripheral producers have upgraded their manufacturing processes. However, most of the design and knowledge-intensive components of this chain continue to be under the command of transnational corporations, mostly in the high-income economies. Pricing pressures are severe, and most component suppliers are confronted with an annual demand for price reduction.

Market growth and expansion of production capabilities are occuring particularly rapidly in China, whose share of global production and trade is increasing accordingly.

The hothouse in which the mass production paradigm had been forged in the first half of the twentieth century was the automobile industry. Over the next century this and related industries came to dominate the domestic manufacturing sectors in the leading industrial countries. By one estimate, in 2000, around 4 million people were employed in the global assembly industry directly, with a further 9 to 10 million employed in supplier industries.[12] The output of the components sector exceeded $500 billion. As the 'automobile society' spread and as production increasingly came to be organized in global value chains, the sector also came to dominate global trade. As table 5.5 shows, by 2002 the sector accounted for more than 13 per cent of global manufacturing trade, and an even higher share of manufactured trade in North America and Europe.

Figure 5.9 presents the basic value chain in the automotive sector. Its key component, and the major driver of this chain, is the design, assembly and marketing of the final product. This is dominated by eleven large transnational firms with operations in a variety of continents – General Motors/Daewoo and Ford/Mazda (with US parents); Volkswagen/Skoda/Seat, Renault/Nissan, Peugeot-Citroën, Daimler-Chrysler, BMW and Fiat (with European parents); and, in Asia, Toyota and Honda (Japanese parents) and Hyundai (Korean). (There are a number of subsidiary assemblers – Mitsubishi and Suzuki in Japan, Proton in Malaysia, Shanghai Automobile in China, Tata in India, and so on – but their presence is largely peripheral at present.) Among these, five firms are especially dominant. Together, GM, Toyota, Ford, Volkswagen and Daimler-Chrysler account for more than 53 per cent of global production. There are extensive equity and technology links between firms (figure 5.10).

Sitting beneath these large transnational producers are the first-tier suppliers and subsystem integrators. Many of these are very large and also operate their own global value chains, such as Delta and Visteon in the USA (formerly owned by GM and Ford respectively), Bosch in

Table 5.5   Share of automotive products in trade in manufactures, 2003 (%)

	Exports	Imports
World	13.2	13.2
North America	17.0	20.8
Latin America	18.0	12.4
Western Europe	14.4	13.9
Central/Eastern Europe, Baltic States, CIS	12.9	12.9
Africa	6.5	11.9
Middle East	3.1	13.7
Asia	9.1	4.8
Australia/Japan/New Zealand	23.3	8.4
Other Asia	2.9	3.4

Source: WTO (2004)

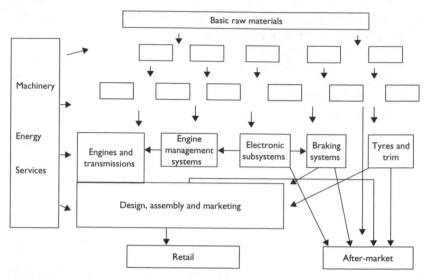

Figure 5.9 The automobile and components value chain

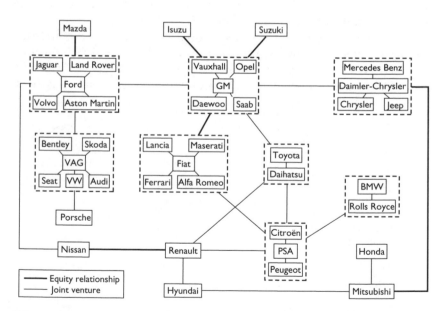

Figure 5.10 The dominating alliances in the global auto industry, c.2000

Source: Dicken (2003)

Germany and Denso and Aisen Seiki in Japan. In turn these first-tier suppliers are fed by second- and third-tier suppliers, as well as by very large producers of basic materials such as steel and aluminium. The whole industry is supported by a myriad of service providers and energy and machinery suppliers. The final market comprises both the retailing of the final product and the very large business in after-sales service (comprising around 20 per cent of the value of all component production).

A key characteristic of this sector, stretching back to Toyota's reorganization of its supply base in the 1970s, is the pressure for 'cost-down'. In this system, each year suppliers throughout the chain are expected to reduce prices, or not to raise prices, in the context of improvements in product specifications. For example, in the wire-harness sector, before the relocation of production to lower-cost producers in Eastern Europe in 2001, UK suppliers were expected to reduce prices by 7 per cent on an annual basis, and by 17 per cent for model changeovers (when new designs could further reduce costs).

In this chapter we are concentrating on the factors driving the global spread of the auto sector and the ability which some middle-income countries have displayed to catch up to the global frontier. We will therefore limit our discussion of the auto sector – which of course deserves much more detailed treatment – to explore this specific agenda.

Factors underlying globalization in the auto sector

Underlying the globalization of the auto and auto components sector has been an uninterrupted growth in scale economies which has forced producers to generate and penetrate ever larger markets. For much of the twentieth century, the primary scale economy lay in production – as a rule of thumb, the bottom of the cost curve in assembly was reached at volumes of 250,000 cars per year, and around 400,000 to 500,000 engines per year. In a context where, for example, total automobile demand in Japan reached 250,000 cars only in 1959, and have begun to exceed these levels in India and China only since the late 1990s, these production scale economies have been very significant. As the twentieth century wore on, some of these scale economies were eroded, since flexible production schedules meant that the bottom of the cost curve could be reached by producing more than one model in a plant ('mixed-model assembly') or by using sub-assemblies produced by first-tier suppliers. This did not mean the end of scale economies, but rather signified a change in their nature, since with the growth in flexibility in assembly came the ability to meet the diverse needs of different customers. Markets segmented (a pervasive cross-sectoral phenomenon, as we saw in the previous chapter), and economies of scale in production increasingly came to be complemented by economies of scope in product – variations (different 'platforms') and variations of variations (proliferation of options within platforms) and, in the more developed forms, mass customization by producing only on a make-to-order basis to meet the needs of individual customers. Whereas scale economies in production led to the development of increasingly large plants, economies of scope led to the development of increasingly large firms (or alliances of firms).

A second factor underlying globalization in this sector has been the growing technological complexity of the automobile. The very large size of the industry, the complexity of the product and the fact that the car is an income-elastic good (that is, unlike foods, demand for it goes up disproportionately as income rises) has made the section an arena for substantial investments in new technologies. New production technologies have consistently been introduced since Henry Ford's moving production line early in the twentieth century. In recent decades this has involved new forms of welding, the development of flexible electronics-based automation technologies and the introduction of complex information processing in the mixed-model assembly of a product containing more than 5,000 components. Materials technology, too, has changed as the industry has striven to achieve lighter, more fuel-efficient and more robust crash-resistant cars. This has led not only to the increasing use of aluminium and plastic, but to the associated introduction of new processing technologies in production. And, particularly as electronic controls have been developed, the final product itself has become much more complex. Stand-alone electronic components in engine-management and braking systems and instrumentation are increasingly being complemented by telecommunications technologies to make the car itself part of a wider information system utilizing global positioning systems and remote diagnostics.

These technological developments have promoted a growth in the scale of firms among the assemblers. But they have also led to the growth of specialized and technology-intensive first-tier component suppliers who increasingly provide the assemblers with sub-assembled modules – braking systems rather than brakes, whole dashboards rather than individual instruments. These first-tier suppliers drive global value chains of their own and are frequently referred to as '0.5-tier-' suppliers to reflect their technological competence, their size and their power relative to the assemblers. Increasingly this has led to the development in the sector of what has come to be called 'global sourcing'. That is, the assembler reaches an agreement with one or two of its '0.5-tier' suppliers to meet its needs in all of its global operations, feeding agreed products and sub-assemblies into all of the assembler's plants.

The third and final factor promoting globalization has been the prevalence of industrial policies in low-income and emerging economies designed to promote this strategic sector. During the height of the import-substituting era, very many economies had introduced policies to promote assembly. For example, even Kenya, with a population at the time of under 15 million, and total vehicle sales of fewer than 15,000, had introduced a policy regime during the 1970s which had led to the establishment of three assembly plants, each operating under contract for a number of vehicle producers. While many of these auto-sector policy incentives were removed during the 1980s and 1990s, a significant number of middle-income countries, such as Brazil, Malaysia, Mexico, Thailand, Turkey and South Africa, as well as large low-income countries such as China and India, retained policies designed to promote their auto and component sectors.

Centralizing, centripetal and centrifugal trends in the auto and components sectors

In the context of these factors driving globalization, the auto sector has been characterized by a number of centralizing, centripetal and centrifugal tendencies. The centralizing element of this equation has seen the consolidation of assembly among a limited number of networked firms (figure 5.10 above). But it is not just assembly that has been consolidated. There has also been a sharp reduction in the number of component suppliers and a consequent growth in their size and concentration. In North America, their number fell from 30,000 in 1990 to 10,000 by 2000, and is projected to fall further to between 3,000 and 4,000 by 2010; Peugeot-Citroën has reduced its supply base from 900 to fewer than 500, and BMW from 1,400 to 600.[13] By 2000, there were eight component suppliers with global sales exceeding $10 billion managing operations in a large number of countries. Six of these were US-owned, one was Japanese and one was German.

A second factor determining geographical spread has been the centripetal consequence of just-in-time production. As we saw briefly in the previous chapter, the last two decades have seen the increasing diffusion of a new form of production organization. The customized and flexible assembly operations which provide competitive advantage in final markets require close coordination on a just-in-time basis with suppliers. Hence assembly is increasingly clustered geographically with component supply, and auto complexes emerge. 'Follower supply' has been a direct complement of the global sourcing which tied assemblers to 0.5 and first-tier suppliers.

But at the same time as these clustered districts are favoured in order to produce tightly controlled production systems, the sector has become progressively beset by significant overcapacity – around 30 per cent in Europe and 25 per cent in the USA in 2003. Hence cost-cutting has become pervasive, in part through cost-down pressures placed on suppliers by the assemblers and other suppliers higher up the production chain, but increasingly also by relocating production to low-cost countries. This is a centrifugal tendency which counteracts the centripetal pressure of just-in-time production, but one which has a predominantly regional character. Mexico (and to some extent Brazil) feeds into the USA, Central and Eastern Europe and South Africa into Europe, and Thailand and China into Japan. This centrifugal trend has of course been strengthened by the industrial policies introduced in low- and middle-income countries designed to promote the manufacture, assembly and export of autos and auto components.

A final globally centrifugal tendency (but one which has its own internal centripetal tendencies) has been the need of the assemblers to tap into rapidly growing markets. The market for automobiles in the high-income world is essentially a replacement market (albeit one which involves significant product upgrading). Between 1990 and 1997 it grew at only 0.1 per cent per annum. By contrast, the market in the emerging economies is expanding rapidly as auto ownership increases – by 7 per cent annually in the same period.[14] This has attracted the assemblers and component suppliers to dynamic new markets emerging in China, India and Eastern Europe.

Globalization and catch-up

Although the automobile was first produced in Europe, mass production and the growth of the mass market occurred in the USA. Until 1950 the US industry accounted for the overwhelming bulk of output, manufacturing not only more than 80 per cent of total global production in the USA, but also accounting for much of the rest of global production in factories in Europe and elsewhere. But after the debris of the Second World War began to settle the European industry took off, rapidly eroding the dominance of North America, but in almost all cases predominantly serving global markets from their European production bases. In turn, Japanese producers began their meteoric rise during the 1970s and 1980s. But because of the trade frictions arising from this rapid growth, Japanese auto firms promptly built up a network of global plants to rival those of their American counterparts. They began in the USA itself, then moved to Europe, and more recently have penetrated Brazil, Asia and elsewhere. As figure 5.11 shows, probably the most significant trend after the 1980s has been the globalization of auto production beyond the USA, Europe and Japan. In particular, production in China and India has grown at very rapid rates indeed. Between 1998 and 2003 the biggest change in global production market shares was a decline of 3.6 per cent in the USA and 2.7 per cent in the EU, and a rise of 3.4 per cent in China, 2.3 per cent in Korea and 1.1 per cent in India. But, given the small size of Chinese and Indian production in real terms, their growth rates over the five-year period was dramatic – 398 per cent in China and 224 per cent in India. In 2003 alone, Chinese production grew by 78 per cent.

This dispersion in global production has not yet been reflected in an equivalent change in global trade patterns, although there are signs that this may be taking place. As table 5.6 shows, a clutch of predominantly middle-income economies, with wage rates much lower than those in the USA, Europe and Japan, is beginning to make rapid inroads into global trade in autos and auto components. It is likely that this growth will be sustained, much as it has in many other sectors, and particularly given the high rates of overcapacity and the consequent high costs of producers in the USA and Europe.

Underlying this change in global market shares, both in production and in exports, is the rapid growth of productive capability in a

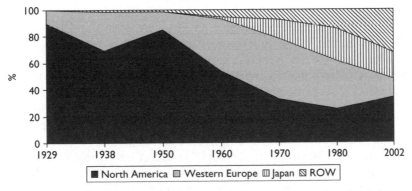

Figure 5.11   Geographical distribution of global auto production, 1929–2002

Source: Calculated from <www.oica.net> and Altshuler et. al. (1984)

Table 5.6   Global exports of autos and components by new entrants, 1990, 1995 and 2002 ($000)

	1990	1995	2002
Mexico	4,708	14,258	30,909
Korea	2,301	9,166	17,300
Czech Republic		1,509	6,403
Hungary	648	659	5,983
Poland	374	996	5,192
Brazil	2,034	2,955	4,979
Turkey	53	642	3,160
Thailand	108	486	2,878
Slovak Republic		344	2,805
China		621	2,677
South Africa		730	2,402
Total global exports	18,960	456,430	620,920

Source: WTO (2004)

selected number of middle-income and low-income economies. This parallels the growth in productive capabilities in other sectors. To illustrate the extent of this catch-up and the role played by government industrial policy, we will focus briefly on the evolution of the South African automobile industry since the mid-1990s. In 2002 the South African auto industry was the fifteenth largest global exporter, and had experienced the seventh fastest growth of exports between 1995 and 2002. (This treats Western European EU producers as a single country.)

Capability growth in the South African auto industry

The South African auto industry had its origins in the 1930s. But it was only in the 1960s that production took place in any significant numbers, fuelled by policies designed to promote domestic supply, then particularly during the 1980s when sanctions against apartheid promoted a siege mentality. Yet policy design in the period before 1990 was poor – local content was measured by weight rather than value (a bizarre choice when the auto industry was trying to produce lighter, more fuel-efficient cars), and little attempt was made to promote exports or reduce model proliferation to encourage scale economies. During the 1990s the Motor Industry Development Programme was introduced, and this represented a sharp reorientation of policy. Although there were many detailed incentives, the primary one was to encourage greater exports and a reduction in model proliferation, and hence an increase in scale economies in production. Effectively, assemblers could import as much as they wanted as long as they covered these with exports. And, crucially, the assemblers could buy export certificates from the suppliers of auto components, thus providing a stimulus towards the export of both cars and components.

In itself, this incentive system provided the carrot for export and output growth. But, to achieve these objectives, the sector had to engage in a rapid and systematic programme of production upgrading. Here they were assisted by the demands of the assemblers who were exporting autos from South Africa – the BMW 3-Series, the Mercedes C-Series, the Volkswagen Golf 4, a Ford engine plant, and Toyota. They were also assisted by government policy designed to upgrade production, which was reflected in the development of a series of 'benchmarking clubs'.

Table 5.7 shows the extent of this catch-up in production parameters, illustrating both the learning path and the distance between South African component firms and their international competitors. These benchmarked data reflect the three key performance indicators that dominate this industry – cost, quality and delivery. The data are drawn from detailed interaction with thirty-two South African component firms over four years, providing longitudinal data on performance enhancement. Performance in 2001 is matched by a sample of twenty-six international firms, for which unfortunately there are no time-series data. The two population samples are largely matched by sub-sector. The comparative sample is split in order to assess the performance of South African component firms in relation to both old and new competitors.

These data show the capability growth which underlies South Africa's exports in this sector. With the exception of delivery reliability to customers, progress for all of these indicators in South Africa has been significant. Despite this improvement, the country's components sector has in most respects some way to go before it reaches the global frontier. However, the upper tier of its component suppliers operates close to the global frontier, and the significant characteristic of the industry is the length of its tail. Although investment in R&D has risen in the South African components sector, and compares favourably internationally, this is somewhat misleading, since most of the R&D involves minor changes to customize components to the local market.

It is striking that the growth of South African auto exports has not been at the cost of the domestic consumer – a frequent criticism directed against active industrial policies. Quality levels are high, and cars are sold interchangeably on the local and export markets. Indeed,

Table 5.7 Learning and comparative advantage in the auto components sector, 1998–2001

Critical success factors	Key performance indicators	N	South African firms					Comparator firms	
			1998	1999	2000	2001	Improvement 1998/9–2001 (%)	W. Europe N=14	Emerging economy N=12
Cost control	Total inventory (days)	32	62.6	54.3	47.6	42.0	32.8	31.2	38.6
	Raw material (days)	32	32.3	27.9	25.2	21.8	32.7	17.2	19.2
	Work in progress (days)	32	12.4	8.9	8.1	8.2	34.3	5.3	8.6
	Finished goods (days)	32	17.8	17.5	14.3	12.1	32.0	8.6	9.5
Quality	Customer return rate (ppm)[a]	23	3270	2638	1406	1240	62.0	549	624
	Internal reject rate (%)	25		4.9	4.2	3.9	20.7	1.9	3.5
	Supplier return rate (ppm)[a]	21		21989	14637	18518	16.0	8319	13213
Delivery	Lead time (days)	17		19.9	19.1	17.9	9.9	16.8	12.0
	Supplier on time & in full delivery (%)	23		78.7	82.1	82.2	4.5	92.2	92.3
	On time & in full delivery to customers (%)	25		92.2	92.8	92.7	0.6	96.1	93.5
Innovation capacity	R&D expenditure (%)	24	1.64	1.70	1.67	2.12	29.5	1.83	2.90

[a] ppm = parts per million

Source: Barnes, Kaplinsky and Morris (2004)

Table 5.8   Comparison of prices, net of import duties and value-added tax, South Africa, the UK and the EU, 2002

	Price in £UK		Price premium	
	UK	SA	UK	EU average
Golf 4	10,064	9,163	12.4	11.1
Toyota Corolla	9,318	7,612	16.5	20.6
Mercedes-Benz	16,496	12,673	21.2	1.3
BMW	16,603	12,070	25.5	12.5

Source: Barnes, Kaplinsky and Morris (2004)

the J. D. Power industry initial quality ratings for the USA in 2002, measured in faults per 100 vehicles, ranked South African BMW products second after Toyota's Tahara plant in Japan. But, perhaps more importantly, stripping out the results of duties and excise tax, cars in South Africa are no more expensive – and indeed are often cheaper – than the equivalent vehicles sold in Europe (table 5.8).

What this brief review of globalization in the auto and the auto components industry has shown is that, as the twentieth century proceeded, the sector became increasingly globalized. Initially the shift was in final markets, from America to Europe and then to the rest of the world. Subsequently the centre of gravity of the sector shifted, initially to Europe during the 1960s and 1970s, and then to Japan in the 1980s and the 1990s. By the millennium, new and significant changes were occurring in the pattern of globalization. The major market growth is now in the emerging economies, and this has led to a rapid geographical dispersion of production. At the same time, the increasing overcapacity in the global industry has led to severe cost pressures, and this has been a factor reinforcing the dispersion into regionally specific low-cost production sites. The complexity of this sector, and its scale economies, has meant that geographical dispersion is much lower than in the textiles and clothing and furniture industries, and indeed many other sectors. But it is significant nonetheless, eroding production in those economies which dominated the industry for the whole of the twentieth century.

5.4   Textiles, clothing, furniture and autos: a portent of the future?

In this chapter we have reviewed the evolution and global spread of three key industries. The textiles and clothing chain is the major exporting sector from low-income economies, particularly from the lowest-income group; the furniture sector is a major export sector, and has grown particularly rapidly since the early 1980s, with trade being widespread among different income-group countries. Unlike these two buyer-driven sectors, the auto industry is driven by key transnational producers. It also plays a dominant role in manufacturing sectors of many high- and upper-middle income economies, as well as in key low-income economies such as China and India.

What common lessons can be learnt from the experience of these three sectors? The first is that global production capability has spread, and, outside of the auto industry, to a very wide number of countries. Second, in each case trade has become increasingly important and, like the global economy in general, trade growth has far exceeded output growth. Third, within this trade growth, there have been an increasing number of participating countries, even in the auto sector, including a developing contribution by low-income economies. Fourth, in all three cases, there is evidence of growing concentration in buying – among retailers and specialized buyers in clothing and furniture, and among assemblers and 0.5-tier component suppliers in autos. Fifth, although production and trade in physical commodities has expanded in each of these sectors, there has been a pervasive tendency for the intangibles of design, branding and marketing to remain located in the high-income countries or, at the very least, in the ownership of firms located in high-income economies. Sixth, the complexity of each of these chains has given a prominent role to key chain governors – network coordinators – whose task it is to allocate responsibilities within the chain and to constrain and/or facilitate different forms of upgrading by different parties in the chain. Seventh, in all three sectors, price competition has become pervasive, particularly in garments, following the reduction of quota restrictions in major markets. And, finally, hovering over all these case studies is the growing presence of China. In textiles and clothing, now that MFA quotas have gone, China is likely to become the location of choice for most global buyers; in furniture, China has developed into the third largest global exporter, having been only the nineteenth largest exporter in 1990 (and registering no exports in 1980); and in autos, its pace of growth has been astonishing.

What are we to make of these three sectoral studies? It might be thought that this experience supports the residual approach to globalization and poverty, since in each sector there is evidence of growing participation by low-income country producers in global markets. But selective use of data can lead to illegitimate conclusions; moreover, the whole is not necessarily the sum of the parts. It does not therefore follow that the global spread of production and trade is leading to the wider distribution of incomes. Nor does it necessarily follow that this growth trajectory is sustainable, that it will spread to other low-income economies, or that the same experience is found in other sectors. Yet much of the analysis of global patterns of production, trade and distribution is all too often pursued at this case-study level. Detailed analysis is undertaken of individual firms, countries, groups of countries and sectors, and then the results are scaled up – almost through sleight of hand – to the global level. It is not surprising, therefore, that the World Bank and others see globalization not just as having an unstoppable momentum, but as providing wide-ranging benefits to all who participate.

In part III, we show how these sector-specific conclusions cannot be extended to the macro-level. The undoubted progress of *some* producers in *some* sectors does not translate into gains reaped by *most* producers in *most* sectors. As a consequence it is difficult to sustain the residual explanation for global poverty. Instead, as we shall see, a significant component of global poverty is relational, a direct result of the workings of the global economy.

Part III

Losing from Globalization

As we saw in the case of China in chapter 2, there are circumstances in which rapid growth, allied to export expansion, can indeed have a significant impact in reducing absolute poverty (although not without growing inequalities). In part II we provided a framework for understanding this process. The ability to target areas of rent, and then to appropriate such rents through the effective management of innovation, provides the basis for sustainable income growth and poverty alleviation. We also showed in chapter 5 that, at least in the case of key sectors, many low-income economies have managed to advance their presence in global production and trade. China was particularly successful in each of these three sectors. While we also noted that, in each of these sectors, price competition was becoming increasingly intense, we were nevertheless able to paint an optimistic picture.

However, very often, optimistic outcomes are predicated on what economists call a partial equilibrium analysis. That is, they do not take account of the full range of interacting factors. It may well be that a partial equilibrium analysis leads to different conclusions from a general equilibrium analysis which takes all factors into account. Take, for example, the case of coffee. It can be shown that, when global prices make it profitable to expand production, it will make sense for an individual farm or even a country to do so; production could be increased with little impact on the global price of coffee. This would be a partial picture. But if all farmers and countries made the same decision – a general equilibrium world – then the global market would be swamped with supplies and the price of coffee would fall. Everyone would be worse off. This is indeed the explanation for events in the latter half of the 1990s, as we saw in chapter 3.

Economists refer to this coffee example as a 'fallacy of composition'. A decision which makes sense for an individual producer loses its logic when all producers make the same decision. And it is here that we must go back to the case studies provided in chapter 5. In each case, some producers did well out of globalization – China in textiles and clothing; China, Mexico and Poland in furniture; and Mexico, Eastern Europe, Brazil, China, Thailand and South Africa in the case of autos and components. But to what extent can this positive performance be generalized? If the very success of these successful globalizers depends on the failure of others treading the same path, the story does not add up.

Part III addresses this problem of adding up, the possible existence of a fallacy of composition. It requires a different methodology, one which takes account of a full range of sectors, and the performance and experience of a range of producers, rather than those of a limited number of sectors and countries who have had a positive experience. In chapter 6, we do this by examining the price performance of more than 10,000 manufactured products, and the way in which this is reflected in the export performance of different types of low-income countries. We will show in this analysis of prices that the specific experience of successful globalizers cannot be generalized. Then, in chapter 7, we provide a theoretical explanation for this conclusion, one that hinges on China's growing impact on the world economy. We will argue that China's success (and, to a more limited extent, the success of other Asian economies) squeezes out the opportunity for many other low-income producers to gain from globalization. This is a direct consequence of systemic overcapacity in the global economy.

Chapter 8 concludes the book by considering some of the outcomes that are generated by these results. Widening inequality and persistent poverty threaten the sustainability of globalization as we know it. They also pose major policy challenges for producers everywhere. For those who are able to manage their innovation processes *better than* competitors, globalization has much to offer. This is the path trodden successfully by many Asian economies, particularly China in the most recent era. But for those producers unable to match this success, including many in the high-income world, and especially for most economies in Africa and Latin America, the fruits of globalization are more uncertain. For these latter countries, it may be necessary to rethink the extent of linking with the global economy.

6

How Does it All Add Up? Caught Between a Rock and a Hard Place

Although the turning point for my own perspective on globalization can be located in a furniture factory in Port Shepstone, South Africa (chapter 1), the seeds of doubt were sown some years before. In 1996 we built an extension to our house in the UK as a consulting room for my wife's practice as a psychotherapist. For some obscure reason, one of the few detailed items which caught my eye when the final bill came was a solid wood pine toilet seat. The cost was £24.99, and it was obtained from a discount builder's merchant. Not long after this, I was in a similar store and was struck to see the price of an almost identical seat at £18.99. Thereafter, with the perverse state of mind of an economist, I have used the price of solid wooden pine toilet seats as a marker of the astonishing fall in the price of many manufactures, charting not just their prices, but also their points of origin. The price of the same toilet seat – solid wood, with brass furniture, packed and retailed in a branded box – is now less than £9.00. More recently, when completing the final drafting of this manuscript, I purchased an electronic wristwatch manufactured and sold under the well-known Lorus brand name of a Japanese manufacturer (and using the same electronic components as the same watchmaker's Seiko brand, selling at more than £50). The watch, formerly manufactured in Japan (I lose watches frequently!), was now made in China. Together with ten four-hour videotapes (also made in China), the total bill was £7.99.

What happens when we try and generalize the experience of producers selling into the global economy beyond toilet seats, watches, videotapes and the three sectors analysed in chapter 5? And what happens when we break down these three sectors into a much finer set of traded products, to take account of the fact that, within textiles and clothing, within furniture and within autos and components, there are a variety of different sub-sectors, each with different characteristics?

We begin in section 6.1 by showing that the global spread of production in the three key sectors is indeed reflected across the range of manufacturing industries. There is undoubted and comprehensive evidence to show the advancing share of low-income producers in global industrial production and trade. However, there has been an ancillary process occurring at the same time – the growing concentration of global buying power (section 6.2). These two developments occurred coterminously, and are closely interlinked (section 6.3). Producers feeding into the global economy are caught between this rock of growing productive capability and the hard place of concentrated buying power, and this results in declining prices and falling margins (section 6.4). It is China's entry and deepening presence in the global economy that largely explains this outcome (section 6.5). India's growing global presence and that of other populous and educated Asian economies suggests that this world of intense competition is unlikely to change, but only to get worse.

6.1   The rock – productive capability diffuses widely

Before reporting trends in global production and trade in manufactures, a 'health warning' is necessary. The calculation of global production shares is based on information collected by the United Nations Industrial Development Organization, drawn from the data supplied by individual countries. This calculates the value of output in domestic prices, which are then translated through prevailing exchange rates into US$ equivalents to facilitate international comparison. However, as we saw in chapter 2 in the discussion of income distribution, this form of translation is very unsatisfactory, since it takes no account of the purchasing power differences between countries. Unlike the measure of comparative income, where purchasing power parity dollars are used, there is no accepted methodology that has been used to measure the comparative value of manufacturing production across countries. This leads to an overvaluation of manufacturing value added (MVA) in many countries where the domestic price of manufactures remains higher than the global price due to widespread tariff protection. There is a second caveat on data which concerns the measurement of global exports. Each country provides data on the gross value of exports in each product grouping. But, as we saw in chapter 1, one of the key characteristics of the recent global economy has been the increasing 'vertical specialization' of trade, that is, the fracturing of production processes which are then parcelled around the global economy. For example, in the Dominican Republic in the early 1990s, on average, the added value in the export of a 'shoe' was less than $0.30; this is because, rather than exporting shoes, Dominican Republic producers were exporting labour, merely sewing together the components imported from other countries, and wrapping them in imported material, paper and boxes. Yet, in international trade statistics, the unit value of shoe exports was not the added value of $0.30, but the gross value of the final product, which was more like $15. This vertical specialization has been growing. Between 1980 and 1998, the share of China's exports that reflects this form of trade grew from 14.9 to 22.6 per cent, and for India from 7.3 to 11 per cent.[1] The unevenness of this verticalization urges caution in comparing export performance across countries and over time.

Manufacturing value added (MVA)

Summary: Major trends in production and trade in manufactures

Manufacturing value added

With regard to the global spread of manufacturing value added, developing countries doubled their share between 1975 and 2000, coming very close to meeting the Lima target of 25 per cent of global value added. The major reason for this rapid growth in global market share was the performance of East Asia in general, and China in particular. Both Latin America (excluding Mexico) and the Caribbean and sub-Saharan Africa saw significant losses in market shares, globally and within the developing world.

Manufactured exports

Manufactured exports grew rapidly from developing countries, accounting for more than 70 per cent of all their merchandise exports by 2000. Even in sub-Saharan Africa and the Middle East and North Africa, exports of manufactures exceeded those of agricultural products. But manufacturing exports have become increasingly concentrated over time in a limited number of developing economies. Once again, the influence of China is particularly marked, in its share of both global manufactured trade and developing-country manufactured exports.

Exports by sector

Considered by sector, there was a pervasive shift in the developing world away from resource-based manufactures to low-tech products. There was also a rapid growth in the export of high-tech manufactures, but much of this was probably due to the labour-intensive and low-tech processes within these high-tech products.

In 1975 the Second General Conference of the United Nations Industrial Development Organization adopted the Lima plan. Its primary target was to double the share of developing countries in global manufacturing value added from 12.6 per cent in 1975 to 25 per cent in 2000. At the time, this target seemed fanciful (about as fanciful as the millennium development goals adopted at the end of the twentieth century which are to halve the proportion of the world's population living in absolute poverty by 2015 – chapter 2). The industrially advanced countries had experienced centuries of industrial growth, and countries such as France and Germany took many decades to push up their share of global manufacturing value added during the nineteenth century. Yet the Lima target aimed to double the share of developing countries in a mere two decades. As we saw in the previous chapter, developing-country productive capacities in manufacturing grew not just in labour-intensive production, but in key sectors such as automobiles and components. This sectorally specific progress was matched across a wide range of other sectors so that by 2000 the Lima target had almost been met, with the share of developing countries in global manufactures rising to 24 per cent (figure 6.1).

This growth in productive capacity was naturally uneven between the types of economy involved (levels of per capita income), their geographical location and their sectoral characteristics. Table 6.1 shows the changing structure of production by their income group and their geographical location between 1985 and 1998. Considered by income group, the major gains were made by the low-income group of developing countries, whose share of global manufacturing output rose from 6.5 to 8.1 per cent. But this was entirely due to the rapid industrial growth in China and India. Other than these two countries, the shares of global manufacturing output rose only for the upper-middle-income group of

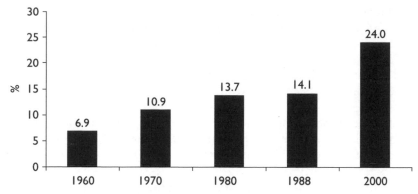

Figure 6.1 Share of developing countries in global manufacturing value added, 1960–2000

Source: UNIDO (1990); UNIDO (2002)

Table 6.1   Share of global manufacturing value added, 1985 and 1998

	Share of the world		Share of developing countries	
By income group	1985	1998	1985	1998
Upper-middle-income	9.0	9.9	46.8	45.7
Low-middle-income	3.7	3.7	19.4	17.2
Low-income	6.5	8.1	33.8	37.1
Low-income excl. China, India	0.9	0.6	4.7	2.9
Least-developed	0.2	0.2	0.7	0.6
By geography	1985	1998	1985	1998
East Asia	4.1	13.9	29.2	57.7
China	1.4	7.0	10.2	29.3
South Asia	0.8	1.8	5.9	7.3
Latin America and Caribbean	6.7	5.2	46.9	21.8
Sub-Saharan Africa	1.0	0.8	7.1	3.4
Middle East, North Africa, Turkey	1.5	2.4	10.8	9.8

Source: Calculated from UNIDO (2002)

countries, and by a smaller proportion than for China and India. Considered by geographical location, the striking feature is the declining share of Latin America and the Caribbean and sub-Saharan Africa, both in global production and as a share of developing-country production. Conversely, there is a dramatic increase in China's share – from 1.4 to 7.0 per cent of global manufacturing value added, and from 10.2 to 29.3 per cent of developing-country manufacturing value added.

Finally, if we group sectors into resource-based, low-technology and medium/high-technology sectors, the major changes in global production have been as follows.

- In the resource-based sector group, the only major change in global share between 1981 and 2000 was that of East Asia (which grew from 4.8 to 13.9 per cent) and, within that, China (from 1.5 to 7.5 per cent).
- In low-technology sectors, once again the major beneficiaries were East Asia (from 5.9 to 14.8 per cent) and China (2.0 to 7.2 per cent); the global share of Latin America and the Caribbean fell from 7.1 to 4.1 per cent.
- In the medium- and high-tech sectors, there has been a familiar pattern of rising shares in East Asia (3.2 to 13.6 per cent) and China (1.3 to 6.8 per cent).

Trade

A similar pattern can be seen when we focus on the participation of developing countries in global trade, as measured by their share of global exports. The Lima declaration did not explicitly target the share of developing countries in trade in manufactures. But it is notable that these grew even more significantly than manufacturing value added, rising from 6.3 per cent in 1975 to 27 per cent in 2000, expanding particularly rapidly during the 1990s. This growing participation in global trade in manufactures reflects the general transition in the export structure of developing countries, with a rise in the share of manufactures, a relatively stable share of agricultural products and a concomitant fall in the share of resources. By 2001, more than 70 per cent of all developing-country merchandise trade was in manufactures (figure 6.2). The only outliers to this pattern were the Middle East and North Africa and sub-Saharan Africa: in both cases manufactures were around 30 per cent of total merchandise exports, exceeding agricultural products but being dwarfed by mineral resource exports. (There is also a growing trend towards the export of services, but these are not the subject matter of this book. However, analogous trends are emerging – see chapter 8.)

Looking at the geography of trade, we see a familiar pattern (table 6.2). By income category, the major gain in share was by the

Figure 6.2   Sectoral shares of developing-country exports, 1981–2001

Source: W. Martin, personal communication

Table 6.2   Share of manufactured exports, 1985 and 1998

	Share of the world		Share of developing countries	
By income group	1985	1998	1985	1998
Upper-middle-income	11.5	14.5	73.6	62.2
Low-middle-income	2.7	3.8	17.4	16.2
Low-income	1.4	5.0	9.0	21.6
Low-income excl. China, India	0.4	0.5	2.7	2.0
Least-developed	0.1	0.1	0.7	0.6
By geography	1985	1998	1985	1998
East Asia	6.8	18.4	51.9	68.7
China	1.0	6.5	7.6	24.0
South Asia	0.6	1.1	4.6	4.1
Latin America and Caribbean	3.2	5.1	24.5	19.0
Mexico	0.5	2.9	3.8	10.9
Sub-Saharan Africa	0.7	0.6	5.6	2.3
Middle East, North Africa, Turkey	1.8	1.6	13.4	6.0

Source: UNIDO (2002)

low-income group. Between 1985 and 1998, it raised its share of global manufactured exports from 1.4 to 5.0 per cent and of developing-country manufactures from 9.0 to 21.6 per cent. But virtually all of this was due to the rapid rise in manufactured exports from China and

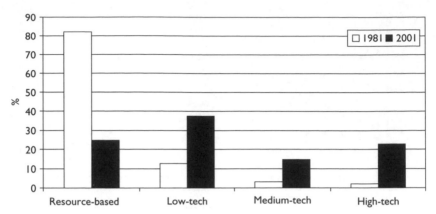

Figure 6.3 Structure of developing-country exports, 1991 and 2000

Source: W. Martin, personal communication

India. China's share of developing-country manufactured exports rose from 7.6 per cent in 1985 to 24 per cent in 2001. By region, the East Asian share grew sharply, while that of Latin America (excluding Mexico), sub-Saharan Africa and the Middle East and North Africa fell. Finally, considered by technological intensity (figure 6.3), the share of resource-based manufactures fell sharply, while those of low-tech manufactures rose. It is also evident that the share of high-tech manufactured exports grew. But much of this was probably in the export of sub-assemblies of high-tech products, which marks the vertical specialization of trade (for example, low-tech assembly of high-tech products).

6.2 The hard place – growing concentration in buying

Summary: Major trends in global buying

Garments, furniture and auto components

In each of these sectors there is detailed evidence of high and growing degrees of concentration in major markets in high-income countries, reflected in increasingly concentrated buying.

Food retailing and food manufacture

In the USA, and especially in Europe, levels of concentration have grown rapidly. In the EU, only in Italy, Greece and Portugal do the five largest firms account for less than half of total retail sales; in Austria, the Netherlands and Sweden the five largest firms account for more than 90 per cent of total industry sales.

Concentration in the retail sector is matched by extensive concentration in food production. In the EU, on average, the largest three firms across seventeen sectors and nine countries account for 68 per cent of total production.

Not just in retailing

Many producers in poor countries sell to specialized buyers rather than to final retailers. Although the evidence is more partial here, it appears as if concentration among specialized buyers is also growing.

Not monopoly but competitive oligopsony

Growing concentration in global buying is not leading to monopoly pricing and super-profits as some theory might predict. To the contrary, retailing is becoming increasingly competitive. The consequence is that global buyers are sourcing dynamically to find the lowest-cost producers (meeting their demanding delivery, quality and product requirements). All of this adds up to fierce cost pressure being exerted on exporters from poor countries.

In chapter 5 we examined the nature of the globalizing trends in three sectors which have become key in the expansion of manufacturing exports from poor countries. In each case, there is evidence of growing concentration in global buying power. These trends are briefly summarized as follows.

- In garments, in the USA, the largest five retailers raised their share of the final market between 1987 and 1991 from 35 to 68 per cent. In both the UK and Germany, concentration was less marked, but the largest five retailers still accounted for around one-third of the final market, and in France, Italy and Japan there has been a pervasive trend for independent retailers to be supplanted by large chains.
- In furniture, there has been a similar process of market concentration. Retail multiples control more than 40 per cent of the UK market, and in Germany a single group and its affiliates controls 60 per cent of the final market.
- In the auto sector, the buyers have concentrated on consolidating their supply base. The number of component suppliers was

reduced by two-thirds in North America between 1990 and 2000, and is projected to fall by a further two-thirds by 2010. In Europe, major buyers have halved their supply base in the past decade. The consequence has been a growth in very large 0.5-tier component suppliers (described in chapter 5) with global buying power of considerable significance – each of the largest eight component suppliers had global turnovers exceeding $10 billion.

What is happening beyond these three sectors? Unfortunately there is not sufficient evidence available to detail the widespread concentration of buying power associated with the global sourcing that has become prevalent in the global economy, and we therefore have to work with very partial data. One area where there is a growing body of material is the food retail sector, which covers predominantly the food sector, but also involves many 'fast-moving consumer goods' such as cosmetics, cleaning materials, unbranded medicines, toys, and basic clothing items. These products account for a considerable proportion of basic household incomes and include a growing number of globally sourced items. For example, in recent years in the major consuming economies fresh fruit and vegetables have moved from being locally sourced into a global industry. Many processed foods, too, are imported, especially those which serve the growing desire for 'ethnic menus'. And the simple toys and clothes sold by these retail chains are almost always imported from low-wage economies.

Consider first the case of the USA. Here, as can be seen from figure 6.4, between 1992 and 2000 there was growing concentration in the retail sector. The share of the five largest chains increased from 26.6 per cent to 42.9 per cent over the eight-year period. However, the level of concentration in the very large US market is dwarfed by the individual country experience in Europe (figure 6.5). There, the median share of the five largest firms was more than 80 per cent across the fifteen countries, and in three of them (the Netherlands, Sweden and Austria) it exceeded 90 per cent of total grocery sales. A number of factors explain this consolidation.[2] Some of these are related to market conditions, such as the demand for a combination of prepared and unprepared foods and the preference of time-conscious shoppers for a one-stop shopping experience that meets a variety of needs. It also reflects the economies of scale that arise from centralized management, bulk shipping and distribution, and inventory management. But, perhaps most relevant for our focus on distributional patterns, it provides retailers with enormous bargaining power. This purchasing power is often directly translated into forcing down the prices paid to suppliers; in other cases price pressure is

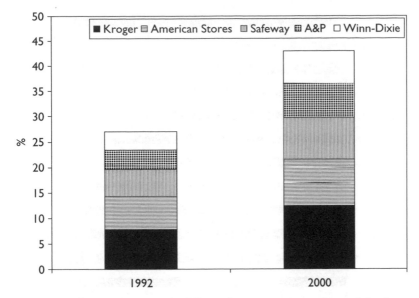

Figure 6.4 Concentration in the US retail grocery sector: share of the five largest firms, 1992–2000

Source: Wrigley (2002)

indirect, with many of the costs of promotion and inventory-holding being borne by suppliers.

These practices were considered in the UK in 2000 by the Monopolies and Mergers Commission, which investigated the purchasing practices of supermarkets. Among other things, the commission looked at pricing practices, and detailed a number which squeezed supplier margins. These included requiring suppliers to make payments or concessions to gain access to supermarket shelf space, and forcing an unfair balance of risk on to suppliers (for example, by requiring compensation from a supplier when profits from a product are less than expected and failing to compensate suppliers for costs caused through the retailer's forecasting errors or order changes). In other cases, suppliers were required to contribute to the costs of buyer visits to new or prospective suppliers, and to purchase goods or services from designated hauliers and packaging and labelling firms.

Faced with the growing power of retailers, there has been an equivalent consolidation process sweeping through the manufacturing industries which supply these grocery chains. Table 6.3 shows the level of concentration in the European food manufacturing sector, covering

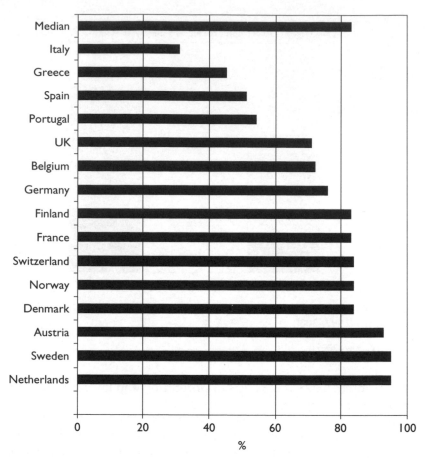

Figure 6.5 Market share of five largest grocery retailers in Europe, 2000

Source: Cited in Bell (2003)

the production of seventeen different products in nine countries, and focusing on the share of production of the three largest firms. In aggregate, across all sectors, the three largest firms accounted for more than two-thirds of production in the nine countries. In only two of the sectors was the average less than 50 per cent, whereas in six of the sectors the largest three firms accounted on average for more than three-quarters of total production.

Hence what we can observe is that, in the high-income consuming countries, there is a growing trend towards consolidation of buying power in the retail grocery sector, and a corresponding increase in concentration in the manufacturing sectors. In many cases these

Table 6.3 Three-firm concentration ratios in EU food processing industries, late 1990s (% share of market)

Product	Ireland	Finland	Sweden	Denmark	Italy	France	Spain	UK	Germany	Average
Baby food	98	100	100	99	96	93[a]	54	78	86	91
Canned soup	100	85	75	91	50	84	–	79	41[a]	87
Ice cream	–	84	85	90	73[a]	52	84	45	72	76
Yoghurt	69	83[a]	90	99[a]	36	67	73	50	76	70
Chocolate confectionery	95	74	–	39	93	61	79	74	–	74
Pet food	98	80	84	40	64[a]	73	53	77	87	79
Breakfast cereals	92	–	52	70	88	70	82	65	67	73
Tea	96	90	63	64	80	82	62	52	55	72
Snack foods	72	70[a]	80	78	71	50	56	73	48	68
Carbonated drinks	85	50	62	–	60	69	79	55	60[a]	71
Pasta	83	97	82	61	51	57	65	37	49	65
Wrapped bread	85	44	47	59	80	70	96	58[a]	9	59
Biscuits	83	73	51	44	55	61	53	42	50	58
Canned fish	–	70	72	49	68	43[a]	33	43[a]	–	55
Mineral water	–	100	74	70	37	–	31	14	22	50
Fruit juice	–	70	50	65[a]	62	26	38	35	46	48
Canned vegetables	–	68	47	50	36	29	–	–	–	47
Average	9	79	69	69	67	63	1	56	5	68

[a] Indicates two-firm concentration ratio

Source: Cotterill (1999)

manufacturers and retailers purchase directly from developing countries. Nowhere is this more the case than with Walmart, whose meteoric growth has made it the world's largest retailer (indeed, the world's largest firm), with sales in 2003 of more than $250 billion. It was founded in 1962 and has been the largest retailer in the USA since 1995. It began its overseas expansion in 1991 and by 2003 it operated in nine countries, including becoming the third largest retailer in the UK. Walmart's key competitive position is as a comprehensive and low-cost retailer, and in furthering this aim it has moved much of its sourcing to China. In 2003 it directly imported $15 billion worth of products from China, alone accounting for 11 per cent of all US imports from China.[3] A similar process of global sourcing and price pressure can be observed in the case of retailers in other countries. For example, one of the most successful UK clothing retailers rebuilt its market share by increasing competition between its suppliers through expanding their number; changing the primary source-country from which garments were being imported; dealing directly with foreign manufacturers rather than through intermediaries (particularly in China); and, perhaps most importantly, introducing a process of what it called 'cross-costing'. This involved obtaining quotes from one supplier, finding another supplier to beat this quote, and then returning to the original supplier to see if they would further reduce their prices.

But, as we saw in chapter 5, producers in poor countries do not always connect with the retailers of their products through direct contact; they often work through buying intermediaries. Here, too, there appears to be a process of consolidating buying power, although this is more difficult to evidence. Keeping our focus on the food value chain (although straying a little from the manufacturing sector), we can observe a similar process of consolidation in the coffee value chain. Figure 6.6 shows the very rapid growth in concentration in the coffee processing sector in Europe, with the share of the largest five producers more than doubling from 21.5 per cent to 58.4 per cent between 1995 and 1998. But it also shows an increase in concentration in the global buying industry, although at a lower pace and to lower levels. This concentration occurred during a period in which (as we saw in chapter 3) global coffee prices plummeted, and this can be directly traced to the simultaneous growth of productive capacity and buyer concentration.

But it is not just in the food industry that concentrated power exerted by specialized buyers has helped to force down global prices. In the shoe sector, for example, local Brazilian buyers played an important role in the rapid growth of exports of shoes to the USA, with a particularly fruitful link being forged between a large local

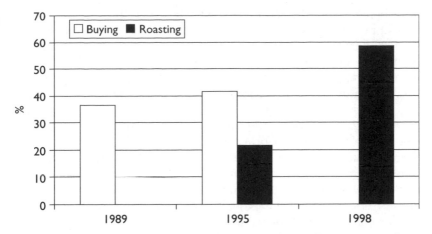

Figure 6.6 Five-firm concentration ratios in European coffee roasting and global buying, 1989–1998

Source: Kaplinsky and Fitter (2004)

buyer and Nine West (which itself began as a trader and then developed its own retail chain in the USA, and subsequently in Europe).[4] As Nine West moved into retailing, it began to focus increasingly on prices. Initially it forced down prices from Brazilian suppliers through its Brazilian buying intermediary. When this proved to be inadequate to its needs, it encouraged its Brazilian buyer in the early 1990s to move its key staff into China, switching an increasing proportion of its imports from Brazil. In some cases its Brazilian buying intermediary utilized the supplier development skills it had developed to help upgrade its Brazilian producers (a process which we described in chapter 4) to assist these Chinese suppliers to improve their productivity and consequently to reduce their prices.

Thus, over the past decade we have witnessed a simultaneous process in many sectors of growing concentration of buying power and intensifying competition. This may seem a little confusing to some of the proponents of free markets. For many years the industrial organization literature characterized the link between 'market structure' (how concentrated is an industry?) and 'market conduct' (how competitive is an industry?) as being one in which concentration resulted in monopolistic pressures. The result of concentration, it was feared, would be monopolization, and hence super-profits. But the process which we have been mapping out is not one of monopoly. Rather, it is one of fierce oligopsony, with a small number of large buyers being locked in intense competition. These increasingly large firms benefit from the economies of scale which this offers – particularly in buying power. But this scale reflects a dual process of growing market share and widening global operations. For example, the consolidation of retail grocery power in the USA described above has not been associated with anything like an equivalent increase in market concentration within metropolitan areas. While the four-firm concentration ratio at the national level rose from 16.9 to 28.8 per cent between 1992 and 1998, the same ratio in the 100 largest cities only rose by 3.7 per cent.[5] In other words, most of this growing concentration occurred through a larger operating footprint rather than through growth in particular markets. A similar process is occurring in global retailing markets – that is, the market presence and buying power of major firms such as Walmart, Tesco, Ahold and Carrefour is developing as much through their growing global presence as through increasing presence in their established markets.

6.3   The rock or the hard place?[6]

To what extent are the rock of growing production capacity in the global economy and the hard place of the concentrated power of global buyers connected? Have they been independent phenomena, occurring at more or less the same time, or has one driven the other, and, if so, in what sequence?

It has been customary to ascribe the success of the Asian exporters who have come to dominate much of developing-country trade with the high-income countries as resulting from the internal dynamic of their economies. In some cases the production surge has been ascribed to the entrepreneurial drive of large, often family-based firms in Korea and Japan. Witness the very rapid growth and massive footprint of firms such as Samsung and Hyundai in Korea and the large Japanese *keiretsu* (such as Mitsubishi and Toshiba). These very large firms have constructed a global presence in a range of sectors, including (in the case of Sony) services as well as manufacturing. In other cases, notably Taiwan, the dynamism of production has been led by clusters of small firms, often working with large enterprises. In all these examples, and despite the protestations of analysts committed to market-led explanations of economic growth, it is clear that the state has played a key role in promoting production capacity. This is particularly evident in China and India, but it was also the case in Korea, Malaysia and Taiwan. In some of these Asian economies, as well as in Latin America in general (and Mexico and the Caribbean in particular), the growth of productive capacity has also reflected the locational decisions by transnational firms. In some cases this began with the drive to penetrate the local market, maturing into outward-oriented production; in other cases, productive subsidiaries were established with the primary intent of serving global markets.

All of these recountings of the growth of productive capacity in the developing world can be seen as various forms of supply-sided explanations. But there is an alternative view which suggests that the primary factor underlying this productive surge lies in demand-sided factors, notably in the growing concentration of buying in the US economy. Whereas much of US manufacturing industry had become highly concentrated by the onset of the Second World War, concentration in retailing only really took off in the 1950s and 1960s, accelerating during the 1970s. Walmart, Kmart and Woolworths, as well as The Gap, Toys-R-Us and The Limited, all trace their origins to the period between 1970 and 1981. The development of what has latterly come to be termed 'lean retailing' was built on the standardization of products and of procedures, in order to sell in very large volumes at low cost. But this required the capacity to buy at low cost and in large volumes. Thus, beginning in the late 1960s, these US retailers began purchasing from Korea and Taiwan, initially through large Japanese trading houses. The evidence suggests that, in the case of both Korea and Taiwan, the origins of the diversified export base which now exists are to be found in the purchases by only a few US buyers of a limited number of products. During the 1970s, nearly 50 per cent of the value of Korea's exports and 25 per cent of the value of Taiwan's exports to the United States were the top ten products. Although this product concentration fell in the early 1980s, it increased again in the late 1980s and throughout the 1990s so that, in 2000, the top ten ten-digit product items accounted for over 30 per cent of the total exports to the United States for both Korea and Taiwan. During the early 1990s (after the Plaza Accord devaluation of the dollar and after the post-Tiananmen Square reforms had begun to bite), the large US retail houses, discount stores and buyers shifted many of their purchases to China.

So, we have two apparently competing explanations for the rise of global productive capacity. The first is rooted in supply-sided explanations of entrepreneurial drive and state support; the second lies in the nurturing effects of concentrated buying power which stimulated and fuelled the rise in production in the Asian economies (and in Mexico, Central America and the Caribbean). Which is correct, and does it matter? On the first question, the answer is probably that these two interpretations reflect two complementary developments, each with its own independent roots. But the important point is that in all likelihood neither development would have been independently possible, at least to the extent to which each developed. Without the demands of these voracious global buyers, the scope for outward-oriented production would have been significantly diminished; conversely, without the availability of large platform producers in low-cost economies, the market power of these retailers would have been reduced. On the second question (does it matter which explanation is correct?), the answer is that, insofar as we are interested in the squeeze on prices associated with global production systems, the answer is no. It is a fact that both the rock of growing productive capacity and the hard place of concentrated buying exist, and are of growing importance. The prices received by global producers are squeezed between these objects, whatever the causal explanations for their existence.

6.4   Between the rock and the hard place – prices are squeezed

Summary: Trends in the global price and terms of trade of manufactures

Price of manufactured exports

After a rapid and sustained growth in the price of globally traded manufactures, the rate of price increase gradually slowed after the 1980s. By the end of the decade, on aggregate, the price of manufactures began to fall.

Between 1988 and 2001 (a period for which we have relatively good-quality data), the lower the income group, the greater the tendency for prices to fall; prices of manufactured products from China were even more likely to fall than those from the lowest-income group of countries. Similarly, the lower the technological content, the more likely prices are to have fallen (although, perhaps surprisingly, the prices of resource-based products were less likely to fall than those of low-technology products). And, within each of the categories of sectors reflecting their technological intensity, prices were more likely to fall the lower the income group of the exporting economy.

Terms of trade in manufactures

Prices of manufactured exports from developing countries as a group have fallen compared with those from high-income countries. This reflects a systematic fall in the barter terms of trade of developing countries in manufactures – that is, the prices of their exports of manufactures have fallen faster than the prices of their imports of manufactures. This is true of their trade with the EU, the USA and Japan. Within this, the performance of the East Asian newly industrializing economies has been less badly affected by these falling terms of trade.

In section 6.1 we showed how productive capabilities have grown in the global manufacturing economy – more and more producers are extending their productive capacity and there have been important shifts in the global geography of production and exporting. In section 6.2 we documented the growing concentration in buying in many of the sectors into which developing-country producers are exporting. These two parallel and complementary forces are increasingly subjecting producers in the globalizing economies to growing competitive pressures. This is reflected in pressure on prices and on the barter trade of developing-country exporters.

Pressures on the prices of manufactured products

At an aggregate level, prices in the global economy grew in the 1960s and 1970s. In some exceptional cases in the developing world this was expressed in hyperinflation, with annual rates of inflation in thousands of percentage points. But inflationary pressures were not confined to the developing world, and even in the industrialized countries of Europe and North America annual price increases exceeded 10 per cent, and often more than 20 per cent in economies such as those of the UK and Italy. But during the second half of the 1980s, and especially during the 1990s, there was a generalized trend towards reining in price inflation, and in most countries in the industrialized world annual price inflation had fallen to below 3 per cent by the turn of the millennium. In exceptional cases such as Japan in the late 1990s, the rule was one of annual price deflation (falling prices) rather than annual price inflation. Therefore, in charting the evolution of price pressures in global manufacturing trade, we need to be aware that the reduction in price inflation reflected not only the competitive pressures in global production and trade, but also complementary macro-economic policies designed to provide more stable economic conditions.

Figure 6.7 shows the trend in the aggregate price of world manufactured exports. It charts the annual rate of price change between 1986 and 2000. As can be seen, there has been a sustained general fall in this price trend, and from 1996 the aggregate price of manufactured products fell on an annual basis. The problem with this data from the IMF, however, is that it is aggregated, and provides little insight into the variations in price performance. It is therefore important to dissect these trends and, by analysing trade into the EU as a surrogate for global trade, it is possible to break them down into the same country and sectoral categories used to analyse the changing geography of production and trade in section 6.1 above.

All world trade is defined in terms of a variety of detailed systems which ascribe a unique code to every traded item. The greater the level of detail required in analysing trade, the more detailed the code numbers that are required. One of the major sources of historical trade data is the United Nation's COMTRADE database. This provides five levels of detail – Standard International Trade Classification (SITC) one-, two-, three-, four- and five-digits, each broken down into different items. However, the problem with using the COMTRADE database for an analysis of prices (defined as the value of trade divided by its volume) is that the commonality of the data begins to break down at the three-digit level. For example, in the case of the furniture trade (SITC 82), at the four-digit level most countries report volume in tonnes, whereas China reports in units.

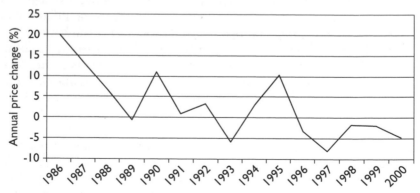

Figure 6.7 World manufacturing export price, 1986–2000

Source: IMF, World Economic Outlook Database, September 2003

With regard to US trade series, some four-digit trade headings provide data only on value, and not on volume. By contrast, the EU uses the Harmonized System (HS) to record its imports and exports. This breaks trade down to a very detailed level – to the eight-digit level in some cases – and also is consistent in the units used to measure the volume of trade. Each of these levels provides greater detail – in the manufacturing sectors, there are 71 two-digit products, 1,008 four-digit products, 4,587 six-digit products and 10,512 eight-digit products. (The eight-digit level is not very helpful for analysing trade across countries since, unlike the two-, three- and six-digit levels, some countries use different codes to report trade of the same eight-digit items.)

The HS system is therefore a much more useful database if detailed analysis of unit price is required. And detail is important, since it is obvious that, the higher the level of aggregation, the more likely detailed price trends will be obscured. We can test this by analysing the extent to which price trends can be identified at different levels of detail of trade disaggregation. Using the Augmented Dickey-Fuller (ADF) unit root tests, the percentage of sectors with discernible price trends between 1988 and 2001 rose from 17 per cent to 32 per cent to 40 per cent at the two-, four- and six-digit levels of disaggregation respectively. Hence this highly disaggregated EU database on manufactured imports is a very useful surrogate for analysing trends in the global price of manufactures. But it suffers from two weaknesses. First, as in the case of all countries using the HS nomenclature, trade data only exist back to 1988. And, second, trade into the EU before 2001 occurred in individual national currencies, and we have therefore had to convert it into a common unit. The unit we use – as do almost all other analyses of the EU's trade patterns – is the dollar, converting the EU data from national currencies through the ECU (until 2000), and then using the Euro (from 2001).

What do these data show? There are sophisticated methods available for tracking the unit price of traded products, most notably the Augmented Dickey-Fuller (ADF) unit root test, which will determine the existence of a price trend, and then the Kalman Filter (KF) to determine the direction and rate of price change. But the problem with the ADF and KF tests is that they require very long time series to determine trends, since they are very sensitive to inter-annual price fluctuations. For this reason we analyse the detailed evolution of world manufacturing prices by comparing prices at the beginning of the period (1988) with those at the end of the period (2001) for the major traded items imported into the EU. (In actual fact, to iron out the possibility of volatile prices, we compare the average for 1988 and 1999 with the average for 2000 and 2001.) We record the percentage of sectors with negative price trends to determine which categories of countries and products are most subject to pricing pressure. This is a blunt tool, but, given the limitations on both COMTRADE and HS data, it provides the least bad method for tracking the evolution of price at a high level of product disaggregation.

Figure 6.8 shows the experience of the four major income groupings of countries exporting manufactures into the EU. It also covers China since, as we have seen, it has been such a dynamic participant in global trade. It is clear from this that, the lower the per capita income grouping, the more likely that unit prices are to decline. Significantly, China's exports are even more likely to be characterized by falling prices than are those of the low-income group of countries.

However, country grouping may not be the best way of showing the vulnerability of producers to growing price pressure. Another way into this is to look at the price performance of different types of products. The presumption here is that price pressures are most likely to be felt in products which benefit least from the innovation rents we discussed in chapters 3 and 4. Hence, in figure 6.9 we observe price trends in relation to the technology intensity of sectors, drawing on the UNIDO classification which we utilized in the analysis of the changing structure of global trade in section 6.1 above, and examining price trends in more than 2,000 six-digit products. This shows that, the lower the technological intensity of these products, the more likely their prices are to fall. Interestingly,

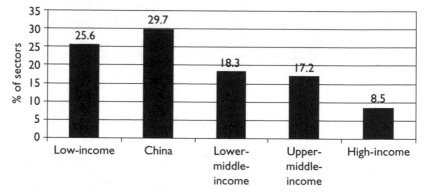

Figure 6.8 Percentage of sectors with negative price trends, 1988/9–2000/1, by country grouping

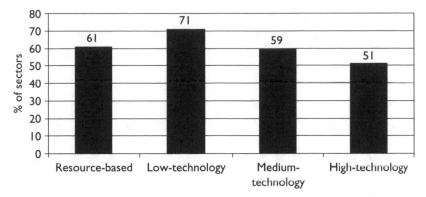

Figure 6.9 Percentage of sectors with negative price trends, 1988/9–2000/1, by technological intensity

the prices of resource-based products (for example, processed vegetable oils) which generally use domestic primary commodities are less likely to fall than those of manufactures which use imported components, and increasingly reflect the vertical specialization of trade.

A final characteristic of price trends brings together the two elements driving the analysis in figures 6.8 and 6.9 above. Is there a tendency for the prices of the different categories of products – measured by their technological intensity – to fall depending on the income group of the exporting country? This information is presented in figure 6.10, and it shows that, in each category of sector, prices are more likely to fall the lower the per capita income grouping of the exporting economy. With the exception of the high-technology sectors, China's relative performance is consistent in the sense that its product prices are less likely to fall than those coming from other low-income countries, but more likely than those from lower-middle, upper-middle and high-income economies.

What can we conclude from all of this? In earlier chapters we argued that the key to sustainable income growth lay in the ability of producers to generate and appropriate rents. With deepening globalization, there is more and more pressure on producers, and hence more and more pressure on incomes. One way in which this pressure manifests itself is through a squeeze on prices: when costs cannot fall faster than prices, then it is likely that incomes will be threatened, and hence that producers will find themselves with falling real or relative incomes (an issue which we considered in chapter 2). An analysis of the price behaviour of global manufacturing exports opens an important window onto these pressures; it is a

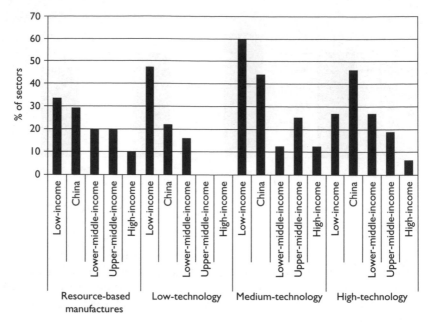

Figure 6.10 Percentage of sectors with negative price trends, 1988/9–2000/1, by technological intensity and country grouping

cloudy window, since in many cases (for example, electronics) costs may indeed be falling faster than prices. Nevertheless the size of the data analysis – more than 2,000 products in the case of the sector analysis – provides some protection against this cloudy perspective. Given this, we can indeed conclude that on aggregate it looks as though, the lower the income grouping of the country, the more likely it is to be facing severe price competition, and the lower the technological intensity of exports, the more likely price pressures are to be severe. Those countries which are low-income and which export low- and medium-technology manufactures are most likely to suffer from competitive pressures.

However, this evidence is not enough to conclude that low-income countries and exporters of low-technology products suffer from globalization. It is true the returns to their exports may be falling. But they are also importers, and simultaneously gain from falling import prices as consumers of manufactured imports. In other words, insightful though the analysis of unit prices may be, it is only part of the story, and for this reason we need now to focus on the terms of trade of the low-income country producers who are the subject of this book.

The terms of trade of manufactures

Summary: Terms of trade trends

Terms of trade of manufactures in aggregate

Considered in aggregate, the prices of developing countries' manufactured exports fell compared with the prices of high-income
country exports of manufactures and knowledge-intensive services – particularly sharply after 1985.

Developing-country barter terms of trade

The barter terms of trade of developing economies (that is, the price
of their actual manufactured exports compared with those of their
actual manufactured imports) fell in their trade with the EU, the
USA and Japan. In both the EU and Japan (where data is available),
the terms of trade of the Asian developing economies fell less
sharply than those of other regions.

In chapter 3 we recounted the less than successful experience of the 25
million coffee farmers who, despite occasional surges in coffee prices
due to natural calamities in prime growing regions, had experienced
a fall in coffee prices since the mid-1960s. When account was taken
of the simultaneous rise in the prices of manufactured imports of these
economies, the resultant purchasing power of their coffee receipts
(their barter terms of trade) fell significantly – by 54 per cent over the
long time-period (1964–2000), and then in peak–trough sub-periods
by 83 per cent between 1977 and 2000 and 25 per cent between 1995
and 2000. It is because of these falling terms of trade in coffee and
other primary products that most poor countries targeted the expansion of their manufacturing sectors in the post-war period and manufacturing exports in the post-1980 period.

As we saw in figure 6.7 above, as the twentieth century wore on,
the price of manufactured products in general also began to fall. But
we also saw in section 6.1 that this fall was uneven between different
types of countries (and indeed different types of products). So, how
did this uneven price performance play out for poor countries in
general? Figure 6.11 begins with a broad approximation. It shows the
price performance of manufactured exports from developing countries against that of manufactured products from high-income
economies. The data are aggregate and as a consequence hide intra-
sectoral differences. Moreover, the figure does not show the true terms

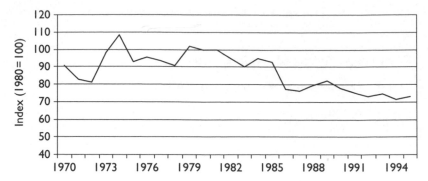

Figure 6.11 Low-income and high-income country 'terms of trade' in manufactures, 1969–1995

Source: Wood (1997)

of trade of poor countries since it does not compare the price of their imports against that of their exports, but rather the price performance of their gross manufactured exports compared with that of high-income economies. Nevertheless, as a prequel to a more detailed discussion of the terms of trade of developing countries in manufactures, it does provide an important backdrop. It shows that, between the post-1970 high point (1974) and 1995, the terms of trade (crudely defined) of these low-income exporters fell by around one-third; between 1985 (when China first entered the global market for manufactures with significance) and 1995, they declined by 21 per cent.

Attempts to calculate the barter terms of trade of poor countries taking into account their actual imports and exports of manufactures are bedevilled by three major problems. First, there are a large number of countries, and although, as we shall see, attempts have been made to separate out the performance of different regions, the calculations are not trade-weighted. That is, the unit prices of manufactured imports and exports into and out of China are given the same weight as those for poor countries with much smaller populations. Second, the unit price analysis is conducted at a very high level of aggregation – in most cases it is at the two-digit product level. This means, for example, using the HS trade database, that the 'unit price' for HS61 ('articles of apparel and clothing accessories, knitted or crocheted') lumps together four-digit items such as HS6111 ('babies' garments and clothing accessories, knitted or crocheted, excl. hats') and HS6112 ('track-suits, ski-suits and swimwear, knitted or crocheted'). (At a greater level of detail, HS61120 and HS611130 both cover 'babies' garments and clothing accessories', but the first category is for cotton and the second for synthetics.) And, third, there is the issue of the currency used to compare trade between many countries (since each country or currency area uses its own individual currency), a problem which we have already highlighted in the analysis of unit prices of EU imports in section 6.1 above. Following convention, almost all studies of terms of trade use the US$ as the unit of comparison. For all these reasons, the estimation of the terms of trade of developing countries in manufactures is necessarily crude.

Maizels has undertaken three separate studies estimating these terms of trade in manufactures, that is, taking account of both the exports and the imports of poor countries.[7] The first looks at the terms of trade of developing countries with respect to the EU; the second focuses on their trade with the USA; and the most recent estimates their terms of trade with Japan. The EU study analysed the period 1979 to 1994 and compared the EU's terms of trade with a range of developing-country groups, as well as the USA and Japan, for both commodities and manufactures. In all cases, the terms of trade performance of countries exporting to the EU was worse for commodities than it was for manufactures. But since it is manufactures which interest us, we show only the results for different countries' terms of trade in manufactures with the EU – that is, comparing the price behaviour of their manufactured exports to the EU with their manufactured imports from the EU. Figure 6.12 displays the results, from which it is clear that both the USA and Japan experienced rising terms of trade in this period. By contrast, the aggregate of all developing countries experienced an annual

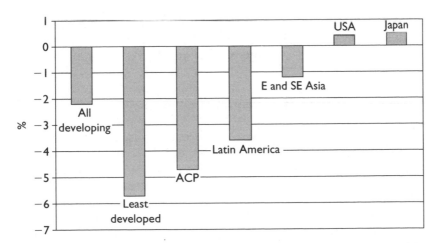

Figure 6.12 Terms of trade in manufactures of countries trading with the EU, 1979–1994 (per cent per annum)

Source: Maizels, Palaskas and Crowe (1998)

fall in their terms of trade in manufactures of −2.2 per cent (compared with −4.2 per cent for manufactures/commodities). The least developed countries saw the greatest fall in their terms of trade in manufactures (−5.7 per cent annually), and East and South East Asia the least significant fall (−1.2 per cent annually).

A similar picture emerges from an analysis of developing-country terms of trade with the USA. Taking 1981 as the base year, these fell by 12 per cent in total by 1997, with a particularly sharp deterioration during the 1980s. However, during the same period, the terms of trade in manufactures of high-income economies with the USA rose by 16 per cent. In other words, while developing-country exporters of manufactures were reducing their prices compared with those of their imports of manufactures from the USA, EU and Japanese exporters were increasing their relative prices. No estimations were made for the differential performance of different types or groups of developing countries in their trade with the USA, but in a subsequent study this was done for Japan. Maizels calculated these terms of trade between 1981 and 2000 for a selection of nine Asian economies (China, Hong Kong, Indonesia, Korea, Malaysia, the Philippines, Singapore, Taiwan and Thailand) and for the EU and the USA. Both groups – low- and high-income – experienced falling terms of trade in manufactures with Japan. By the end point, the terms of trade decline was 20.7 per cent for low-income countries and 13.6 per cent for high-income exporters.

6.5 Is China's growing participation in the global economy an explanation for falling prices and falling terms of trade?

Summary: China and the global economy

China's extraordinary growth performance since 1990 has been closely related to its engagement with the global economy after 1985. It has reflected a combination of historically unprecedented rates of investment and sustained productivity-enhancing innovations.

China has become a major exporter of manufactured goods and accounts for a significant and growing share of imports into high-income countries of most of the products exported by low-income economies.

Its success in the US market has been associated with a rising balance of trade surplus in China's favour.

In previous sections of this chapter we have shown how relatively poor economies and those producing relatively low-technology products are caught between the rock of growing competition in production and the hard place of increasing buyer concentration. We also observed that the 1990s saw a decisive shift in the sourcing patterns of the US buyers who have played such a prominent role in these developments, procuring many of their purchases from China rather than from Hong Kong, Korea, Singapore and Taiwan. In this section we will show how China's role in the global system of production and buying has grown and how it has come to play an important role in the distribution of returns from this pattern of global production and consumption.

The rapid growth of the Chinese economy in recent years has been exceptional. Between 1990 and 2002 the economy grew on an annual basis at 9.7 per cent;[8] by 2001 China's GDP had risen to 12.1 per cent of global GDP, and its per capita GDP was 58 per cent of the global average per capita GDP (in all cases taking account of the purchasing power of China's currency).[9] Underlying this expansion has been a surge in investment – by 2001 China was investing almost 40 per cent of its GDP annually, double the level of other low-income economies (figure 6.13). In 1976, when Korea had a similar per capita income to that of China in 2003 (measured in PPP terms), the share of its investment to GDP was only 26 per cent. Much of this investment came from abroad, and foreign investors crowded into China as a production platform for the global economy. In 1998 and 1999, China gobbled up 23 per cent of all foreign direct investment going to the

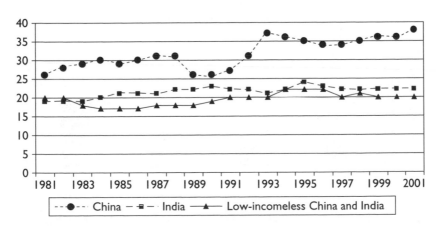

Figure 6.13   Investment as a share of GDP, 1980–2001 (%)

Source: Martin and Manole (2003)

developing world, and this rose in 2002 to 33 per cent; if the share of Hong Kong is added to that of China (since much of Hong Kong's FDI inflows were directed towards production on the mainland), the combined share rose from 30 to 41 per cent of all FDI going to the developing world.[10] But, of course, China's rapid economic growth does not only arise from this high rate of investment – it also reflects significant improved productivity across a range of sectors and in a range of different types of enterprises, with particularly rapid growth in foreign-owned enterprises during the 1990s (figure 6.14).

With this rising productive capacity came China's significant entry into the global market in the mid-1980s. Until 1985, the pattern of China's exports had been stable – about half was manufactures, with the balance pretty evenly split between natural resources and agricultural products. But the post-1985 export surge was built largely on manufactures, so that in a short period of time manufactures had become dominant. In 1991 they accounted for almost 90 per cent of total exports. The pace of manufactured export growth speeded up through the 1990s after the abolition of the two-tier exchange rate in 1994, and in the five years between 1997 and 2002 manufactured exports doubled. By comparison, during the high points of their export-growth spurts, it took Germany ten years to double exports in the 1960s and seven years for Japan in the 1970s. By 2002 China accounted for more than 20 per cent of all developing-country exports, and by 2003 it had become the world's fourth largest exporter after the USA, Japan and Germany.

The bedrock on which this export growth was built was a combination of severe price competition and growing production excellence and product quality.[11] The surge in export growth after the mid-1980s was

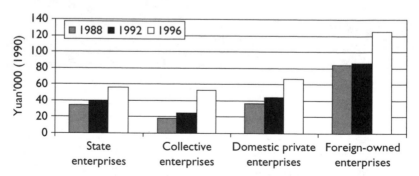

Figure 6.14 China's productivity growth in different types of enterprises, 1988, 1992 and 1996 (1990 constant prices)

Source: Jefferson et al. (2000)

accompanied by a significant fall in China's terms of trade of around 25 per cent. This fall was greater for trade with Japan, the EU and the USA than it was for trade with other developing countries and reflected a combination of falling export prices (see section 6.3 above) and the production of new low-priced products, particularly the rapid push into the low-tech assembly of high-tech electronics products.[12] These expanded rapidly, and the value of high-tech exports more than doubled, from $25 billion in 1999 to $58 billion in 2001.[13] The scale of many of these factories and cities dedicated to exports is shown in box 6.1.

Box 6.1   China's global export platforms

- Shunde in the Pearl River Delta styles itself as the microwave-oven capital of the world, with 40 per cent of global production in a single giant factory.
- Shenzhen makes 70 per cent of the world's photocopiers and 80 per cent of its artificial Christmas trees.
- Dongguan has 80,000 people working in a single factory making running shoes.
- Zhongshan is the 'home of the world's electric lighting industry'.
- Pou Chen has two shoe plants, employing 110,000 people making 100 million pairs of shoes a year.
- Flextronics (a Singapore firm) has a Chinese plant which doubled its payroll to 12,000 in a year, making Xbox electronic games consoles. In 1999, only 5 to 10 per cent of suppliers were local; by 2003, 50 to 70 per cent of inputs were locally sourced.

Source: Roberts and Kynge (2003)

All of this has translated into China's growing dominance in global markets in many sectors, particularly for those buyer-driven sectors which, as we observed in chapters 4 and 5, have been targeted for export growth by most poor countries. Table 6.4 shows how significant its presence has become in the USA, Japan and the EU in key sectors of relevance to developing-country exporters. Between 1980 and 2002, its share of total manufactured imports in the USA (including many products which China does not produce or export in significant numbers) rose from virtually nothing to 14 per cent. In the buyer-driven consumer products sectors which have not been subject to major import quotas, its share of total imports has grown dramatically, particularly in the case of Japan and the USA. In footwear and

Table 6.4 Share of imports from China – EU, Japan and the USA, 1995 and 2002

	EU		Japan		USA	
	1995	2002	1995	2002	1995	2002
All manufactures	2.2	4.0	5.3	6.8	7.6	13.8
Textiles	2.5	4.6	31.3	47.5	11.6	15.8
Clothing	7.9	11.5	56.6	78.1	14.9	15.1
Other consumer products	6.4	9.5	19.7	31.6	25.5	36.5
Footwear	6.7	9.7	47.3	67.4	52.3	68.2
Travel goods	40.4	45.1	32.9	45.2	47.4	64.2
Toys and games	26.0	35.8	26.4	63.5	48.4	66.6
Furniture	7.0	6.2			11.2	34.0

Source: WTO (2004)

toys and games, where its presence has not been hindered by import quotas, it now accounts for more than two-thirds of all imports into both the USA and Japan, and for two-thirds of imports of travel goods into the USA. The pace of its growing presence in the clothing and textile sectors has hitherto been constrained by import quotas, but, as we saw in chapter 5, these are soon to be abolished and it is expected that China will become the premium source of supply in both these sectors.

An indication of the significance of China's growing share of US imports is the size of the US trade deficit with both China and 'Greater China' (China, Hong Kong and Taiwan). Figure 6.15 illustrates how this has ballooned since 1995, reaching $103 billion and $114 billion respectively by 2002. It is notable that, in the earlier period, many of China's exports to the USA were indirect, reflecting the 'triangular manufacturing networks' described in chapters 5 and 6. However, as the 1990s wore on, an increasing proportion of a rapidly growing volume of imports from the sub-region came directly from China.

In summary, in this chapter we have charted the forces which are squeezing the incomes of low-wage economy exporters of manufactures. They are caught between a rock and a hard place, that is, between growing production capabilities around the world and the increasingly concentrated power of global buyers. This has led to a squeeze on the prices of their manufactured exports and, despite their gains on the prices of imports of manufactured products, to declining terms of trade with the major consuming regions of the world. A major cause of this price pressure has been the rapidly growing presence of China in global markets for manufactures. It is not just the extent of this pressure on prices which is a source of concern in regard to our focus on global incomes and distribution, but the trends. What

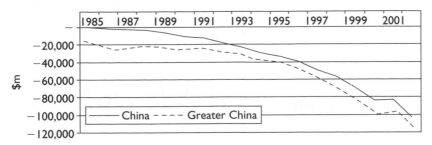

Figure 6.15 US current account deficit with China and Greater China (China, Hong Kong and Taiwan), 1985–2001 ($m)

Source: From data in Cheong and Geng (2003)

we have seen in this chapter suggests that, if anything, these pressures are likely to worsen as the early decades of the twenty-first century wear on.

But does this necessarily spell gloom for poor countries? Will the growth of production capacity not inevitably lead to an equivalent expansion of global consumption that might rescue these low-income exporters from the trauma of declining prices? These issues are considered in the following chapter.

7

Does it All Add Up?

As we have just seen, the combination of growing productive capabilities in the global economy and the concentrated power of global buyers has led to significant and sustained pressure on the prices of manufactured products, particularly those emanating from low-income economies and those products embodying a low technological content. It might be concluded that this automatically translates into a squeeze on the profit margins of the exporters of these manufactures, and hence on their incomes. But this is not necessarily the case. As we shall see, there are circumstances in which falling prices can indeed be associated with rising – rather than falling – margins and incomes. In other words, although on their own falling prices may be suggestive of problems for particular producers, the story is more complicated.

As we saw in chapter 6, the key to the outcome of falling prices is to be found in the fact that producers do not only sell their output. They also are consumers – of final products, of intermediate products and of raw materials. But even this evidence on the *relative* price of inputs and outputs does not unlock the door to understanding the impact on incomes and distribution. This is because, in addition to the price of inputs and outputs, we need to take account of their volume, and of productivity change in production. The discussion of aggregate global supply needs to be linked with global aggregate demand.

In considering these issues, we begin with a brief excursion into the theory of the terms of trade (section 7.1), since this provides an important backdrop for assessing the overall outcome of global specialization. This will be followed by a review of some of the major factors which might lead to a win–win outcome from deepened globalization in the production and exchange of manufactures (section 7.2). It begins with a discussion of the theoretical explanation for such mutual gains and considers some of the evidence to back these assumptions. In section 7.3 we question this win–win outcome by focusing on the realism of these abstract theoretical assumptions in the context of the real world of the early twenty-first century. We conclude with a pessimistic view that, while the workings of the global economy may be positive for some producers, they are unlikely to work to the benefit of many other producers. In these circumstances, a significant degree of poverty and inequality are relational outcomes of globalization. They arise as a direct consequence of excess global capacity and constrained global consumption, and lead to a race to the bottom in real incomes.

7.1   A brief excursion into the theory of the terms of trade

---

Summary: The terms of trade

The terms of trade reflect relative prices of exports and imports, and have three components.

- The barter terms reflect the prices of products being exported and imported.
- The income terms of trade take account of the volumes of imports and exports as well as their prices. An increase in demand that is proportionately greater than the fall in relative product prices translates into rising income terms of trade. This may result in an enhanced capacity to import, despite falling barter terms of trade.
- The factoral terms of trade reflect not just prices, but also factor productivities. Rising factor productivities may outweigh falling product prices, and may allow for incomes to be enhanced despite falling barter terms of trade.

In themselves, falling prices may not be a bad thing. By lowering the cost of consumption, they provide benefits to the consumer and hence enhance incomes; and, to the extent that they reflect cost-reducing improvements in productivity, they need not harm producer incomes. The key to assessing the impact of falling prices on incomes is the question of *relativity*: how much do the prices received by exporting countries fall *relative* to the prices of the products which they import; how much do the prices received by producers fall *relative* to the prices of the inputs into their production processes; and how much do the prices received by producers fall *relative* to the cost reduction enabled by productivity improvements? It was these issues which Prebisch and Singer considered when they first brought attention to the problem of falling terms of trade in the early 1950s. They were concerned with the impact of falling prices on the *inter*-country distribution of income (since in principle the problem of falling prices could apply to production and trade within a country), and particularly on the impact on poor economies. As we saw in chapter 3, they argued that the prices of developing-country exports were systematically falling *compared* to the price of their imports and provided five major explanations why the terms of trade would fall against developing-country producers, particularly those producing primary products such as agricultural commodities and metals and minerals.[1]

The first reason was that many of these (exported) products were inputs into the production of (imported) manufactures. Hence, a fall in the price of a primary commodity which is an input into a manufacturing product would have different implications for the producer of the commodity and the purchaser of the manufacture. For example, if the copper inputs into a telephone system comprised 10 per cent of the final product costs, a halving of the copper price (their export) would lead only to a 5 per cent fall in the price of the final telephone (their import). Second, Singer and Prebisch argued that, as incomes grow, the demand for the products produced by low-income economies would rise less than that for products embodying higher technology. Moreover, the demand for these lower-technology and more basic products would be much more price sensitive. Hence, an increase in demand for the output of low-income country exports would only come from a large and disproportionate fall in prices. Allied to this was a third explanation, that many of the commodities exported by low-income countries were subject to synthetic substitution, and hence to declining demand. An example of this is the development of synthetic rubber used in the manufacture of auto tyres. Fifth, and this takes us back to chapter 3 when we discussed the question of innovation and technology rents, the output of low-income economies generally embodied products with low barriers to entry. Thus, these products would be subject to a greater squeeze on prices and margins than products which were more difficult to produce and which had greater technological content. And, finally, products emanating from high-income countries were more likely to be priced on a cost-plus basis. The power of organized labour meant that there would be much more resistance to falling prices in high-income countries than in poor countries, where a large 'reserve army of labour' would make it more likely that wages could fall as a result of competitive pressures, and hence that their product prices would fall. It is clear from this set of reasons that Prebisch and Singer believed that the falling relative prices experienced by developing countries reflected a combination of product-specific factors (demand characteristics, technological content) and country-specific factors (the determinants of wage and price formation).

The final explanation offered by Singer and Prebisch is important, since it has a bearing on the discussion of a win–lose outcome to globalization in section 7.3. They argued that the primary underlying determinant of the terms of trade decline for low-income economies was to be found in the nature of the labour markets in the low- and high-income economies. They would have liked to reflect this by comparing the price of all low-income exports with those of all low-income imports, but this created insuperable data problems. Therefore, *as a surrogate*, they chose to measure the terms of trade for commodities (read, low-income economy exports) against manufactures (read, high-income economy exports), and it is this that becomes the focus of extensive discussions on the empirical reality of relative price changes.[2]

Hidden in this discussion of changing relative prices of different types of products is a variegated analysis of terms of trade. The data produced in chapter 6 referred to the '*barter terms of trade*', that is, the unit price of exports compared to the unit price of imports – how many kilos of coffee might have to be exported to import a kilo of fertilizer? But what happens if a fall in the barter terms of trade of a country leads to a massive increase in demand for coffee? This may be either because falling prices stimulate demand, or because its price competitiveness may allow it to sweep up a market in a foreign country. In this case, we need to take into account not just the unit price of exports, but also the volume of those exports. Falling unit export prices in this case may be associated with a large increase in demand, such that the '*income terms of trade*' increase, that is, total incomes increase in the exporting country despite falling relative prices. And, third, there are the '*factoral terms of trade*', which refer to the incomes arising from different inputs into production – wages for labour, profits for capitalists. This generally reflects the productivity of production. Falling product prices may be outweighed by rises in labour productivity or capital productivity, allowing wages or profits to rise as product prices fall.

We can see from this that the impact of falling product prices on income distribution – both within countries and between countries – reflects a complex amalgam of events which include the degree of price fall, the nature of demand for different types of products, patterns of cost-reducing productivity growth, and the extent to which demand growth relates to the degree of price fall. It is not possible to document all of these factors, and of course they vary across different products (particularly if we use the very fine eight- and ten-digit product codes described in chapter 6) and across different countries. For this reason, we consider below some of the major factors that might have a bearing on these outcomes in the contemporary period. We begin with those factors which suggest a positive scenario to global specialization (section 7.2), reflecting the discussion in part II. We then proceed to examine those with a less positive outcome (section 7.3).

7.2   Win–win: it really does add up

Summary: The win–win outcome to globalization

There are powerful arguments that globalization allows for income growth for all. This is premised on a view that specialization, allied to the scale of global markets, provides for enormous gains in productivity. When producers specialize across countries in areas of comparative advantage, and then trade, all can benefit. These benefits feed through in the following ways.

- The growing diffusion of productive capacities has provided the opportunity for many producers to gain incomes from global production and exchange.
- The adverse barter terms of trade observed in chapter 6 are outweighed by demand expansion and rising income terms of trade.
- Global citizens gain as consumers, as world prices fall and cheapen the price of improved-quality goods.
- The expansion of manufactured exports by China and other dynamic Asian economies might have squeezed out some other low-income producers from final product markets, but it has created an enormous demand for food and industrial raw materials.

Think about the life-cycle of a closely knit family in an economy rich enough to offer gainful employment and to provide the space for extended education and retirement. At any one stage there are income-earning family members and those who are either too young to work, too infirm to work, are involved in education, or are considered too old to work. Everyone's needs are met by specialization of activity and by the transfer of incomes. Those in work provide the incomes to support the young, the sick and the old, in the knowledge that in the past they benefited from these transfers and that in the future they in turn will be recipients of intra-family income transfers. Extend this model beyond the family to the wider economy and, again, a story can be told in which specialization of task, allied to income transfers, provides for a world of mutual gain.

This simple model underlies much of our thinking about the benefits accruing from globalization, a win–win world for all who participate. Adam Smith, one of the founding fathers of modern economics, set the scene when in *The Wealth of Nations* he wrote about the benefits of specialization. Smith begins his treatise with the following words: 'The greatest improvement in the productive powers of labour, and the greater part of the skill, dexterity, and judgement with which it is any where directed, or applied, seem to have been the effects of the division of labour.'[3] In the case of pin manufacture, he famously contrasted the productivity of craft production unaided by mechanization (where each worker produced fewer than twenty pins a day) with a factory involving both specialization and machinery in which each worker produced 2,000 pins a day. For Smith, there were three components to this division of labour which facilitated productivity growth. The first was familiarity and specialization of task by the individual labour; the second was that specialization meant that workers did not waste time by downing tools and picking up new tools as they performed multiple tasks; and the third was the specialization of machinery manufacture which led to the development of capital goods firms producing equipment to mechanize production.

A necessary corollary of this division of labour is the development of markets in which products can be bought and sold. (This, of course, lies at the centre of Smith's model of economic growth; and as is well known, Smith believed that the functioning of markets provided the 'invisible hand' which squared the circle of individual greed and social welfare.) For Smith, a key component of the link between markets and specialization was scale – 'as it is the power of exchanging that gives occasion to the division of labour, so the extent of this division must always be limited by the extent of the market.'[4] The larger the market, the greater the opportunities for specialization and productivity gains. To draw a link to the current period, heavy investments in fixed equipment and R&D mean that it is often only the global market which provides sufficient scale for the true fruits of the division of labour to be realized.

Although Adam Smith argued that international trade was an important component of economic growth, the benefits of specialization and the division of labour *between countries* is most closely associated with David Ricardo, writing some fifty years after Smith. Ricardo's famous example setting out the case for mutual gain from international trade was based on potential trade between Portugal and England in cloth and wine. He used a fictitious example, estimating the number of labour hours in the production of wine being 90 and 120 respectively and that of cloth as being 80 and 100 respectively.

These figures showed that, because of higher productivity, Portugal had an *absolute advantage* in the production of identical quantities of both wine (90 hours compared with 120 hours in England) and cloth (80 hours compared with 100 hours in England). However, it was relatively more efficient in the production of wine than cloth, where it held a *comparative advantage*. In other words, although it was absolutely better in the production of both commodities than England, it was *relatively* better than England in wine production than in cloth production. Therefore, he argued, if Portugal specialized in wine and England in cloth and they traded their outputs, then both countries would gain.

It is this combination of division of labour and inter-country specialization in comparative advantage that provides the intellectual underpinnings for the mutuality of gains arising from globalization. But woven into this framework is a critical assumption that 'markets clear', that is, that what is produced is consumed in an unproblematic way. Ricardo was explicit about this, leaning on the work of the eighteenth-century French economist Jean-Baptiste Say, who argued that supply necessarily creates its own demand:

> In an economy with an advanced division of labour, the means normally available to anyone for acquiring goods and services are the power to produce equivalent goods and services. Production increases not only the supply of goods but, by virtue of the requisite cost payments to the factors of production, also creates the demand to purchase these goods. 'Products are paid for by products' in domestic as well as in foreign trade; this is the gist of Say's Law of Markets.[5]

A final plank in the construction of a case for the mutual gains arising from globalization and specialization is the argument that comparative advantage is dynamic, and this requires firms and countries to graduate from low-technology and labour-intensive sectors to higher-technology and more capital-intensive sectors. In the 1930s, the Japanese economist Akamatsu developed a 'flying geese' model to describe the proposed dynamic trajectory of the region in Japan's 'Greater East-Asian Co-prosperity Sphere'. More recently, Balassa developed the idea of a stepladder, with second-tier newly industrializing countries filling the sectors vacated by Japan and the first-tier newly industrializing economies as their wages rose and as they, in turn, moved into higher technology sectors.[6]

What evidence is there to support this win–win outcome to globalization? We can take as read the success of a significant number of economies – predominantly in Asia – who have gained from globalization (chapter 1). In the following discussion we draw on the issues raised in the analysis of global prices presented in chapter 6 to show that this price performance may indeed reflect a process of growing interchange in global product markets which provide for mutual gain. We begin by observing the increment to incomes that consumers gain as the costs of imported input and consumer products falls. We then consider the evidence on income terms of trade, and conclude by examining the impact of China (and other dynamic economies) on the growth in global demand for raw materials.

The availability of cheaper products of a higher quality

One country's exports are another country's imports. So the flip side of declining product prices that reduce the returns to exporters is the declining product prices that enhance the incomes of importers. One of the features of advancing globalization has been the decline or eradication of obstacles to importation. Some of these were barriers which affected import volumes, such as non-tariff quota barriers or outright prohibitions; other barriers – tariffs – made imports more expensive for consumers. Recent decades have seen successive rounds of trade reform in a wide range of countries, and these have been particularly significant in low-wage developing economies which had previously pursued import-restricting policies designed to protect local producers.

The sweeping away of these barriers has meant that a wider variety of goods has been available, at lower prices, and frequently of a much higher quality. The prices of many basic consumption goods used by the poor have fallen particularly rapidly, as we saw in chapter 6. This means cheaper and better quality clothes and shoes, as well as construction materials for basic housing. But consumers do not gain only from cheaper final products; they also gain from the lower prices of machinery and equipment, and raw material inputs and components.

Referring back to the three sectoral studies in chapter 5, for example, the South African-based auto assemblers would not have been able to achieve such significant exports without access to imported compon- ents. Similarly, the expansion of furniture exports from a variety of countries depends on access to cheap and high-quality wood, glues, fabrics and dyes, and that of clothing exports to the availability of world-class cheap textiles. The falling price of all of these types of imported inputs has been one of the major factors driving the fall in global inflation rates referred to in chapter 6.

Rising income terms of trade

As we saw in chapter 6, developing countries' barter terms of trade have fallen with respect to their trade with the EU, the USA and Japan. In other words, the prices of products which developing countries exported to these high-income countries fell relative to the prices of the products they imported from these countries. But has the volume of their trade grown faster than this decline in the barter terms of trade – have their income terms of trade grown so that their *capacity to import* has expanded over time? Figure 7.1 shows the data for the

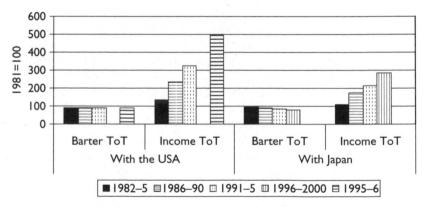

Figure 7.1 Developing countries' barter and income terms of trade with the USA and Japan, 1982–1996 (1981 = 100)[a]

[a] An index below 100 reflects a decline in relative export/import prices (the barter terms of trade) and falling import capacity (income terms of trade); conversely, a rising index reflects rising relative prices (barter terms of trade) and growing import capacity (income terms of trade).

Source: Drawn from Maizels (1999, 2003)

USA and Japan (unfortunately there are no matching figures for developing countries' trade with the EU). It is evident from this that rapid volume growth of exports has meant that, despite falling relative prices, overall receipts from trade with these major purchasing countries have grown rapidly. In their trade with the USA, total export receipts of developing countries grew consistently, reaching a level in 1995–6 which was five times that in 1982–5. In their trade with Japan between 1982–5 and 1996–2000, the trend was also upwards, although to a lower extent than that with the USA, increasing by almost 300 per cent.

Two points of caution on this result are important, however, and we shall return to them in the following chapter. First, the data for the USA is aggregated for all developing countries, and that for Japan refers only to trade with Asian-region developing countries. There is no indication whether the income terms of trade have risen for all developing countries, or for all groups of developing countries. Second, the rise in export volumes of course involved the commitment of resources to exporting. It is possible that, had the same resources been directed towards investment in other products or in products destined for different markets (including the domestic market), the resultant income would have grown even more rapidly. Nevertheless the evidence does suggest that, *at least in the aggregate*, the tendency of manufactured export prices to decline did not result in a fall in aggregate export revenues.

China is not just a competitor in external markets

In chapter 6 we not only documented the price pressure on manufactured exports in general and on developing-country exports in particular. We also argued that this was closely associated with, and probably caused by, the massive increase in China's exports of manufactures. However, by definition, manufactures involve the transformation of inputs into outputs – in the case of automobiles, for example, more than 5,000 components are involved, and each of these in turn requires the input of a variety of raw and semi-processed materials. The advance of global value chains over the last two decades of the twentieth century resulted in a significant increase in global trade in components, and hence in a growth of import intensity in export production in almost every country. For example, in the case of China, the proportion of export revenue which reflected direct imports into production processes rose from 8 to 12 per cent between 1980 and

1998, and in the case of direct and indirect imports (that is, taking account of the imports going into the production of domestically sourced inputs) it rose from 15 to 23 per cent in the same period.[7]

Consequently, with rapidly growing production destined for both the domestic and the export market, it is not surprising that China has become a very large market for the exports of other countries. In many cases, it has imported manufactured products, particularly capital goods from Japan. In addition, as we shall see in the following chapter, Chinese exports of products such as consumer electronics have involved the assembly of components sourced from the East Asian region. However, from the perspective of the wider global economy, it is China's sourcing of commodities and semi-processed commodities which represents a particularly significant impact on the global economy.

Focusing on basic metals as an example, China's demand for imports has been fuelled by three factors. The first has been the rapid growth of domestic demand for household consumer goods and autos (which, as we saw in chapter 5, has grown at a dramatic pace). Secondly, there has been very substantial investment in infrastructure, in both the public and the private sector, and this has been particularly basic-metal intensive. And, thirdly, many of China's exports have been of metal-based products. Consequently, China's share of global demand for the main base metals (aluminium, copper, iron ore, nickel, steel and zinc) grew from 7 to 10 per cent of global demand in 1993 to 20 to 25 per cent in 2003. In the case of steel, its share has grown from less than 10 per cent in 1990 to more than 25 per cent in 2003, equivalent to three times that of Japan, and more than either the EU or the USA (around 20 per cent each). Between 2000 and 2003, China's share of the increase in global demand for aluminium, steel, nickel and copper was 76 per cent, 95 per cent, 99 per cent and 100 per cent respectively. As figure 7.2 shows, its projected utilization of these basic metals is likely to expand even further in the future, in part because of its relatively low per-capita consumption of these materials (table 7.1). Bear in mind, China accounts for more than 20 per cent of global population, and it is inevitable that, as incomes improve and the minerals intensity of consumption grows as it has in other countries, this will continue to lead to rising demand for imported materials.

This thirst for mineral imports is also reflected in the food sector, where falling land availability (a consequence of rising industrialization) and stagnant agricultural productivity have led to rising food imports. In the first half of 2004, China had a trade deficit on foodstuffs of $3.7 billion, including imports of 4.1 million tonnes of foodgrains. It is predicted that this deficit will soar in the future – in the case of foodgrains, to around 40 million tonnes by 2007.[8]

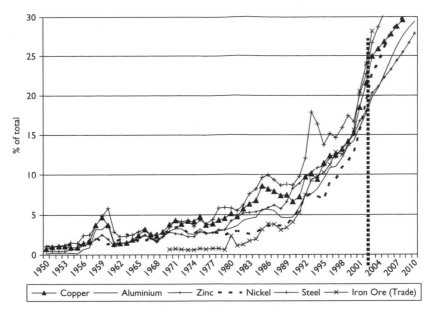

Figure 7.2 Actual and projected global share of China's consumption of base metals, 1950–2010

Source: Macquarie Research Metals and Mining, personal communication (2004)

Table 7.1 The scope for China's increased consumption of basic metals, 1955–2003

	Kgs per capita			GDP per capita
	Aluminium	Copper	Steel	(US$ 1995)
Japan				
1955	0.6	1.2	80	5,559
1975	10.5	7.4	599	21,869
Korea				
1975	1.0	1.3	84	2,891
1995	15.0	8.1	827	10,841
China				
1990	0.7	0.6	59	342
1999	2.3	1.2	108	756
2002	3.3	2.0	160	933
2003	4.0	2.4	200	1,103

Source: Macquarie Metals and Mining, personal communication (2004)

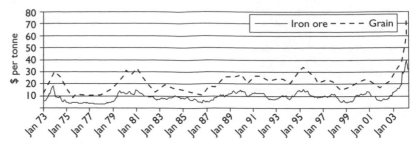

Figure 7.3 Shipping freight rates, 1973–2003

Source: Chandlers, personal communication

An indication of the impact which China's thirst for material and food inputs can have on the global economy may be seen in the global shortage of shipping capacity. As figure 7.3 shows, beginning in 2001 shipping freight rates began to escalate. For both iron ore and grain, they reached levels which were more than double the previous highs in 1973 and 1995 respectively (although these rates are not price-deflated). The cause? As a major ship-chandler observed, 'Chinese iron ore, steel and soybean demand was unquestionably the main reason ocean freight rates for dry bulk commodities hit all time highs earlier [in 2004].'[9]

7.3   Win–lose: perhaps it does not all add up?

Summary: The win–lose outcome to globalization

The positive case for globalization is premised on assumptions of full employment, the immobility of capital and the availability of resources allowing the losers to restructure and catch up.

But each of these assumptions is flawed.

- Even in China, the massive expansion of industrial capacity is job-destroying. This has not surfaced as a policy issue in the USA and the UK because their growing balance of payments deficits have hitherto allowed them to expand employment, including in non-traded labour-intensive services. The medium- and long-term prognosis is more serious given the size of the reserve army of labour in China, India and elsewhere in low-income economies.

- Capital is highly mobile, is profit-oriented, and has gravitated to Asia in general, and China in particular.
- The aid resources allowing other low-income economies to catch up with the high-income economies and Asia are both falling in aggregate and privileged to countries of geo-strategic interest to the USA and Europe.

Thus, instead of a win–win world of specialization and trade, the global economy is beset by growing structural surplus capacity in production, and by a large surplus of increasingly educated labour. Export optimism fails to take account of the fallacy of composition.

At the beginning of section 7.2 we traced the theoretical case for a win–win outcome to globalization back to the pioneering writings of David Ricardo in 1817. Building on Adam Smith's insights on the benefits of specialization, exchange and scale, Ricardo provided a framework for realizing the gains from specialization and exchange between countries. However, there are three crucial assumptions in Ricardo's schema which have a bearing on this win–win outcome, and which are relevant not only to Ricardo's theoretical model but also to real-world outcomes from contemporary globalization.

The first is the existence of full employment in both exporting and importing economies. Without this it makes less sense for each country to specialize in its area of comparative advantage, especially if (as in the case of Ricardo's original example of wine and cloth) a country has an absolute advantage across a range of products. In other words, in Ricardo's example, if Portugal had the resources to produce enough wine and enough cloth for its own needs, it would have made more sense for it to produce both products rather than to trade its wine for England's cloth. (In the contemporary world, why would it, for example, benefit China or high-income economies to purchase products from Africa if they could produce these more effectively themselves, and had the resources to do so?) A second linked and key assumption is in regard to the mobility of capital. Ricardo argued that, if capital (and skilled entrepreneurship) was mobile, then in the case that a country such as Portugal had unemployed resources and an absolute advantage in all products it 'would undoubtedly be advantageous to the capitalists of England, and to the consumer of both countries, that under such circumstances, the wine and the cloth should both be made in Portugal, and therefore that the capital and labour of England employed in making cloth, should be removed to Portugal for that purpose.'[10] In other words, it would not only pay 'Portugal' as an economic entity to produce all the products it needed, but it would also provide English entrepreneurs with a higher rate of profit if they produced in Portugal and exported the output to England. (In the contemporary period, transnational firms and global buyers will gravitate to the site of least cost, wherever this might be.) And, third, although Ricardo was not explicit on this, the pursuit of the dynamic comparative advantage which Balassa and others argue is necessary for a win–win outcome to globalization requires income transfers to facilitate producers moving from one activity to another. (In the current period, with rapid changes in global sourcing, producers need assistance to make the transition to new processes, new products, new functions, and new sectors.)

What evidence can we bring to bear to explore the validity of these three assumptions in the contemporary global economy, and how might this affect the distributional outcomes of the globalization of production and trade?

Questioning the assumption of full employment

As we saw, Ricardo's framework of comparative advantage rested explicitly on Say's assumption of full employment. This assumption that labour markets have a tendency to clear continues into the twenty-first century, and is validated by Keynesian macro-economic policies that have been so influential since the depression years of the 1930s. Keynes departed from the thinking of his day by problematizing the phenomenon of unemployment. But he did so in a framework which saw unemployment as a manageable and *temporary* departure from a world of full employment. He argued that Say's assumption that supply created its own demand was essentially true, but that there was often a temporary misalignment between supply and demand which required active state intervention to resolve.

There is, however, an alternative body of thinking on labour markets which, instead of assuming a systemic tendency towards full employment, argues that there is a systemic tendency towards a reserve army of labour. This is to be found in the writings of classical economists such as Malthus and Marx. It was Marx, in particular, who argued that technological change would lead to a disproportionate saving of labour inputs as output grew much more rapidly than labour demand. But the labour-surplus economy is also a central component in the thinking of one of the most celebrated development economists of the twentieth century, W. A. Lewis. Lewis argued that in most developing countries there was a dual economy – one segment comprised a modern sector with near-full employment, and the second comprised a sector characterized by heavily disguised unemployment, where people undertook all kinds of work at very low (and often zero) productivity. Lewis believed that over time the modern sector would soak up labour from the secondary low-productivity sector, and that in the long run there would be a tendency towards full employment. This, he believed, had occurred in the rich countries, which, faced with a labour shortage, could either encourage immigration (which he thought politically unlikely) or export capital to countries which continued to have a labour surplus: 'When the labour surplus disappears our model of the closed economy no longer holds. [However] in the real world . . . countries which achieve labour scarcity continue to be surrounded by others which have abundant labour . . . available . . . at a subsistence wage.'[11] Lewis's analysis of the cane sugar industry showed that, despite sustained productivity growth, wages of sugar workers failed to grow between 1870 and 1954 because of the reserve army of labour. One final observation of Lewis is worth keeping in mind – his model, he argued, applied only to unskilled labour, since it was evident to him that skilled labour was indeed a scarce input, in both rich and poor countries alike.

To summarize: in contrast to the neo-classical and Keynesian worldviews, there is an alternative body of thinking about economic progress which believes that the central tendency is towards structural unemployment, underwritten by a reserve army of labour. In a closed economy there may be circumstances in which labour markets become tight. But, once global barriers are reduced, either migrant labour saturates the labour market in countries formerly characterized by near-full employment, or imports from labour-surplus economies have the same effect. The net effect of either of these outcomes will be to depress the incomes of all of those whose livelihoods depend on the work which can be performed by this surplus labour force. This may be either because wages in the formerly tight labour market are depressed, or because the global labour pool forces widespread unemployment.

Our argument is that this is precisely what is happening in the current phase of globalization, and that the full effects of what will become a major phenomenon are being hidden in the rich countries only by the trade deficits which allow labour to be absorbed into the non-traded service sectors of their economies. Moreover, the spectre of a global reserve army of labour is emerging to affect medium- and long-term employment and wage rates as the large labour surplus in China, India and elsewhere is made available to support global production networks.

Let us consider the evidence, beginning with the recent period. A striking feature of the massive recent expansion in manufacturing output and trade globally has been that it has been a process of jobless growth. More than that, as we shall see, it might be termed a process of job-destroying growth. From the perspective of the high-wage economies this is perhaps not surprising, since they have been experiencing linked processes of offshore-outsourcing and labour-saving technical change. But it is surprising when, as in the case of low-income exporters of manufacturers, employment displacement is associated with a very rapid growth of industrial production and manufactured exports.

During the 1990s there was a vigorous academic debate among economists as to how much the job loss in the USA and the EU was due to trade with developing countries. Authors such as Wood had argued that much of this job displacement (and the concomitant worsening of income distribution) was a result of the rapid rise in imports from developing countries.[12] The riposte to this trade-based explanation was that it was rapid labour-saving technical change rather than the swift growth of imports in labour-intensive sectors that explained the loss of jobs in manufacturing.[13] In fact these two explanations are not entirely disconnected, because to some extent the spur for labour-saving technical change was the growing threat of import competition.

Whatever the reason for this job displacement in manufacturing, it has indeed been significant. Table 7.2 shows that in the fourteen largest OECD economies – the economies with high wages threatened by imports from low-wage economies – employment in formal-sector manufacturing fell by 8 per cent between 1995 and 2002. But what is

Table 7.2   Employment in formal-sector manufacturing, 1995–2002

	Employment ('000)				Index of employment (1995=100)			
	OECD 14[a]	China	India	Brazil	OECD 14[a]	China	India	Brazil
1995	85,623	98,030	6,500	9,438	100	100	100	100
1996	84,508	97,360	6,800	8,739	99	99	105	93
1997	83,003	96,120	6,900	8,381	97	98	106	89
1998	81,728	83,190	6,800	7,882	95	85	105	84
1999	81,266	81,090	6,700	7,420	95	83	103	79
2000	81,486	80,430	6,600	7,478	95	82	102	79
2001	80,535	80,830	6,400	7,565	94	82	98	80
2002	78,761	83,080	6,500	7,556	92	85	100	80

[a] USA, Canada, Germany, UK, Japan, Russia, Italy, France, Taiwan, Korea, Spain, Netherlands, Austria, Sweden

Source: Calculated from Carson (2003)

perhaps even more surprising is that, contrary to expectations, there was an even more significant fall in employment in China (by 15 per cent), and in Brazil, the third largest developing-country manufacturing sector (by 20 per cent). In India, the fall in manufacturing employment of nearly 5 per cent occurred between 1996 and 2002. The overall picture for these seventeen largest manufacturing economies was a decline in total employment in formal-sector manufacturing from 200 million to 176 million, a fall of 12 per cent in seven years.

The picture for China is particularly surprising since, as we saw in chapters 1 and 6, it has been such a successfully growing economy. It is also an especially important economy due to its size, with a formal-sector employed labour force larger than that in the combined fourteen largest OECD economies. Figure 7.4 shows how the rapid growth in employment during the first half of the 1970s gave way to a process of employment displacement during the 1990s, particularly in state-owned enterprises and township and village enterprises (TVEs). Figure 7.5 shows that, as China entered the global economy after the early 1980s, this labour displacement was particularly acute in manufacturing. But it is also evident in mining. Even these numbers underestimate the extent of real labour displacement in China, since many people in the state-owned and township and village enterprises remain on the books but are effectively unemployed. This is because there remains a residue of enterprises which continue to keep workers on their payroll (so that they can get access to social security services) even though there is no sense in which they are actually working productively.[14]

Nevertheless, despite this widespread job displacement in manufacturing, unemployment has not surfaced as a major issue in most of the high-income world. After all, the US economy, the world's largest,

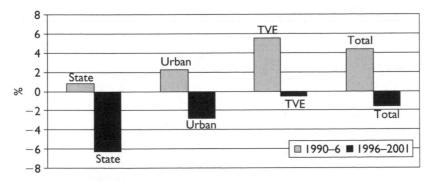

Figure 7.4 China's growth in employment (% per annum), 1991–2001

Source: Rawski (2003)

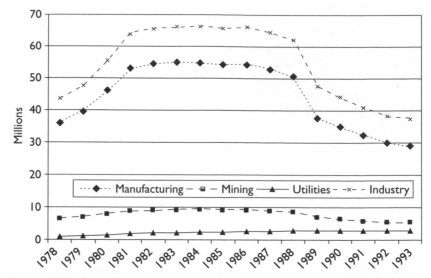

Figure 7.5 The evolution of sectoral employment in China, 1978–1993 (million workers)

Source: Rawski (2003)

continues to experience relatively low rates of unemployment, as do those of the UK and (to a lesser extent) the EU. Although the rate of unemployment grew in most of the major OECD economies during the early years of the twenty-first century (table 7.3), this was nowhere near the rates of the depression years in the 1930s, when unemployment reached and often exceeded more than 20 per cent of the active labour force.

However, this rosy picture on employment is masked by an important structural feature of the global economy, in that two of the very largest economies (the US and the UK) have been fuelling both domestic and global employment growth through a rapid descent into balance of trade deficits (figure 7.6). Moreover, despite earnings on the export of services, in both the USA and the UK there have also been sustained balance of payments deficits. This has been particularly evident for the USA, where the deficit on the current account increased rapidly from around 2 per cent of GDP in 1997 to more than 5 per cent in 2003; in the UK, the current account deficit averaged more than 2 per cent of GDP between 1999 and 2003. The growth of these trade and payments deficits coincides with the massive growth during the 1990s in China's manufactured exports and India's service-sector exports (largely of software). It is notable that the US trade

Table 7.3   Standardized unemployment rates in the major economies, 2001–3 (%)

	2001	2002	2003	2004
All OECD	6.5	7.0	7.1	6.9
Seven largest OECD	5.9	6.5	6.7	6.4
EU 15	7.4	7.7	8.1	8.1
USA	4.7	5.8	6.0	5.5
UK	5.0	5.1	5.0	n/a

Source: <http://www.oecd.org/dataoecd/41/13/18595359.pdf>

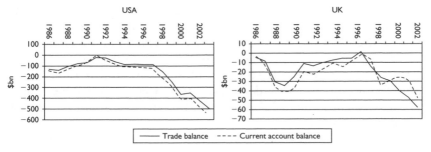

Figure 7.6   Balance of trade deficits, USA and UK, 1986–2003

Source: <www.OECD.org>

deficit in 2002 of $424 billion was almost as large as its total for manufactured exports ($569 billion) and significantly exceeded the total of China's manufactured exports ($293 billion) and those of Japan ($388 billion).

These trade deficits have allowed consumers in these two countries to go on a buying spree. In the USA, for example, on aggregate, from the late 1990s, private consumers have been spending around 5 per cent more than they have saved, and net personal savings rates in the UK have also fallen. Much of this consumption boom has been in labour-intensive personal services, and this has helped to maintain domestic employment, despite the decline in manufacturing employment. But it has also helped to sustain employment in those countries exporting to the USA and the UK (particularly in Asia, and especially in China), as well as in other countries (such as continental Europe and in East Asia) which have exported machinery and equipment and other inputs to those countries with sustained trade surpluses. In effect, these balance of payments deficits have had the same effect on an international plane as the Keynesian deficit financing used by governments to stimulate domestic demand during the Great Depression of the 1930s. Were the surplus countries such as China, Japan and

India to 'cash in' these surpluses (leading perhaps to devaluations of the dollar and sterling or, through other measures, to reduce demand, and thus for imports), then domestic demand – and employment – in the USA and the UK would fall. (This is analogous to governments deciding to balance their books after a sustained period of deficit financing.) The sustained nature and size of these savings and balance of payments deficits in the USA and the UK are such that this situation cannot continue. The short- and medium-term prognosis on global employment is thus not good.

The long-term prognosis is probably even worse. Figure 7.7 shows the size of the global labour force, from which it is evident that the number of people available to work in low-income economies dwarfs that in the high-income, high-productivity economies. Much of this developing-country labour force, as Lewis indeed argued, is either unemployed or works at very low productivity and is often in the informal sector. In many developing countries, the effective rate of unemployment is high. In some countries such as South Africa it is more than 30 per cent.

But it is in China, and to a lesser extent in India, that the numbers are so startling. The two countries have labour forces of 770 million and 470 million respectively. As we have seen, China's formal-sector manufacturing employment (83 million in 2002) is already larger than that of the fourteen largest high-income economies combined (79 million). Yet, a variety of observers concur that there are something like 100 to 150 million people in China currently working at very low levels of productivity who are waiting to be absorbed into the global economy. This surplus labour force, as can be seen in relation to figure

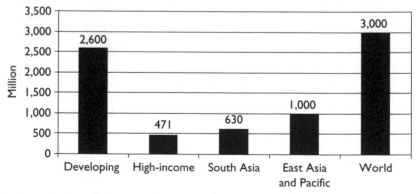

Figure 7.7   The global labour force (2002)

Source: World Bank (2004)

7.7, is equivalent to more than one-quarter of the total labour force in all high-income economies. Yet this labour surplus does not show up in Chinese labour statistics:

> The officially released low (formal) unemployment figures, however, do not reflect the severity of the actual high unemployment . . . [which] . . . takes place in urban China not in the form of open unemployment, but rather in the form of lay-offs. Laid-off workers, according to an official definition, are those who loose [sic] their jobs as their employing units encounter economic difficulties, while still maintaining their nominal employment relationship with their employees.[15]

Rawski concludes that '[e]xpansion of formal employment during the 1990s is entirely attributable to increases in rural jobs . . . [and] employment prospects deteriorated dramatically after 1995, with large numbers pushed out of the formal sector.'[16] One of the consequences of the opening-up, argues Rawski, is that the barriers to domestic migration have dropped sharply, so that up to 100 million people moved their place of residence during the 1990s.

The Chinese labour market is a segmented one. Recent figures (although the numbers should be treated with great caution) suggest a conflicting picture on the evolution of real wages. Some observers conclude that the effect of this labour surplus has been to reduce wage pressures: 'Unlike the situations in Japan and the newly industrialising Asian economies, where the supply of labour quickly hit the limits with wages shooting up, China's market wages for the unskilled labour in major manufacturing centres such as Guangdong have been stagnant at a subsistence level around $100 a month for more than a decade.'[17] However, others dispute this. In Guangdong in 2002, with a sample of 21,543 firms (of which roughly half, 46.5 per cent, were exporters), average wages were $138, those for exporting firms were $145, and those for non-exporters were $120.[18] What appears to be happening is that enterprises that are moving into higher value-added products and technologies are indeed raising wages in the coastal regions, albeit at a rate which is much lower than the growth in GDP. In addition, new migrant workers are streaming into the coastal regions and keeping marginal wages low there. At the same time, the vast interior is being opened up, and new investments which require low wages to compete globally are moving into the hinterland. As the Japanese managing director of a Chinese subsidiary observed, 'If we run out of people we just go deeper into China.'[19] It is this labour market segmentation which explains the fact that, despite rising wages in some parts of the economy, the US International Trade Commission concluded that global apparel production was likely to shift to China when clothing protection is removed in the major high-income economies (chapter 5).

All of this accords with Lewis's (and indeed Marx's) model, except that Lewis had argued that the reserve army would be gradually absorbed. If the numbers we have documented above are correct, this absorption will take a very long time, particularly as technology is becoming ever more labour-saving in nature. But, secondly, Lewis also argued that this reserve army of labour was predominantly unskilled in nature, and it is here that the global picture is changing structurally. Many developing economies have invested substantially in skill development. For example, table 7.4 indicates the extent of this skill development in China. Almost all children of school age are enrolled in schools, with high levels of progression to secondary and senior secondary education. The aggregate numbers having completed schooling are very substantial, and the quality of education (as reflected in teacher–pupil ratio) compares well with that in many high-income economies. But China, although probably much more advanced than other low-income economies, is not unique. India has a long history of tertiary education, and this has been borne out in recent years by the very strong growth of information technology exports. In large part this reflects the globalization of sourcing in software, which closely parallels that in autos, furniture and clothing documented in chapter 5. The consequence is that the job displacement previously experienced by the manufacturing sector in the USA has now begun to affect professional services also. As figure 7.8 shows, whereas historically electrical engineers and computer scientists experienced an unemployment rate less than half that of the US labour force in general, by 2001 this pattern no longer held, and they experienced similar rates of unemployment to those in the economy in general. In other words, the reserve army of labour of Marx and Lewis is no longer confined to unskilled workers.

Questioning the assumption of capital immobility

In Ricardo's world, countries continued to trade because investment was immobile. But if it were mobile, and if Portugal had unused resources, then Ricardo believed that capital would move to Portugal in the search for higher profits. The result would be expanding activity in Portugal and declining production in England. Abstracting from this theoretical mind-construct of Ricardo, a similar story can be developed for the actuality of the contemporary world. Given the

Table 7.4   Development of the Chinese educational system, 1985–2002

	1985	1990	1996	2000	2002
% of school age in primary education	96.0	97.8	98.8	99.1	98.6
% of primary school graduates entering junior secondary school	68.4	74.6	92.6	94.9	97.0
% of junior secondary school graduates entering senior secondary school	41.7	40.6	48.8	51.1	58.3
Numbers in technical secondary schools	61,000[a]	1,567,000	3,348,000	4,125,000	3,962,000
Number of students studying abroad	2,124	2,950	20,905	38,989	125,179
Numbers of students with university education			6,140,000		
with three years of college education			9,620,000		
completing specialized secondary school			17,280,000		
completing senior secondary school			72,600,000		
completing junior secondary school			263,000,000		
completing primary school			420,000,000		

Table 7.4 (continued)

	1985	1990	1996	2000	2002
Number of full-time teachers					
Higher education	247,000	395,000	403,000	463,000	618,000
Secondary schools	3,171,000	3,492,000	4,040,000	4,723,000	5,030,000
Primary schools	5,499,000	5,582,000	5,736,000	5,860,000	5,779,000
Pupil–teacher ratio					
Colleges and universities	5.0	5.2	7.5	12	14.6
Secondary schools	17.2	14.6	16.4	18.2	18.7
Primary schools	24.9	21.9	23.7	22.2	21
Number of books published	21,621	80,224	112,813	143,376	170,962

[a] 1980

Source: China Statistical Abstract (1997) China Statistical Yearbook (2003)

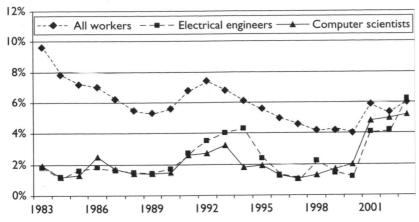

Figure 7.8 US unemployment rates, 1983–2003

Source: Hira (2004)

lower costs of production in a region – across a range of sectors – and given the mobility of investment capital, production will become increasingly concentrated geographically. In reality this has meant a flow of investment resources to the Asian region in general, and to China in particular. It is this which has partly buttressed the changing distribution of global manufacturing value added evidenced in chapter 6.

Although much of the capacity expansion in low-income economies in general and China in particular was financed domestically, a considerable proportion was externally sourced, by a combination of indirect private portfolio investments into stock markets and direct foreign investment into enterprises. For example, throughout this period, inward flows of investment accounted for more than 10 per cent of all gross fixed capital formation in China.[20] Table 7.5 shows the extent and distribution of these flows of foreign direct investment between 1991 and 2002. Following the 1997 Asian crisis, the proportion of FDI going to the developing world fell, as investor confidence was dented. But a striking feature of these investment flows was their concentration. For almost all of this period, more than half of total FDI going to the developing world went to Asia, and a rising proportion of this was directed to Hong Kong and China, playing a significant role in its expansion of manufactured exports. Indeed, China and Hong Kong absorbed between one-third and two-fifths of all FDI going to the developing world for most of this period.

Table 7.5　The size and geographical distribution of flows of foreign direct investment, 1991–2002

	1991–6 average	1997	1998	1999	2000	2001	2002
World annual flow ($bn)	254,326	481,911	686,028	1,079,083	1,392,957	823,825	651,188
Developing economies' share of world total (%)	36	40	28	21	18	25	25
Africa as % developing	5.0	5.5	4.7	5.3	3.5	9.0	6.8
Latin American and Caribbean as % developing	29.6	37.9	42.9	47.2	38.8	40.0	34.5
Asia as % developing	64.9	56.5	52.3	47.3	57.7	51.0	58.6
China and Hong Kong as % developing	34.5	28.8	30.6	28.3	41.7	33.7	41.0
India as % developing	1.2	1.9	1.4	0.9	0.9	1.6	2.1

Source: Data drawn from UNCTAD (2003)

Income transfers to fund restructuring

In a world of rapidly changing global specialization, and even more rapidly changing technology, no country can hope to sustain income growth without the capacity to change. This, as we saw in chapters 3 and 4, requires particular abilities at the level of the enterprise; it also requires that governments provide a policy framework which promotes industrial restructuring. Such a framework includes the development of a stable macro-economic operating environment with low rates of inflation, currency stability and affordable investment. It also requires the effective provision of resources necessary to cope with particular market failures across a range of sectors, for example, in supporting training, R&D and investments in information technology. And, in some cases where governments are particularly effective, industrial restructuring can also be facilitated by sector-specific policies that target particular branches for concentrated support, as in South Africa's Motor Industry Development Programme, which helped to consolidate the auto sector's export growth (chapter 5).

However, underlying these policies designed to promote restructuring (particularly in the case of the poorest countries) is the availability of a pool of funds on which governments can draw, which are not short-term in nature, and which do not have to achieve a commercial rate of return. Aid flows – transfers from rich-country governments and international institutions to poor-country governments – potentially provide just this form of restructuring resource.

During the late 1960s and early 1970s the rich countries committed themselves to increase aid flows to the developing world in order to assist long-term growth processes. The spur for this was in part the massive transfer of resources from the USA to Europe designed to aid reconstruction in the immediate post-war period – Marshall Aid Fund transfers to Europe accounted for more than 2 per cent of US GDP between 1951 and 1955. Spurred by President Kennedy in 1961, the United Nations unanimously committed its rich-country member states to a flow of official government aid equivalent to 0.7 per cent of their GDPs. As figure 7.9 indicates, however, after a period of growth between 1956 and the late 1980s, the absolute level of transfers of aid from rich-country governments to developing countries actually fell during the 1990s. This occurred despite a growth in the GDP in rich countries, so that aid transfers in aggregate fell from 0.33 per cent of GDP in 1986–92 to 0.22 per cent between 2000 and 2003. To make matters worse, much of this aid destined for 'developing countries' was targeted at countries that met key strategic

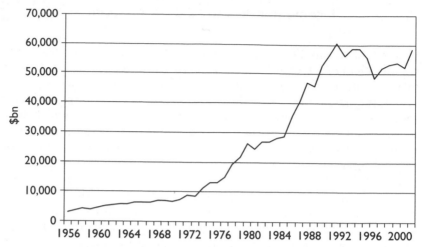

Figure 7.9   Global aid flows to developing countries, 1956–2003[a]

[a] Includes debt-forgiveness

Source: Data drawn from <www.oecd.org>

interests. For example, in 2003 the major beneficiaries of US aid were almost all a reflection of geo-strategic considerations – in order of importance they were Egypt, Russia, Israel, Pakistan, Serbia and Montenegro, Colombia, Ukraine, Jordan, Peru and Afghanistan.[21] Similarly, the bulk of EU aid is destined for the European periphery (North Africa and Central and Eastern Europe) rather than those countries in greatest need. Compounding these problems, the developing world (and particularly those economies which require the greatest assistance with restructuring) is mired in debt, so that most of the new, incoming aid funds are destined for the repayment of past inflows (since much 'aid' does not come in grant form, but as loans that need to be repaid).

What relevance does this pattern of aid flow have for the analysis of the poverty and distributional implications of developing countries producing for global markets? The point is that the funds available for capacity expansion have been severely skewed geographically. FDI has dwarfed aid flows and has gone predominantly to Asia in general, and China in particular. The compensating flow of official aid transfers has fallen in aggregate (and especially as a proportion of production), and has gone largely to countries that are strategically linked to the USA and Europe. What has not happened has been the systematic targeting of large flows of funds to facilitate the restructuring required by the poorest countries, and those in Africa and Latin America and elsewhere which, as we saw in chapter 2, have suffered so badly over the past two decades.

Structural excess capacity

As we have seen, the rising flow of investment ambitions in the developing world has coincided with the search for new production outlets by foreign investors and for new sources of supply by global buyers. The consequence has been a significant growth in capacity in many sectors which in many cases exceeds all feasible demand. For example, in the auto sector, global production capacity exceeded global demand by more than 25 per cent in 2003.

There are two major reasons for this systemic overcapacity. The first, and narrower reason, is the political will which sustains sunken investments despite their low profitability.[22] This has been the case in a number of sectors in the rich countries. Most markedly it occurs in agriculture, where each of the major triad economies (the USA, the EU and Japan) provides substantial subsidies and effective protection to domestic producers, forcing global prices down to sub-economic levels. But it also occurs in manufacturing. For example, in the steel sector, many governments have responded to the threat of job displacement by providing various forms of protection, including in the case of the USA through the use of anti-dumping tariffs, despite the lack of evidence that countries were exporting to the USA at prices below costs. The scrapping decisions which help to bring supply into balance with demand have thus been undermined by the adverse political reaction to capacity reduction.

But, more broadly, there are periods in history in which investment surges. This longer-run perspective on investment is most closely associated with the writings of Joseph Schumpeter, who provided a theoretical framework for explaining the longer-term rhythms of the global economy (which are often referred to as Kondratieff long waves, named after a Russian minister of agriculture who was one of the first to observe the existence of long cycles of economic activity). Schumpeter argued that these long-run variations in investment and growth were associated with major clusters of technological innovations, such as the railways and steel in the nineteenth century and electricity and chemistry at the turn of the twentieth. But, more recently, Perez has suggested that the growth-generating power of these surges of investment lies in the capacity of new technologies to provide a new paradigm for the rejuvenation of all existing economic activities (the present information revolution is a clear example of this).[23] It is the depth and breadth of the changes involved that would generate major surges of transformation in the world economy, lasting about half a century. In connection with this, Perez provided a coherent explanation for the relationship between investment and production.

Perez distinguishes four phases of each of the major technologically based 'great surges'. The first of these is that of 'irruption', when the new technology arrives, generally with a 'big bang', offering massive potential for use and profit, in a world characterized by the maturity and market saturation of the industries of the previous surge. This is followed by a second phase, when there is a 'frenzy' of intensive diffusion involving a major financial bubble and ending in its collapse. In the third phase this diffusion is extended to encompass greater and greater markets, sectors and territory. It is the expansive 'synergy' phase. Finally, phase four is one of 'maturity', when the potential of the previously new technology is diminishing and the gestation period of the new wave begins.

Why the distinction between the second and third phases if they both involve processes of diffusion? The answer is to be found, Perez argues, in the disjuncture between financial and productive capital. In the first phase there is a close correspondence between the interests of the new technological entrepreneurs and the financiers. But towards the latter part of the second phase they move out of synch – finance capital gets locked into wild speculation pursuing irrational short-term gains. It overinvests massively in the new sectors, and we observe bubble economies – the dotcom bubble of the late 1990s and the bubbles of earlier great surges (for example, canal mania, railway mania and the 'roaring twenties'). The collapse leads to a period of crisis, a 'turning point'. During this phase, productive capital is obliged to make long-term investments for expansion of production and markets and thus needs to harness a less impatient financial sector to suit its requirements. Then, in the fourth phase, as the cycle matures and the opportunities dwindle, financial capital begins to separate out from the dominant firms of the declining paradigm and to search for new opportunities, facilitating the gestation and irruption of the new cycle.

Perez's model is concentrated on what has historically happened in the core countries of the world economy. In that sense, she holds that the collapse of the NASDAQ in 2000 ended the frenzy phase. The years since then would be the time of instability between the second and third phases, when control of the economy should move from financial to production capital, probably with the support of adequate regulation.

But, extending Perez's argument to the global economy, this is not what has happened. Globalization has permitted financial capital to spread its action across the world and to continue pressing for short-term returns, creating imbalances and overinvestment distortions both in core and in peripheral countries. The financial instruments that have been created provide virtually unlimited investment funds, supporting ventures which cannot conceivably be justified by historic returns on investment. Capital is thus widely available to support new ventures, funnelled either through the foreign direct-investment flows or the indirect portfolio investment flows documented above, or through the creation of finance in countries such as Japan, Korea and China, whose banking systems have lent money to enterprises which have no prospect of repaying their loans. Lack of effective bankruptcy laws in China (enabling the scrapping of excess capacity) means that banks are reluctant to enforce liquidation, since they will lose all assets. In 2002 the official figure for all China's bank loans showed that 23 per cent were non-performing, but the real figure was said to be around 40 per cent.[24]

This overcapacity is reflected at a global level in a number of sectors. But it is in China where this frenzy of investment has been carried to the most extreme lengths, and where growing overcapacity is becoming a major problem. For example, in the first ten months of 2002 China made 24 million air-conditioners, but sold only 14 million. At the same time, leading firms were expanding capacity even further – Midea, for example, doubled capacity from 3 to 6 million units in 2003. As a result prices fell at 15 per cent per annum and Midea increased its exports between 2001 and 2002 by 70 per cent (to $340 million) and planned to increase further to $500 million in 2003. In the production of microwaves, where there was a similar pattern of excess capacity, prices fell from an average of yuan 2,000 ($240) in 2001 to yuan 500 ($60) in 2003. The price of a 29-inch colour television fell from yuan 6,400 ($770) in 1997 to yuan 2,000 ($240) in 2002, again on the back of excess capacity.[25]

Here we can see the link to the picture of falling global product prices documented in chapter 6. Heavy investments, often in very large-scale capital-intensive plants, have been fuelled by easily available credit lines. Political pressures limit the scope for capacity reduction, and the consequence is that many products are being traded globally at marginal costs, with an effective write-off of much of the capital investment that went into the growth in production capacity. Although there is no general evidence on global capacity growth or capacity utilization,[26] there is micro-evidence which suggests that this is a serious systemic problem, that it underlies the price pressures we have documented in global trade, and that it is suggestive of a substantial squeeze on producer profit margins and/or on the margins and profitability of the banks which provided the resources for capacity expansion.

The fallacy of composition

Almost all theories of economic growth are concerned with supply-sided issues. How can the rate of investment be increased to ensure that production capacity grows? How can the productivity of investment be improved so that the returns from investment are maximized? What can be done to improve labour skills? What types of infrastructure are required to promote the efficiency of investment, and how can infrastructural investments be increased? How can entrepreneurship be promoted and innovation increased? It is assumed in all of this that the demand side of this story is solved, that there will be willing consumers *who have the incomes* to consume all that is produced. Thus, the demand side of the growth process has been assumed to be unproblematic, an assumption which accords with that of Jean Baptiste Say discussed earlier in section 7.2.

In the discussion above on the growing reserve army of labour in the global economy we have already questioned whether the feasible growth of consumption in the global economy can possibly provide work for the global labour force. But there is a subsidiary demand-related issue which also bodes ill for sustained global income growth as globalization proceeds. This is referred to as the 'fallacy of composition', that is, what may make sense for an individual decision-maker loses its efficacy if the same decision is made by a number of parties.[27] For example, if a single country devalues its currency, it becomes more price-competitive in global markets. But if other countries devalue as well ('competitive devaluations') the logic of this action falls away. (In fact this is exactly what happened during the 1930s among the industrially advanced economies, and helps to explain the failure of the USA to capture the competitive benefits of the declining value of the dollar in 2003–4, since many Asian exporters such as China linked their currencies to the dollar, and devalued against the Euro and other currencies at the same time.)

At the beginning of the 1980s, Cline questioned the extension of the East Asian model of rapid growth as a fallacy of composition. He argued that, if all countries replicated the share of manufactured exports in their external trade of the four 'Asian tigers' (Hong Kong,

Korea, Singapore and Taiwan), the result would be an unsustainable crowding-out of competitors in external markets. In Cline's words, 'Elevator salesmen must attach a warning label that their product is safe only if not overloaded by too many passengers at one time: advocates of the East Asian model would do well to attach a similar caveat to their prescription.'[28]

In actual fact, Cline was demonstrably incorrect about developments at that time. Although, with the recent exception of China, few developing-country exporters were able to replicate the extraordinary export performance of the East Asian tigers, as we have seen, developing-country manufactured exports did indeed grow very rapidly. In many cases, this growth was made possible by rising incomes in the major markets; it was also facilitated by the collapse of production capacity in many key labour-intensive sectors in the high-income economies, such as footwear, apparel and furniture. But in many cases, as we saw in chapter 5, import penetration in major consuming economies is close to 100 per cent. So, in future, the gains of one low-income country exporter will no longer be at the cost of production in the importing high-income economies, but at the cost of other low-income economy exporters. It is this which leads to a very gloomy interpretation of the consequences of removing trade barriers in the clothing and textile sector. Cline's gloomy prognosis may well have been correct, but the consequences are coming to be realized only now that China – an economy of enormous size – is entering the global economy in so many sectors of production.

7.4 Striking the balance between optimism and pessimism

At the outset of this chapter we observed that unfortunately the evidence is not available to allow for an unambiguous judgement on which of the contrasting outcomes will emerge from the sustained fall in product prices of many manufactures that we documented in the previous chapter. This is partly because of theoretical disputations, partly because of the non-availability of data, and partly because we are in the midst of this significant structural change in the global economy, and it is still not clear how events might work out. In sections 7.2 and 7.3 we presented the case for and against a positive win–win outcome to the growing global specialization of production and trade.

To summarize the discussion briefly: the case for a win–win outcome to globalization is predicated on the productivity improvements arising from a growing global economy. This allows, and indeed induces, producers and countries to specialize and exchange their output across national boundaries. This raises producer incomes. Consumers also gain from the better quality products and from the lower prices which, as we documented in chapter 6, are an outcome of these global production systems. Although China has indeed captured a growing share of global markets for manufactures, at the same time its manufacturing output requires machinery and equipment and inputs of food and raw materials from other countries. A virtuous circle results.

The contrary view – one which we believe our evidence supports – is a little more complex, and considerably more pessimistic. The mutual gains from specialization and trade are predicated on a world of full or near-full employment which makes it profitable for producers and countries to specialize in areas of their relative capability. Once this assumption is removed, it does not follow that there will be a space for all producers in a system of global production and exchange, and some countries may not be able to find markets for their products. If they do, this may be at the cost of significant reductions in the prices of those products. The mobility of productive capital reinforces the dominance of global production and exchange by the relatively efficient producers and economies, who in the current era are based in Asia in general, and China in particular. The relative decline in the volume and the pattern of the distribution of aid resources does not allow the relatively inefficient producers to catch up.

This situation is unlikely to change, since there is a structural excess capacity in the global economy, not just in productive capacity, but also in the labour market. Moreover, technological change is increasingly labour-saving (or, the other side of the coin, there is a structural shortfall in consumption). Rising exports of manufactures from high-income economies to balance imports of manufactures from low-income countries are unlikely to change this. This is because the exports of manufactures by high-income to low-income economies creates less employment than is displaced by imports of manufactures from low-income economies; by one estimate, these imports displace 5.7 times more jobs than are created in export expansion.[29] Moreover, even though in some high-income economies (notably the UK) knowledge-intensive service exports are increasing, the rate of improved productivity in these services has been growing rapidly.[30]

At the worst, the so-called gains from outward oriented manufacturing may reflect a fallacy of composition. In other words, it may make sense for an individual country such as China to expand massively its exports of manufactures, but if the same path is adopted by all low-income economies, everyone will lose. However, even at best, in a world of excess capacity and structural unemployment, some countries such as China may succeed in this outward orientation. This will leave little space for other less efficient producers – notably those in Africa and large parts of Latin America.

If this more pessimistic view is the more likely outcome, it suggests that Lewis's two-sector model, on which Singer and Prebisch drew fifty years ago, remains a powerful explanation of differential income standards and trends in the high- and low-income worlds.[31] Except that it is a two-sector model which is played out at the global level. And, unlike Lewis, who believed that the productive sector would ultimately draw in the labour surplus from the less productive sector, we instead find ourselves in a Marxian/Malthusian world in which the labour surplus is endemic to the functioning of the system.

As we shall see in chapter 8, there are indeed many beneficiaries from this process of ongoing global integration. But there are also many casualties, and it is this which helps explain the incidence of persistent poverty and rising inequality that besets the global economy and that we documented in chapter 2. If so, what are the implications for the sustainability of globalization itself? And what are the implications for policy, particularly for those policies designed to alleviate global poverty and return us to a more equal world? This is the subject matter of the concluding chapter.

8

So What?

We began this analysis of the relationship between globalization, poverty and inequality in a furniture factory in Port Shepstone, a small town of 30,000 people, 70 miles south-west of Durban on the east coast of South Africa. The managing director had complained that he could not cope with global competition – the price received for the identical bunk beds he exported had fallen from £74 in 1996 to £48 in 2000. A neighbouring firm, also producing bunk beds for export, reported a similar problem – the prices it received had declined from £69 in 1996 to £52 in 1999. And the region's largest exporter of wooden doors reported a price fall of 22 per cent between 1996 and 2000.

At first this looked like a story of individual entrepreneurial failure. But, on closer inspection, the picture which began to unravel was much broader, and much more significant. As we have shown in previous chapters, falling prices have become a systemic feature of modern globalized production systems. In this chapter we ask the 'so what?' question. That is, what are the wider implications of the pattern of falling prices, persistent absolute poverty and growing inequalities which we documented in earlier chapters? We will respond to this question by addressing two sets of implications. The first are the implications for policy (section 8.2). Not all regions and types of economies have been affected in the same way in the recent era of globalization. There is thus no justification for a one-size-fits-all policy agenda, as, for example, is being pushed through the global economy in the form of the Washington Consensus.[1] Similarly, since locational externalities have become an increasingly important component of modern competitiveness, different regions will need to respond in different ways in their policies towards insertion in the global economy. The second set of issues raised by our analysis in section 8.3 concerns the very sustainability of globalization itself. To what extent is the stubborn persistence of absolute poverty and the growth in inequality likely to threaten the continued outward expansion of the global economy?

8.1   A brief synopsis

In chapter 1 we began this enquiry by observing that the current phase of globalization, beginning after the Second World War and gathering speed during the 1980s and 1990s, is not unique. The latter half of the nineteenth century had witnessed a similarly historically significant increase in global integration. However, this was followed by nearly four decades of inward orientation between 1914 and 1950. The globalization of the latter twentieth-century period was distinct in a number of ways. It was characterized by the very rapid expansion of global trade in manufactures, fuelled by the systematic reduction in the barriers to trade. Increasingly, this trade was in semi-processed manufactures, produced in coordinated global production networks. While global financial flows were important in both periods, they were much more volatile in the twentieth century. As for the migration of people, global movements of unskilled workers dominated the early period, while the latter twentieth century saw movements of skilled workers. The global flow of foreign direct investment has been important in many parts of the world in recent years, but, nevertheless, much of production destined for global markets is undertaken by locally owned firms benefiting from the global mobility of finance.

Chapter 2 focused on the two dimensions of poverty, the absolute and relative standards of living, and documented the trends over the past three decades. In relation to absolute poverty, using the widely accepted (albeit ambiguous) measure of $1 per day in purchasing power parity dollars, the evidence suggests that, while there was a decline in the proportion of the world's population living in absolute poverty, there remains a stubbornly large number of at least 1.2 billion people who remain below this very basic poverty line. Considering relative poverty, the overwhelming evidence is that inequalities have risen, particularly within countries, and on a range of dimensions. Chapter 2 concluded by addressing the relationship between these poverty patterns and globalization. Is poverty a residual phenomenon, as the World Bank suggests, in which case the appropriate response is for all countries to deepen their participation in the global economy as rapidly as possible? Or is the relationship more troubling and problematic – a relational one in which the stubbornly large number of the global poor and growing inequalities are in large part an outcome of globalization itself?

Part II (chapters 3, 4 and 5) began to unravel these questions by examining the processes at work that determine the distribution of income arising from global production networks. Chapter 3 provided a theoretical underpinning to the analysis, drawing the link between incomes and 'rents'. Rents arise from scarcity, having something, or being able to do something which others do not have, or cannot do. Incomes can be high and sustainable if producers are able to appropriate rents and to protect themselves from competition by constructing and/or taking advantage of barriers to entry. Chapter 4 focused on the determinants of successful innovation management, that is, developing the capabilities to catch up to the global frontier, to construct barriers against competitors and to take advantage of these barriers. But effective production is only one part of the story of global production networks – the other is the role played by global buyers, and this too was analysed as a factor determining the distribution of rewards in the current era of globalization. In chapter 5 we showed how the combination of effective innovation management and concentrated global purchasing was changing the geography of production in three sectors of considerable significance to low-income economies – clothing and textiles, furniture, and automobiles and components. In each case, global production networks are making growing use of low-income production platforms, concentration is growing in the buying of global products, and price pressures are becoming intense.

In part III (chapters 6 and 7) we have attempted to build a general picture from the partial firm- and sector-specific empirical material presented in chapters 1 to 5. How does it all add up? Does it matter that some firms and low-income economies have been able to carve out growing shares in global markets? Based on an analysis of global trade in manufactures, chapter 6 sought to answer the first of these questions. It showed that the combination of growing production capabilities and the intensification of concentration in global buying has led to a systematic squeeze on the prices received by producers. While there has been an increasing tendency for the prices of all manufactures to fall in recent years, this fall has been accentuated for low-income economies, for low-technology sectors and for sectors in which Chinese producers are concentrated. The massive surge in efficient investment in China and its increasingly skilled labour force have made it a major driver of these falling prices and of global overcapacity in a range of sectors.

As for the subsidiary question of how this matters, chapter 7 considered whether the global economy could adjust to this massive increase in productive capacity, the associated concentration in global buying power and the impact on product prices. It concluded that, despite the uncertainty of many of the signals which may be used to deliver a judgement, on balance it is likely that the outcome will be deleterious for very many people in the world. *That is*, the macro-story does not add up, and the sector-specific trends on overcapacity and intensifying competition are supported at the general level; *that is*, that the global resource army of labour, the surfeit of investable funds and the mobility of global investors mean that global integration provides a win–lose outcome on many dimensions; *that is*, that the gains of some are at the cost of others; and *that is*, that for many in the global economy, poverty and inequality are not residual, but relational to globalization.

8.2 Implications for policy

One of the key conclusions of our analysis has been that the impact of globalization on poverty and inequality is heterogeneous. It follows from this that policy needs to be heterodox – one size does not fit all. Before we discuss these variegated implications for policy, it is first necessary to understand in more detail how different types of economy and different regions of low-income economies have fared in the recent era of globalization. After this, we outline a framework for thinking about different types of heterodox policy, in the first instance with regard to the promotion of innovation and growth, and then in relation to the ways in which different types of countries and different regions relate to the global economy.

The impact of globalization on different regions and types of low-income economies

Summary: Regional impact of globalization

Broadly speaking there are significant differences in regional experiences with globalization. Asia has gained, while Latin America and the Caribbean and (especially) sub-Saharan Africa and Central Asia have lost.

In East Asia, the locational imperatives of modern production systems mean that countries which together participate in regional value chains have been able to reap complementary and systemic gains.

The heterogeneity of the global economy argues against one-size-fits-all policy prescriptions.

Drawing on chapter 2, table 8.1 summarizes developments in relation to the numbers of people living in absolute poverty (defined as less than $1 per day at purchasing power parity prices) in key low-income regions of the global economy during the heightened decade of globalization in the 1990s. Table 8.2 provides matching data on the growth of regional per capita incomes. The story is quite clear. East Asia appears to be a winner, with regard both to the falling number of people living in absolute poverty and to growth performance. As we have seen in previous chapters, this is largely a consequence of China's extraordinary growth in GDP (at around 10 per cent annually) and manufactured exports (expanding at 17 per cent per annum) during this decade. South Asia does less well in regard to the poverty outcome than to economic growth (where it is a relatively strong performer). The significant casualties are Latin America and the Middle East and North Africa (both a greater number of absolutely poor and low growth rates), and especially sub-Saharan Africa (a large growth in the numbers of absolutely poor and declining per capita incomes for most of the 1980s and 1990s) and, to a lesser extent, Eastern Europe and Central Asia.

China's growth and export surge play a major role in explaining the success of the East Asian region and have had a beneficial impact on surrounding countries for two reasons.[2] The first is that China has sourced raw materials and capital goods as inputs into its manufacturing processes from the region. Secondly, and especially in the case of electronics, its exports of final products have drawn on an extensive web of semi-manufactured components produced in the region in the form of regional value chains. In understanding this regional performance we can refer back to the discussion in chapter 4 on the determinants of effective innovation. Proximity in industrial clusters facilitates beneficial spillovers between firms and allows for more effective logistics through inter-firm just-in-time production. These have become critical elements in achieving the systemic efficiency underlying competitive advantage in the contemporary economy. Reflecting this, in many sectors key chain governors – TNCs or their agents in triangular production networks (see chapter 4) – coordinate production through a network of producers located in the region.

Table 8.1   Numbers living in absolute poverty, 1990 and 2001 (less than PPP$1 per day, millions)

	1990	2001
East Asia & Pacific	470	284
South Asia	467	428
Latin America & Caribbean	48	50
Eastern Europe & Central Asia	6	18
Middle East & North Africa	5	7
Sub-Saharan Africa	241	314
World	1,237	1,101

Source: <http://www.developmentgoals.org/Poverty.htm/povertylevel>

Table 8.2   Growth in per capita incomes, 1970s, 1980s, 1990s and 1998–2002 (constant $1995) (% per annum)

	1970s	1980s	1990s	1998–2002
East Asia & Pacific	4.5	5.7	6.4	5.3
South Asia	0.3	3.3	3.4	3.1
Latin America & Caribbean	3.3	−0.7	1.6	−0.7
Middle East & North Africa		−1.8	1.1	1.2
Eastern Europe & Central Asia			−2.6	4.0
Sub-Saharan Africa	0.5	−1.0	−0.5	0.6
World	2.0	1.4	1.0	1.2

Source: World Bank (2004)

Components are produced in Indonesia, the Philippines, Korea, Taiwan and other countries, and then shipped to China for further processing and assembly before their exportation to final markets.

As a consequence of these imports of raw materials, equipment and intermediate inputs (much of which is processed for exports to other regions), China's trade deficit with East Asia grew from $4 billion in 1990 to $40 billion in 2002, and the region's share of China's merchandise imports grew from 55 to 62 per cent in the same period.[3] Both Lall and Abaladajo and Shafaeddin conclude that the major intra-regional casualties – that is, countries with which China has competed – have been Japan and the lower-income economies producing low-technology and labour-intensive products such as clothing and luggage goods. But the losses of these economies have not been absolute. They have only been relative to the sharper gains reaped by economies such as Korea, Taiwan, Singapore and China. Both sets of authors concur that there are warning signs that these complementary production arrangements which have grown up during the 1990s may well turn into competitive relations in the future.

The contrast with other developing countries which have not been drawn into this complementary regional production system is striking. Consider, for example, the case of Brazil, an example of a middle-income economy with a history of industrial production and manufactured exports. It has come to be caught in a pincer movement between competition from low-wage and efficient competitors from below and higher-wage and efficient competitors from above.[4] This has had important and adverse implications for the distribution of income among Brazilian wage earners. Comparing the period before and after 1992 (when trade was liberalized significantly and Brazil could be said decisively to have entered the globalizing economy), the impact of this competition can be seen clearly.[5] Between 1992 and 1999, despite an increase in the level of education in the labour force, real wages fell by 15.9 per cent in traded sectors and 8.1 per cent in non-traded sectors. The fall was greater the higher the degree of tradedness. The ratio of wages in the traded goods to the non-traded goods sectors was constant during the 1980s, with a value of 74 per cent in 1992. But, after its deepening participation in the global economy, this ratio fell to 69 per cent in 1995 and to 64 per cent in 1999. Moreover, although wages fell disproportionately in the traded-goods sectors, it also fell in the non-traded-goods sectors, a consequence of declining wages and surplus labour in those sectors directly affected by imports. Significantly, the only category of the Brazilian labour force not to have experienced a decline in real income was the college-educated skilled group. Although there are no similar structured studies of wage evolution in comparable middle-income economies, such as Mexico, India and South Africa, it is likely that the outcome there will be much the same as that in Brazil.

As for the transitional countries in Europe and Central Asia, the outcome of their experience with deepening globalization is compounded by the fact that this integration occurred at the same time as they undertook far-reaching reforms to deregulate and liberalize their economies, and to restructure their delivery of social services. So it is not clear how much of this adverse poverty and distributional outcome is due to globalization and what share is as a result of the impact of economic reform in the domestic economy. In virtually all these cases, distribution has become considerably more unequal, and living standards have fallen. In many cases morbidity has grown and life expectancy has declined sharply. As in the case of Brazil, the adverse performance of these countries must be seen in the context of the destruction of much of their historic industrial competences, squeezed between low-income and low-cost, and high-income and technologically sophisticated competitors in the global economy.

By contrast, the especially adverse performance of the very low-income, predominantly agricultural economies in sub-Saharan Africa and elsewhere must be seen in a somewhat different light. In these cases it is not so much that existing producers are being squeezed out of global markets or are having to lower their wages in order to survive. Rather it is that the intensity of global competition prevents them from entering global markets in the first place. With the exception of South Africa, few African economies have been able successfully to expand their exports outside of the commodities and clothing sectors, despite this being an explicit objective of economic policy. And in the case of clothing, as we saw in chapter 5, their participation in external markets is extremely fragile and likely to be rapidly eroded as quota protection is removed after January 2005.

We have considered the differential impact of globalization on incomes, poverty and distribution as a regional issue. Insofar as the different regions are characterized by roughly similar economic structures, this is broadly speaking an accurate reflection of the outcome of globalization. However, there are important intra-regional variations. In sub-Saharan Africa, South Africa and Mauritius are very dissimilar to their neighbours, and confront different types of problems in competing in the global economy. In Latin America, Costa Rica has shown a demonstrable capacity to manage innovation more effectively than many of its similarly small Central American neighbours, and Chile has shown greater economic flexibility than other regional economies with similar resource potential (such as Argentina and Brazil). In Eastern Europe and the former Soviet Union, Poland and the Czech Republic have fared less badly than their neighbours. However, although the nature of economic structure in individual economies speaks powerfully of their capacity to cope with the competitive pressures of globalization, regional factors continue to play a dominant role in determining the economic outcome of deepened globalization, as is so powerfully evident in the case of East Asia.

Heterodox policies in a globalizing world

Summary: One-size-fits-all and heterodox policies

The Washington Consensus policies of the World Bank and the IMF represent a one-size-fits-all approach to growth and poverty alleviation. They are premised on a residual explanation for global poverty and inequality and fail to meet the challenge either of the hetero-geneity of country and regional experience or of the need to address the relational determinants of global poverty and inequality.

Given this relational perspective, there is a need for active and integrated policies to allow countries to gain from globalization. This requires addressing three types of policies – functional policies affecting the climate for investment and production, horizontal policies which address cross-sectoral market failures, and selective policies which target sectors, firms and regions.

Given this uneven experience with globalization, it is necessary for countries and regions to respond with appropriately contextual policies, reflecting their individual comparative advantages, constraints, opportunities and trajectories. This, however, is not the position in which many countries find themselves. Increasingly, policy agendas are being formed in low-income countries as a consequence of external influences. In some cases, these may be ideological in nature, influencing the worldview of key domestic actors. For example, after the military coup in Chile during the early 1970s, policy was formed by a group of young economists who had studied together at the University of Chicago with a leading proponent of market economics, Milton Friedman. In other cases, the policy agenda is directly dictated by international financial institutions such as the IMF, the World Bank and the WTO, often backed by pressure from large donor countries such as the USA.

Williamson has characterized this policy agenda as the Washington Consensus.[6] It is a policy agenda which, in its ideal type, strips governments of the responsibility for and capability of influencing either the allocation of resources to promote and influence growth or the distribution of income. Even in its amended form[7] the central tenets of the policy agenda are unchanged – Rodrik refers to this as the 'Augmented Washington Consensus'.[8] This approach towards markets (including global markets) reflects the residual explanation for global poverty – allow growth and global integration to take place without interference, and all will be well, for all. However, the substance of the analysis in earlier chapters is to show that, left to market forces alone, as the Washington Consensus proposes, globalization will neither solve the problem of absolute poverty nor result in a more equal world. On the contrary, it is likely to exacerbate both – poverty, inequality and globalization are relational. Thus, to achieve a different outcome requires active policies to promote and sustain innovation.

What might such a policy framework consist of? One approach is to enhance the capacity to innovate through a programme of active and integrated policies. Based on the experience of the successful latecomer industrializing economies of East Asia, Lall and Teubal identify three categories of policy.[9] The first are 'functional policies' designed to improve the efficiency of market operations. For example, where innovation is stifled by monopoly, competitions policy may promote an environment more conducive to investment. So too will a macro-economic policy that provides for a more stable economy – rapid and/or fluctuating inflation discourages investment, and a volatile foreign exchange rate undermines the capacity to export. Many of these functional policies are within the agenda of the Washington Consensus, for example, the promotion of macro-economic stability. But other components, such as policies designed to inhibit surges of inflowing hot money that require controls on capital flows, run counter to its policy prescriptions.

The second type of policies that can be identified are a group of 'horizontal policies' which respond to generalized market failures and cut across sectors. For example, the mobility of labour often means that firms will underinvest in training, since they face the danger of competitors bidding away their skilled employees. Another example relates to incentives to promote research and development (R&D). It has long being recognized that R&D is a public good, that is, it is difficult to appropriate. Thus, as we showed in chapter 4, intellectual property laws limit the operations of markets and are designed to promote invention and innovation. These cross-sectoral policies are more likely to run against the tenets of the Washington Consensus than are the functional policies, but are much less controversial than the third category of policies, referred to by Lall and Teubal as 'selective policies'. These comprise policies which are designed to promote specific sectors, specific firms or specific regions. For example, they may provide sector-specific tariff protection against imports or, as we saw in chapter 5 in the case of South Africa's auto industry, incentives to promote sectoral exports. In Korea and Taiwan, selective support provided subsidized finance and preferential licensing to particular sectors. In Malaysia during the 1980s and 1990s, and now in China, the apparatus of government was designed to promote 'national champion' firms. It is these selective policies that are anathema to the proponents of the Washington Consensus. But, arguably, it is these very same policies that have been influential in explaining the success of precisely those East Asian economies which have been able to benefit in the recent era of globalization.[10]

The extent to which individual countries can successfully implement these innovation and industrial policies depends on the capabilities of their government bureaucracies. In general, the weaker the state, the less firms will be able to benefit from the policy rents that we outlined in chapter 4. Effective policy design and implementation is also bottom-up rather than top-down, incorporating close interaction with a range of non-government stakeholders.[11] These heterodox policies will reflect differing degrees of emphasis between as well as within each of the three categories in different economies. But what these individually crafted policies will have in common is their integration, recognizing the synergies between these categories, so that, for example, those designed to promote macro-economic stability do not undermine those targeted at the promotion of individual sectors.

Learning from the past

Summary: Learning from the past

The design of a policy agenda which recognizes the relational character of global poverty and inequality must learn from the strengths and weaknesses of post-war import substitution. Its strength was that it provided a protected environment to foster the growth of dynamic capabilities. But it had three key weaknesses.

- In many low-income economies, the scale of protected markets was too small to allow for the innovation-enhancing benefits of competition. In the current era of World Class Manufacturing these are economies of scope rather than in production, so it is large markets rather than large factories that are indicated.
- There is considerable learning that arises from exports. But exports from low- to high-income economies lock producers into process capabilities, at the cost of product and value-chain role-changing capabilities. Trade with other low-income economies provides more scope for the development of a fuller range of capabilities.
- A major weakness of import substitution was the creation of unproductive policy-induced rents. Policy design must recognize the danger of creating these unproductive rents by ensuring a competitive environment.

In all these cases we have made the generic observation that there is an enhanced need for policies designed to interfere with the operations of markets. This relates to both domestic and external markets. This is not the first time such policies have been indicated. The three decades after the Second World War, the first stage of the recent era of globalization, were decades in which similar policies were implemented. This is referred to as the era of import substituting industrialization. Such policies have been much maligned, despite the fact that it is unquestionable that they lay behind the modern success of industrial powerhouses such as Germany, the USA, Japan, Korea and China. But that agenda did have three key weaknesses that must be recognized and addressed if a new phase of protected and facilitated growth is to be pursued.

The first of these is that, in most cases, domestic scale was too small to allow for efficient production. In many sectors, productivity gains arise from what has been termed 'Verdun's Law'. That is, there are heavy fixed costs to an investment, irrespective of scale. This means that, as capacity utilization increases, so the marginal and the average costs of production decline and productivity increases. In other words, economies of scale are pervasive and significant. In the era of mass production, when inflexible production systems dominated, much of these scale-inducing factors were the fixed costs of buildings and machinery. Scale economies in this case arose from enhanced plant size. But in the era of flexible World Class Manufacturing (see chapter 4), the economies of scale are in scope rather than in production – often plant sizes either are static or even decline, but can produce a greater variety of products. For example, in modern auto factories, the scale economies arise not so much from the growth of the size of individual assembly plants, but from the capacity to produce a range of autos on the same line in multiple plants. In these circumstances scale economies arise from the costs of product development. Hence, the new policy agenda will need to provide the capacity to spread knowledge-intensive investments in process and product over a larger volume of sales, albeit perhaps in smaller and more distributed plants.[12]

The second lesson that needs to be understood from previous experience is the importance of serving external markets as a source of learning. As we saw in chapters 4 and 5, firms in low-income economies can absorb a great deal about process efficiency when they sell into high-income markets. However, at the same time, they are constrained in the capacity to build product development capabilities, or to realign their role in global value chains. Hence, the challenge is to fashion an insertion in global markets that promotes a more rounded capacity to innovate, and this may indicate the need to target different markets, including for large economies, to place greater emphasis on the domestic market.

Most of the products exported by low-income economies – not just manufactures, but also agricultural products such as horticulture – are destined for high-income consumers. They are clearly superior to the products manufactured during the previous phase of import substitution, even for low-income consumers. But, if attention were to be given to the needs of these low-income consumers as a prime objective in product design, how much more effective might these products be in meeting consumer needs? A clear case in point is the automobile, where variants targeted at low-income consumers are stripped-down versions of high-income models rather than purposely designed vehicles. They are therefore unnecessarily costly and are inappropriate for driving on poor roads, and require a costly service infrastructure with the capacity to diagnose and repair complex electronic components. More basically, what sorts of fruit and vegetables are being produced for external markets in East Africa? Sophisticated systems exist to produce ready-packed, short shelf-life salads for Europe. By contrast, the production systems required to turn out products for low-income consumers domestically and in the region languish and are not subject to modern methods of innovation management.

Here we can see a link between a policy agenda designed for outward orientation and the growth of regional markets. Both for reasons of realizing scale economies and because of the learning capacity provided by exports, there is a need in most low-income economies – bar the very largest such as China and India – to produce for external markets. But the most viable external markets are likely to be similar rather than dissimilar markets, and markets which are in some way protected from the gales of global competition. Naturally this is not the first time that this opportunity has been identified. For example, during the 1980s a group of Latin American countries attempted to gain through linking together in the Andean Pact. But, as in the case of other regional integration initiatives, this proved to be a failure. On the other hand, there are many cases to the contrary, including of course the EU and the East Asian production system that we observed above.

A final lesson to be learnt from the era of post-war import substituting industrialization is the need to foster competition, and to avoid the creation of monopoly rents. The historical experience of Japan with regard to technology importation during the 1960s and 1970s is important here. The Japanese created a policy regime in which all technology importation had to be licensed, a common feature of the post-war economy. However, unlike what was happening in most of the developing world, the Japanese Ministry of International Trade and Industry (MITI) would only sanction the importation of technology if it involved more than one competing firm. In fact, virtually all other instruments of industrial and technology policy were fashioned to promote intense competition, even if it sometimes simultaneously required cooperation (for example, in basic research, or in marketing). It is in this failure to develop and sustain a competitive environment that many developing economies fell down in their promotion of protected industrialization. This suggests a further argument for regional integration in that it provides the scale that allows for the development of protected and competitive markets.

It is essential that any new policy agenda must avoid the creation of unproductive rents. The extensive licensing systems utilized in many economies, particularly in India during the 1960s and 1970s, encouraged what has come to be called 'rent-seeking behaviour'.[13] This led not only to corruption (buying licenses), but also to the diversion of entrepreneurial energy in the search for ways around and through often amazingly complex industrial policies. One important lesson from recent history is that industrial policies do not necessarily involve the endogenization of rent-seeking behaviour. Not just Korea and Taiwan, but also countries such as China and South Africa show clearly that intelligent policy design can promote a world of effective and efficient innovation management.[14] But much of this runs against the current of the Washington Consensus and the policies being promoted in low-income economies by the IMF, the World Bank and many high-income country donors.

Policies towards the global economy: the new regionalism?

Summary: The new regionalism?

However effective policy design may be in enhancing innovative capabilities, the underlying structural problems with the global economy of surplus capacity and intense competition remain.

Consequently, for some regions and many countries, a much more selective approach will be needed towards participating in the global economy, involving selective disengagement.

As long as the US economy continues to fuel global consumption, East Asian economies will continue to gain from global integration. However, their very success denies the same opportunity to Latin America, Africa and Central Asia.

There are two implications of this for the external policy of low-income economies outside of East Asia.

- The necessity of tapping wider markets to achieve economies of scale and scope indicates the need for the development of stronger intra-regional economic ties.

> • In many important respects, low-income economies hold antagonistic interests. East Asian economies will benefit from a 'level playing field'. Other low-income economies, particularly those in sub-Saharan Africa, will only prosper with an uneven playing field, but one tilted in their direction.

In chapter 2 we suggested three approaches towards poverty alleviation and income distribution in the context of globalization. The first is that growth and global integration will eat away at residual poverty. The second (discussed in chapters 3, 4 and 5) is that the ability to grow and to alleviate poverty and inequality depends upon the approach adopted towards globalization – the issue is not whether to participate in the global economy, but how to do so. The third approach (the subject of chapters 6 and 7) is that there are structural problems with the global economy which mean that the full integration of all economies will drive living standards down for the majority – a race to the bottom. Rejecting the first of these – the residual explanation for global poverty – does not mean that all economies have to choose either the second or the third approach. Which is relevant depends on the type of economy involved – what may be appropriate for some will be inappropriate for others.

The logic of this choice will to a significant extent be regionally determined. In chapter 4 we showed that a key component of competitive success has been what economic geographers refer to as 'locational externalities', that is, spillovers between firms and groups of firms which are located in a particular region. We saw how this can arise from the availability of a pool of skilled labour, the benefits of having a range of suppliers and customers in close proximity, opportunities to exchange knowledge in informal gatherings, and the greater ease of building the trust which facilitates the capture of relational rents in closely knit communities. With the advance of World Class Manufacturing and shortened lead times and reduced inventories, proximity provides additional competitive advantages. Clusters of firms and regional systems of innovation and production are of critical importance in the contemporary global economy.

Using a broad brush, let us look at the implications for the way in which different regions may need to restructure their relations with the global economy. In the case of East Asia, insertion in the global economy has been a relatively successful experience, particularly for sectors in which producers participate in regional value chains. Should the global economy remain stable, then there is little need for these economies to reorient external policies. But if, as seems more likely, there is a decline in extra-regional demand as the USA (and the UK) rein in consumption, then the East Asian economies may need to focus on the local regional market. Moreover, there are some very populous economies in the region – notably China and Indonesia (and India in South Asia) – where the domestic market provides significant potential for growth. The desirability of a greater inward focus in these large countries is reinforced by the growing political tensions that are emerging as a result of the unequalizing consequences of participating in the global economy.

But not all East Asian economies have benefited or are likely to benefit from globalization in the same way or to the same extent as China. Some of the countries have been excluded from this virtuous circle of regionally integrated production and trade. These are the low-income economies which specialize in the production of simple final products such as footwear, clothing and luggage goods, where there is little scope for integrated production networks and where one country's advance in external markets may be at the cost of another's. For these East Asian countries, the indicated policy agenda might be closer to that relevant to the middle-income economies in Latin America, to Central Asia, to India and to South Africa (see below), whose existing production capabilities do not allow them to compete effectively in the global economy. They have been squeezed by competition in external markets and through imports, and do not operate effectively in competitive regional production networks.

This category of 'squeezed economy' applies to much of Latin America (particularly Brazil and Argentina), to the economies of Central Asia, to North Africa, to those economies in Eastern Europe which are not part of the EU (currently Turkey is the most prominent example), to India (excluding some services) and to South Africa. Once again, as a generic challenge, it is necessary for each of these economies to foster the upgrading of production capabilities across the spectrum through effective innovation policies, even though this may require them to run against the stream of the Washington Consensus. More specifically, these economies will experience decreasing returns from competing in external markets because of the competitive pressure arising from China's increasingly successful participation in these major markets, backed often by the regional production network in East Asia. Consequently, in addition to maintaining the capacity to promote production through active and selective innovation and investment policies, some form of selective disengagement may be required from the global economy for these economies, notably selective protection against imports. In addition, closer attention may have to be paid to promoting regional markets, a subject which we will address below. The exceptions in this category of countries are the economies of Eastern Europe and that of Mexico, which may gain from their location and close integration with dominant regional economies (the EU and the USA and Canada respectively).

The final category of economies are those whose prospects are determined not so much by the destruction of existing capabilities, as by their inability to enter global markets in the first place on account of the severity of competition. This is a competition which is expressed not just in final product markets in North America and Europe, but also by an inability to attract foreign capital and FDI. These economies are 'failed globalizers' not because they have not tried to join in, but because of their inability to compete. They are the economies where the World Bank's injunction to participate more actively, based on its residual approach to global poverty, is most poignant. It includes most of sub-Saharan Africa, much of the Pacific, much of South Asian manufacturing, parts of Latin America and even the low-income economies of East Asia. For this group of economies, as elsewhere, there is the clear need to adopt policies which foster the growth of domestic innovation capabilities. But even more than the middle-income economies discussed above, they require the capacity to protect nascent domestic capabilities, and to target and stimulate local and regional consumption.

There are two conclusions for external policy that follow from this analysis. First, going back to the lessons which we have learnt from a previous phase of protected and policy-facilitated innovation and growth, there are dangers of disengaging from the global economy and turning inwards into a single economy. With the exception of China, India, Indonesia and Brazil, few low-income countries have an adequately large market to allow for the capturing of the economies of scope and scale that characterize modern production systems. Their small size also does not allow them to foster the competition required to sustain innovation. Hence the combination of the benefits provided by outward orientation, the requirements for greater scale and the locational externalities in modern production systems indicates the need for greater intra-regional integration. There are already signs that many countries are beginning to grasp this regional nettle. There is growing momentum in Africa behind NEPAD (New Partnership for African Development) and in Asia for a stronger role to be given to ASEAN (Association of South East Asian Nations). In Latin America, there has been a revival of interest in both the Andean Pact and in Mercosur, driven by economies such as Brazil which has suffered from intense competition in global markets. This is not an easy path, since to be successful it requires not just an economic but also a political commitment.

The second implication for external policy is that low-income economies may hold antagonistic interests. For example, as we saw in the case of the clothing sector, in the context where the clothing industries in most high-income countries have been reduced into insignificance, the export gains of some low-income economies (notably China and India) will be at the cost of others (Bangladesh and sub-Saharan Africa). The less competitive low-income economies can gain from globalization only if competition from the more successful low-income economies is restrained. This runs against two important strands of thinking in the institutions of global governance such as the WTO. First, what low-income countries require is not a level playing field – this will drive them into a race to the bottom. Instead what they need is a tilted playing field, but one which is inclined in their direction. And, second, the tilt in this playing field should be directed not only against high-income economies, but also in many crucial cases against other low-income economies. The idea of a common set of interests which underlies much development discourse and theories of imperialism is mistaken. The policy divisions may be as much between low-income economies as between low- and high-income economies.

8.3   So what for the sustainability of globalization?

Summary: Is globalization sustainable?

Three factors question the sustainability of the current phase of globalization. In each case they reflect endogenously determined contradictions arising out of the very success of globalization.

- Global value chains are energy intensive. The need to combat global warming requires a higher price for energy, and this will undermine the profitability of these globally extended chains.
- The persistence of poverty leads to a resentment by the dispossessed. In a world of urban slums, this surfaces in a variety of millenarian religious-based political movements. Focusing on the ideological and cultural hegemony of global capitalism, they are likely to attack the expressions of the global economy, and hence undermine its communication systems.

> • As in the nineteenth century, the rapid adjustments forced by changing global specializations induce anxiety and have significant distributional impacts. This sets off political opposition to globalization. The fact that in the current era articulate and organized professionals are as likely to be affected as the unskilled is likely to make this opposition to continuing globalization more effective.

In recent decades globalization has been so rapid and significant that it is not uncommon to see it characterized as an inevitable and inexorable process. The gains to be made are so substantial for the powerful parties who drive globalization that it is difficult to see the limits of this push to deeper integration. New technologies are continually being introduced which are likely to enhance these gains further. In the most recent period this applies particularly to the falling costs of transferring knowledge and information. But these innovations follow post-Second World War technological advances which reduced the costs and speeded up the transfer of goods across national boundaries. The almost absolute military dominance of the USA backing the global ambitions of the US corporate sector is an added factor underlying the inexorable progress of globalization.

Yet it is important to keep a sense of history. Projecting forward on the basis of past growth is a process full of pitfalls. Marie Jahoda criticized the environmental doomsayers during the early 1970s (when a variety of environmental disasters were predicted) by arguing that they ignored feedback loops; societies respond to environmental degradation by changing consumption habits and/or by utilizing new technologies. To illustrate the absurdity of blind projection she calculated that, if the increase in the training of technical staff by the Americans in response to the surprise launching of the first satellite by the Russians in 1957 was sustained, by 1992 there would be two scientists for every man, woman and dog in the USA![15]

In other words, the fact that global processes extended so rapidly in the last decades of the twentieth century is no guarantee that the shift will be sustained in the twenty-first century. This is self-evident. But it is also backed up by historical experience. As we saw in chapter 1, the nineteenth century was similarly a period of global integration, followed by what Williamson has termed an 'implosion into autarchy'.[16] This tension between integration and subsequent disintegration is not confined to the 100 years between 1850 and 1950. It recurs through history. For example, the Roman Empire commanded the space around the Mediterranean Basin and Western Europe for 450 years, and was followed by the Dark Ages. There is growing evidence that, between 1421 and 1423, Chinese ships had circumvented the globe, mapped distant shorelines in some detail, and had traded with many distant economies. But it was followed by a turning inward and a retreat into autarchy for more than 400 years.[17]

In the nineteenth century, Marx and Lenin drew on Hegel's thinking on dialectics to develop a theory of history. Briefly, they argued that history is driven by the continuous conflict between opposing forces and used this to develop a theory of historical progress ('dialectical materialism'). There are many objections to this theory of history, not least because it posits strong 'systems' with discrete boundaries and because, somehow, 'history' conveniently stops at the stage of communism when there is only one class. But one important insight which they do offer is the idea that each system is characterized by 'internal contradictions' and that it thus 'sows the seeds of its own destruction'. What they meant by this is that a dominant characteristic in history is that the very extension of any economic and political system sets up oppositional forces which undermine its continuing viability. That is, the roots to change are endogenous to the socio-political-economic system.

Of course we need to take great care in drawing on this framework. Change occurs for a multitude of reasons, often through factors which are exogenous to the economic system, for example, through environmental catastrophes. But nevertheless there is an important insight in this historical schema which helps us explain the fragility of the current global system – the idea that the routes to change are not just largely endogenous to the system, but often arise out of its very success, a response to the dominant forces which drive the system forward. There are three such endogenous internal contradictions that are currently emerging to threaten the sustainability of globalization.

The first of these concerns the environmental footprint of contemporary globalization. Figure 8.1 illustrates the extent of 'food-miles' in our modern consumption basket. Global sourcing has become increasingly widespread, in the case of a selection of products from a single UK supermarket, flying in fruit and vegetables from Brazil, Guatemala, Israel, Kenya, Peru, Thailand, the USA, Zambia and Zimbabwe. In so doing, supermarkets have been able to abolish seasonality in our food consumption, with a range of attractive, (over) packaged (and often tasteless) products available 364 days a year. This snapshot in figure 8.1, just a selection of available fruit and vegetables, tells only part of the food-miles story. How much of the packaging, the print and inks, the components of the supermarket trolley, the lorries which deliver the products, the building materials in the chain

Figure 8.1 Food-miles in the shopping trolley

and so on similarly depend on global supply chains? In each case, the different components of the chain have to be transported (and some times retransported) over extensive distances. This example of extended and growing global supply chains in fresh fruit and vegetables is, as we have seen in chapters 1, 5 and 6, replicated at an increasing rate across a wide range of sectors.

All of this global sourcing is at a cost to the environment. Some of this is a direct outcome of global transport, as in the case of the Exxon Valdez oil-spillage in Alaska during the 1990s. But the bulk of this negative environmental impact is indirect, particularly through the link between increased energy consumption and global warming. For much of this intricate system of global production depends on the low price of energy which makes it profitable to ship low-value-added commodities and components around the world. Despite the claims of the hydrocarbon lobby to the contrary, we now know that there is growing evidence of global warming, and that this is predominantly a consequence of increased carbon emissions. We also are beginning to realize that one consequence of climate change is its disproportionate negative impact on poor people and low-income economies.[18]

If we are to respond appropriately to global warming, then energy will have to be priced at its true environmental cost. But, if so, what will be the impact of this on the profitability of globalized production systems? How many activities which are currently profitable will be unattractive should energy prices be increased significantly? To what extent is the current pattern of globalization environmentally sustainable? On the other hand, it is possible (and perhaps even probable) that, despite the logic of forcing energy prices to a level which reflects its true environmental cost, the power of the hydrocarbon lobbies to block an increase in prices makes this an unlikely outcome. In this case, energy-intensive global value chains are likely to worsen global warming and hence exacerbate poverty and inequality. This outcome, as we will see in the following discussion, challenges the sustainability of globalization. So either way – be it through higher energy prices or through the impact on poverty and inequality – the energy intensity of globalized production systems poses a threat to the sustainability of globalization.

A second type of endogenous internal contradiction is more speculative but potentially as threatening to the sustainability of globalization. It reflects the social and political threat arising from poverty and inequality. The background to this potential internal contradiction is to be found in the changing geography and demographics of the global population. Davis has recently produced an important analysis which helps to explain the rise of various forms of fundamentalist millenarianism in recent years.[19] He draws on estimates that in 2004, for the first time in history, more than half of the world's population will have been living in cities. The growth of cities from the industrial revolution was historically tied to the development of industry. Consequently, argues Davis, until the late twentieth century, politics was based largely on class affiliations. However, modern cities are slums, populated by the dispossessed and unemployed. In these environments politics takes a new form, with the marked growth of various forms of millenarianism, expressed largely in fundamentalist religious affiliations – Pentecostal churches in Africa, Latin America and the USA, Hindu fundamentalism in India, and Islamic fundamentalism in Asia and North Africa. In very recent US political discourse, this is referred to as the 'religiosity' of contemporary politics.[20]

How does this relate to the sustainability of globalization? The link is to be found in the cultural and social hegemony of contemporary globalization and its links to the growth of millenarian movements in low-income economies. Through its 'cultural' extension of TV, films, printed media and, especially, advertising, globalization has spread a pattern of behaviour and values which has become increasingly offensive to many around the world, and has been used as a political rallying call by the leaders of many of these fundamentalist faiths.

Curiously, many of the leaders of this fundamentalism were themselves privileged beneficiaries of globalization, but they drew on the support of masses of the 'losers', who were excluded from many of the fruits of globalization. Their response has been to attack the many manifestations of globalization, beginning with the World Trade Center (the name itself evokes the hegemony of global processes), and moving to tourist centres associated with Western values (nightclubs in Bali). But where will it end, and what impact will it have on the very sustainability of globalization itself? What impact might attacks on its infrastructure have on the sustainability of globalization? It is unfortunately not too fanciful to envisage strategically placed bombs in shipping containers – indeed the USA is currently taking active steps to reduce the likelihood of such attacks. Nor can we rule out the possibility of suicide attacks in prominent airports, tourists being taken hostage, or strikes against foreign business people. The point is that these are not likely to be stochastic events, but are more predictable since they feed into the social and political culture of 'religiosity politics'.

More importantly for our analysis, they are an outcome of the very success of globalization in two important respects. First, as we saw in chapter 7, the displacement of labour which results from reducing impediments to trade has contributed to the growth of slums. And, second, the extension of global product markets has depended on the development of global brands. These brands are backed by advertising, not just the explicit 'in-your-face' hoardings which increasingly dominate the cityscape, but also the more subtle subliminal offerings such as 'product placements' of key global brands in films. Much of this branding is culturally specific, with an emphasis on sexuality which is anathema to many religious groups.

There is a third endogenous factor which might undermine the sustainability of contemporary globalization, and which has been the subject matter of preceding chapters in this book. This is that globalization forces alterations in economic specialization. The result is frequent and significant change in employment patterns, in work organization and institutional design. Perhaps more importantly, it has also led to significant changes in the pattern of income distribution. There are two key consequences of these related changes. The first is that life appears to have become more insecure for many, including for articulate professionals in the high-income economies. Some years ago Robert Reich, a sometime Secretary of State for Labor in the Clinton administration, wrote insightfully on this issue. He observed that the USA had a large and growing 'underclass'; on top of this underclass, by definition, was an 'overclass'. This, said Reich, was not new. But what was new was the character of the in-between category – 'the anxious class'.[21] To a significant extent this growing anxiety and unease is a direct consequence of the imperative for continual 'reinvention' forced by global competition. Jack Welch, former CEO of General Electric (GE) in the USA, was widely considered to be one of the select number of truly influential management innovators during the 1990s. His philosophy was to force a regular turnover of staff in all GE subsidiaries, however well they were performing, and managers were expected to evaluate and 'weed out' the least-well-performing group of employees on an annual basis. In the early years of the millennium, GE promoted a '70:70:70 policy' – 70 per cent of activities to be outsourced; 70 per cent of this outsourcing to be off-shored (that is, sent abroad); and 70 per cent of this offshoring to go to low-wage economies. It is an agenda of uncertainty, distrust and fear. This is echoed in the world-view of the head of Intel, Andy Groves, who wrote a best-seller entitled *Only the Paranoid Survive*.[22] In each case the prognosis was change – 'reinvention', 'reorganiza-tion', 'business process engineering' – an ongoing agenda not just in the private sector but even in state-owned bureaucracies such as the UK's National Health Service and educational systems. It is a world of insecurity, fear and anxiety, and one which threatens to engender opposition to globalization, the more so as the professional classes in the high-income economies are now being threatened by the off-shoring of their own jobs to India and other lower-wage economies.

It is not just that the changes induced by globalization have led to widespread fear and anxiety (including among the articulate profes-sional classes in high-income economies), but, as we saw in chapter 2, it has also resulted in growing inequality. The rich are increasingly confident and bold, with a widespread tendency to flaunt their wealth, reflected as we saw in chapter 4 in the growth of 'positional con-sumption' in many product markets. We know from previous eras in economic and political history that the impetus for social change comes not so much from changes in absolute deprivation as from rel-ative deprivation, and it is this which perhaps above all threatens the sustainability of globalization.

The lessons of the nineteenth century provide an important back-drop in understanding these possible developments in the early twenty-first century. As we saw in chapter 1, following five to six decades of growing global integration, the world economy turned inwards after 1914, and the outward momentum was regained only in the decades after 1950. In between saw a period of internal focus and a reduction in economic integration. This reversal of global processes followed directly from the very success of late nineteenth-century integration and can be explained by four factors which reflect the impact of globalization on distribution.[23] First, cheap grain imports into continental Europe led to a decline in agricultural profits. This resulted in the imposition of tariffs against agricultural imports in much of Europe. Second, there was a mass migration of unskilled Europeans into the USA as 60 million people, often literally walking across Europe, made their way there between 1820 and 1914. This forced down relative wages in North America and led to growing controls against migration. In the UK, for example, there were no controls on immigration until the Aliens Act of 1906. Third, the competitiveness of European manufactures threatened the survival of the USA's nascent manufacturing sector. This resulted in the imposition of tariffs against manufactures. And, finally, the demand for growing markets and resources led to the expansion of colonialism. This spurred the imperialist rivalries which helped to fuel the First World War. In each case, the seeds of change are to be found in the very workings of the nineteenth-century global economy, and arose as a direct consequence of its success. As the CEPR review of this period observes, '[t]he experience of the First World War was clearly important in destroying the liberal economy of the pre-1914 era. However, the late nineteenth century record does clearly show that left to its own devices, globalization can undermine itself politically, and distribution matters not just for its own sake, but also because of the political responses it provokes.'[24] Williamson concludes of this transition towards inward-orientation, 'the forces of globalization had a significant distributional impact within participating countries. [Moreover], it also suggests that these distributional events helped create a globalization backlash.'[25] 'European countries staying open to trade absorbed the biggest distributional hit; European countries retreating behind tariff walls absorbed the smallest distributional hit.'[26]

To conclude the story, therefore, while many have gained from globalization, there remains a substantial number of the world's population – roughly one-quarter – who continue to live in absolute poverty. At the same time, inequality has increased, across and within countries. Some of this poverty and inequality arises as a consequence of the failure of communities to participate in globalization, a residual category of non-performers. This is the view backed by the World Bank, the IMF and much of contemporary economic theory, for whom the response is clear – join in. But we have argued in this book that a significant component of absolute poverty and worsening distribution arises as a direct consequence of globalization – they are relational phenomena. In these circumstances, the logic for these victims is to be much more selective in their engagement with the global economy.

Whatever the normative conclusion ('what ought countries to do?'), there are reasons to question the sustainability of the late twentieth-century era of globalization. Like the earlier phase of nineteenth-century internationalization, globalization is threatened from within. That is, there are a number of factors, endogenous to the global system, which undermine its future viability. The current deepening of globalization is likely to run out of steam as a result of its own internal contradictions. For some this will be a setback, undermining their growing absolute and relative wealth. For others it might prove to be a relief, providing the opportunity to develop new paths of social and economic development.

Notes

1 Global Dynamics

1 Joffe, Kaplan, Kaplinsky and Lewis (1995).
2 Wood (1994, 1998); Lawrence and Slaughter (1993); Borjas, Freeman and Katz (1997).
3 Dicken (2003).
4 Calculated from World Bank (2004).
5 Griffith-Jones, Gottschalk and Cailloux (2003).
6 Although the most common current referencing to this phenomenon is to the writings of Feenstra (1998) (who refers to this as the 'vertical disintegration of trade') and Hummels, Rapaport and Yi (1998) ('vertical specialization in trade'), the origins to the literature are to be found in the 1970s (Helleiner 1973) and early 1980s (Froebel, Heinrichs and Kreye 1980) ('the New International Division of Labour').
7 These financial flows, particularly those which were short-term in nature, often had a severely destabilising impact on recipient economies owing to their tendency to surge (Griffith-Jones, Gottschalk and Cailloux 2003).
8 In actual fact Baldwin and Martin's data reflect the ratio of the current account (goods and services) to GDP rather than capital flows. However, as they point out, these net exports and imports of goods and services are necessarily reflected in flows of finance, and therefore these data form a good indicator of financial flows during these periods (Baldwin and Martin, 1999: 8).
9 Chiswick and Hatton (2001); CEPR (2002); World Bank (2002).
10 See, for example, Baldwin and Martin (1999); Bordo, Eichengren and Irwin (1999); Crafts and Venables (2001); Dicken (2003); Obstfeld and Taylor (2002).

2 Globalization and Poverty

1 Cited in Townsend (1979: 33).
2 Cited in Townsend (1979: 32–3).
3 Townsend (1979: 31), italics added.
4 Baulch (2003: 7).
5 Ravallion (2003: 745).
6 Sala-i-Martin provides a less convincing explanation for these differences, based on the exclusion of the former Soviet Union from his database and the fact that the World Bank focuses on consumption rather than income. But, when correcting for this, Sala-i-Martin estimates consumption from the national accounts of each country and appears not to grasp the significance of Ravallion's observation that he and the World Bank are using household survey data rather than estimates of income distribution.
7 Pogge and Reddy (2002: 4).
8 Jones (1997); Beaudry, Collard and Green (2002).
9 Milanovic comprehensively takes apart Sala-i-Martin's widely cited work by exposing the extensive and illegitimate methodological assumptions which he makes, almost all of which underestimate the extent of poverty and bias the calculations of global income inequality to suggest a picture of falling inequality (Milanovic 2002).
10 Ibid.
11 Dunford (1994).
12 Gottschalk, Gustafson and Palmer (1997); Streeten (1998).
13 Kohl and O'Rourke (2000).
14 Hartog (1999).
15 Kaplinsky (1998).
16 Cline (1997).
17 Rodrik (1999).
18 In the extreme case where a single individual commands all income, the gini coefficient is equal to 1; where income is perfectly distributed and everyone gets an equal share, the gini is zero.
19 UNDP (1999).
20 Wood (1994, 1997, 1998).
21 '. . . until about 1985, China achieved a remarkable reduction in the incidence of poverty. [But] [a]fter the mid 1980s the rate of reduction in poverty drastically slowed down and arguably was halted or even reversed' (Khan 1999: 2).
22 China Poverty Alleviation Office, *The Guardian*, 20 July 2003.
23 Freeman and Perez (1998).
24 The three quotes in this paragraph are drawn from World Bank (2002), pp. ix–x, 37 and xi respectively.
25 Williamson (1990).
26 This argument has been extensively made with respect to widening

inequality in high-income economies, notably the USA (Lawrence and Slaughter 1993).

27 This contrast between poverty as a residual and poverty as a relational outcome of globalization is drawn from Bernstein (1990).

3 Getting it Right

1 Prebisch (1950); Singer (1950).
2 Sutcliffe (1971: 103).
3 However, given inflation in the US economy, this did not translate into higher purchasing power of wages in the USA.
4 Ricardo (1973 [1817]: 33).
5 Freeman (1976).
6 Lundvall (1992); Nelson (1993).
7 Barker (1977).
8 *Management Review* (1996).
9 Hoffman and Kaplinsky (1988); Womack, Jones and Roos (1990); Cusumano (1985).
10 Womack and Jones 1996.
11 Kaplinsky (1995).
12 Jaikumar (1986).
13 *Financial Times*, 25 April 2001.
14 Best (1990); Pyke, Becattini and Sengenberger (1990); *World Development* 27, 9 (1999) [special issue on industrial clusters in developing countries].
15 For example, Krueger (1974); Lal (1983).
16 For Japan, see Best (1990); for Korea, see Amsden (1989); for Taiwan, see Wade (1990); for Singapore and Malaysia, see Mathews and Cho (2000); and for South Africa, see Barnes, Kaplinsky and Morris (2004).
17 Yoffie (1983).
18 Gereffi (1999).
19 During the early 1990s there was a vigorous debate in the USA on the dangers of foreign ownership of productive assets. Reich (who subsequently became the Secretary of State for Labor) argued that ownership was much less important than the location of high-value-added activities, and here the USA had a major advantage in its best-in-class tertiary educational system and its physical infrastructure. He argued that these should become the primary arenas for the US government's industrial policy (Reich 1991).
20 Singh (1995).
21 King and Levine (1993).
22 Albert (1993).
23 Griffith-Jones, Gottschalk and Cailloux (2003); Teunissen, Joost and Teunissen (2003).

24 Kaplinsky (1982).
25 Chang (2002).

4 Managing Innovation

1   Womack and Jones (1996); Lipietz (1987); Piore and Sabel (1984); Pine (1993). Much of the discussion in this section is drawn from the work undertaken with Justin Barnes, John Bessant and Mike Morris.
2   Hill (1987).
3   Hamel and Pralahad (1994).
4   Teece and Pisano (1994).
5   Leonard-Barton (1995).
6   Wheelwright and Clark (1992).
7   Kaplinsky (1994: ch. 2).
8   Monden (1983); Schonberger (1986); Kaplinsky (1994).
9   Schonberger (1986); Bessant (1991); Kaplinsky (1994); Womack and Jones (1996).
10 Schmitz (1999).
11 Economic theory makes the distinction between a world where a single producer (monopoly) or buyer (monopsony) commands the market and one where a limited number of producers (oligopoly) or buyers (oligopsony) influence market outcomes. The key determining characteristic of oligopoly and oligopsony is that the market is sufficiently personal for the actions of individual participants to be affected by the potential response of individual known competitors.
12 Williamson (1985).
13 Gereffi (1994, 1999).
14 Gereffi (1999).
15 Sturgeon (2002); Gereffi, Sturgeon and Humphrey (2004).
16 Gereffi, Humphrey and Sturgeon, 2004; Gibbon and Ponte (2004).
17 Porter (1990).
18 Data provided by Mil Niepold of Verite.
19 Cusumano (1985); Womack, Jones and Roos (1990); Hoffman and Kaplinsky (1988).
20 Bessant, Kaplinsky and Lamming (2003).
21 Kaplan and Kaplinsky (1998).
22 Schmitz and Knorringa (2000).

5 The Global Dispersion of Production

1   The data for the USA, Germany, France and Japan in this section is drawn from Gereffi and Memedovic (2003); the data on the UK comes from Gibbon (2002).
2   Calculated from WTO (2004).
3   Fernando (2003).

4 *Financial Times*, 21 July 2004.
5 These two quotes are drawn from USITC (2004), pp. xi and xiii respectively.
6 The UK and EU data is drawn from Gibbon (2002), and the US data from Gereffi and Memedovic (2003).
7 Readman (2004).
8 Ibid.
9 Ibid.
10 SITC is the Standard International Trade Classification used to categorize global trade. These data are calculated from <www.unctad.org>.
11 Schmitz (1999).
12 Dicken (2003: 355).
13 GPN (2003).
14 Humphrey (2001).

6 How Does it All Add Up?

1 Martin (2003).
2 USDA Economic Research Service (2000: 18–22).
3 *Fortune*, March 2004: 44.
4 Schmitz (1999).
5 USDA Economic Research Service (2000).
6 Much of the material in this section is drawn from Hamilton, Feenstra and Petrovic (2004) and Hamilton and Feenstra (forthcoming).
7 Maizels, Palaskas and Crowe (1998); Maizels (1999); Maizels (2003).
8 World Bank, World Development Indicators (2003).
9 Cheong and Geng (2003).
10 Calculated from UNCTAD, *World Investment Report* (2003).
11 A survey of seventy German metalworking firms in 2004 reported that, while 40 per cent of these businesses judged Eastern European products to be inferior to their own, only 17 per cent felt that this was true of Chinese equivalents (*Financial Times*, 23 August 2004).
12 Zheng and Zhao (2002).
13 Liu (2002).

7 Does it All Add Up?

1 Prebisch (1950); Singer (1950).
2 For a summary of these debates, see the various contributions in Sapsford and Chen (1998).
3 Smith (1976 [1776]: 13).
4 Ibid.: 31.
5 This is Blaug's summary of Say – Blaug (1985: 149).
6 Balassa (1989).
7 Martin and Manole (2003).

8 *Financial Times*, 23 August (2004).
9 Tom Cutler, Clarksons, personal communication.
10 Ricardo (1973 [1817]: 136).
11 Lewis (1958 [1954]: 435).
12 Wood (1994). More recently, Rowthorn and Coutts (2004) have suggested that, between 1992 and 2000, internal factors such as technological change and the falling income elasticity of demand for manufactures accounted for two-thirds of employment loss in manufacturing in twenty-three high-income economies, and trade with low-income countries for around one-third of employment loss.
13 Lawrence and Slaughter (1993).
14 Gu (2003).
15 Gu (2003: 2).
16 Rawski (2003: 4–5).
17 Cheong and Geng (1993: 129).
18 Rawski, personal communication.
19 Roberts and Kynge (2003).
20 The data in this section are drawn from UNCTAD (2003).
21 <http://www.oecd.org/dataoecd/42/30/1860571.gif>.
22 Brenner (1998).
23 Perez (2002).
24 *Financial Times*, 5 February 2003.
25 Ibid.
26 But see Brenner (1998), who does provide evidence of excess capacity in the USA and elsewhere for the mid-1990s.
27 Mayer (2002); UNCTAD Trade and Development Report (2002).
28 Cline (1982: 89).
29 Rowthorn and Coutts (2004).
30 Triplett and Bosworth (2003).
31 During the 1980s, Singer returned to this theme: 'It will be noted that some of the . . . explanations for a deteriorating trend in terms of trade of developing countries relate as much or more to the characteristics of different *countries* – their different levels of technological capacity, different organization of labour markets, presence or absence of surplus labour, etc. – as to the characteristics of different *commodities*. This indicates a general shift in the terms of trade discussion away from primary commodities *versus* manufactures and more towards exports of developing countries – whether primary commodities or simpler manufactures – *versus* the exports of industrial countries – largely sophisticated manufactures and capital goods as well as skill-intensive services including technological know-how itself' (Singer 1987: 628). When new datasets became available, he pioneered the empirical work on the declining terms of trade of low-income economies in manufactures which he had prefigured in an article published in 1971 (Singer 1975 [1971]); Sarkar and Singer 1991).

8 So What?

1 Williamson (1990).
2 Lall and Abaladajo (2004); see also Shafaeddin (2002).
3 Lall and Abaladajo (2004).
4 These issues were presciently addressed by Wood (1997).
5 Arbache, Dickerson and Green (2004).
6 Williamson (1990).
7 Kuczynski and Williamson (2003).
8 Rodrik (2002).
9 Lall and Teubal (1998).
10 Amsden (1989); Wade (1990, 1996); Barnes, Kaplinsky and Morris (2004).
11 Morris and Robbins (2005); Rodrik (2004); Schmitz (2004).
12 Kaplinsky (1990).
13 During the early 1970s influential critiques of import substituting industrialization were made by Bhagwati and Desai (1970) and Little, Scitovsky and Scott (1970). Subsequently, Krueger (1974) and Lal (1983) provided the architecture of a generalized assault on active industrial policies, followed up in the 1990s by the World Bank, as reflected in its review of the 'East Asian Miracle' (World Bank 1993).
14 For Korea, see Amsden (1989); for Taiwan, see Wade (1990); for the various economies in the East Asian region and the promotion of the electronics industry, see Mathews and Cho (2000); for the South African auto industry, see Barnes, Kaplinsky and Morris (2004).
15 Jahoda (1973).
16 Williamson (1998: 61).
17 Menzies (2002).
18 Yamin (2004).
19 Davies (2004).
20 Hadden and Long (1983); Bromley (1991).
21 Reich (1991).
22 Groves (1996).
23 The first three of these are discussed in CEPR (2002: 38–9).
24 Ibid.: 39.
25 Williamson (1998: 51).
26 Ibid.: 62.

References

Albert, M. (1993) *Capitalism against Capitalism*. London: Whurr.

Altshuler, A., M. Anderson, D. T. Jones, D. Ross and J. Womack (1984) *The Future of the Automobile*. Boston: MIT Press.

Amsden, A. (1989) *Asia's Next Giant: South Korea and Late Industrialization*. New York: Oxford University Press.

Arbache, K. S., A. Dickerson and F. Green (2004) 'Trade liberalisation and wages in developing countries', *Economic Journal*, 114, pp. 73–96.

Balassa, B. (1989) *New Directions in the World Economy*. New York: New York University Press.

Baldwin, R. E, and P. Martin (1999) 'Two waves of globalization: superficial similarities, fundamental differences', *Working paper 6904*, Cambridge, MA: NBER.

Barker, T. C. (1977) *The Glassmakers: Pilkington, the Rise of an International Company, 1826–1976*. London: Weidenfeld & Nicolson.

Barnes, J., R. Kaplinsky and M. Morris (2004) 'Industrial policy in developing economies: developing dynamic comparative advantage in the South African automobile sector', *Competition and Change*, 8, pp. 153–72.

Baulch, B. (2003) 'Aid for the poorest? The distribution and maldistribution of international development assistance', *CPRC Working Paper No. 35*.

Beaudry, P., F. Collard and D. A. Green (2002) 'Decomposing the twin-peaks in the world distribution of output-per-hour', *Working paper 9240*, Cambridge, MA: NBER.

Bell, R. (2003) 'Competition issues in European grocery retailing', *European Retail Digest*, 39.

Bernstein, H. (ed.) (1990) *The Food Question: Profits vs. People*. London: Earthscan.

Bessant, J. (1991) *Managing Advanced Manufacturing Technology*. Oxford: Blackwell.

Bessant, J., R. Kaplinsky and R. Lamming (2003) 'Putting supply chain learning into practice', *International Journal of Production Management*, 23, pp. 167–84.

Best, M. H. (1990) *The New Competition*. Cambridge: Polity.

Bhagwati, J., and P. Desai (1970) *Planning for Industrialization: Indian Industrialization and Trade Policies since 1951*. Oxford: Oxford University Press.

Bhalla, S. S. (2002) *Imagine There's No Country: Poverty, Inequality, and Growth in the Era of Globalization*. Washington, DC: Institute for International Economics.

Blaug, M. (1985) *Economic Theory in Retrospect*. 4th edn, Cambridge: Cambridge University Press.

Bordo, M. D., B. Eichengren and D. A. Irwin (1999) 'Is globalization today really different from globalization a hundred years ago?', *Working paper 7195*, Cambridge, MA: NBER <www.nber.org/papers/w7195>.

Borjas, G., R. Freeman and L. Katz (1997) 'How much do immigration and trade affect labor market outcomes?', *Brookings Papers on Economic Activity*, 1, pp. 1–85.

Brenner, R. (1998) 'Uneven development and the long downturn: the advanced capitalist economies from boom to stagnation, 1950–1998', *New Left Review*, 229.

Bromley, D. G. (ed.) (1991) *Religion and Social Order: New Developments in Theory and Research*. Greenwich, CT: JAI Press.

Bugliarello, G. (1999) 'Science and technology policy and intellectual property: seeking new global linkages', in A. Akhunov, G. Bugliarello, and E. Corti, *Intellectual Property and Global Markets: An East–West Dialogue*. Burke, VA: IOS Press.

Carroll, L. (1916) *Alice's Adventures in Wonderland and Through the Looking-Glass*. Chicago: Rand McNally.

Carson, J. G. (2003) *US Weekly Employment Update*. New York: Alliance Bernstein.

CEPR (2002) *Making Sense of Globalization: A Guide to the Economic Issues*. London: Centre for Economic Policy Research.

Chang, H.-J. (2002) *Kicking Away the Ladder?: Development Strategy in Historical Perspective*. London: Anthem Press.

Cheong, Y. R., and X. Geng (2003) 'Global capital flows and the position of China: structural and institutional factors and their implications', in J. J. Teunissen (ed.), *China's Role in Asia and the World Economy*. The Hague: FONDAD.

China Statistical Abstract (1997) New York: Praeger.

China Statistical Yearbook (2003) New York: Praeger.

Chiswick, B. R., and T. J. Hatton (2001) 'International migration and the integration of labour markets', IZA Discussion paper no. 559 <http://papers.ssrn.com/sol3/papers.cfm?abstract_id=322541>.

Cline, W. R. (1982) 'Can the East Asian model of development be generalized?', *World Development*, 10, 2, pp. 81–92.

Cline, W. (1997) *Trade and Income Distribution*. Washington, DC: Institute for International Economics.

Cornia, A. C., and J. Court (2001) 'Inequality, growth and poverty in the era of liberalization and globalization', *Policy Brief No. 4*. Helsinki: Wider.

Cotterill, R. (1999) *Continuing Concentration in Food Industries Globally: Strategic Challenges to an Unstable Status Quo*. Storrs, CT: University of Connecticut, Food Marketing Policy Centre.

Crafts, N., and A. J. Venables (2001) 'Globalization in history: a geographical perspective', <http://ideas.repec.org/p/cep/cepdps/0524.html>.

Cusumano, M. A. (1985) *The Japanese Automobile Industry: Technology and Management at Nissan and Toyota*. Cambridge, MA: Harvard University Press.

Davis, M. (2004) 'Planet of the slums: urban involution and the informal proletariat', *New Left Review*, 26, pp. 5–34.

Dicken, P. (2003) *Global Shift: Reshaping the Global Economic Map in the 21st Century*. 4th edn, London: Sage.

Dunford, M. (1994) 'Winners and losers: the new map of economic inequality in the European Union', *European Urban and Regional Studies*, 1, 2, pp. 95–114.

Feenstra, R. C. (1998) 'Integration of trade and disintegration of production in the global economy', *Journal of Economic Perspectives*, 12, 4, pp. 31–50.

Fernando, L. (2003) *Kenya: Capacity Building for Garment Exporter to Meet the 2005 Challenges*. Geneva: International Trade Centre.

Freeman, C. (1976) *The Economics of Industrial Innovation*. London: Penguin Books.

Freeman, C., and C. Perez (1988) 'Structural crises of adjustment', in G. Dosi et al. (eds), *Technical Change and Economic Theory*. London: Frances Pinter.

Frobel, F., J. Heinrichs and O. Kreye (1980) *The New International Division of Labour*. Cambridge: Cambridge University Press.

Gereffi, G. (1994) 'The organization of buyer-driven global commodity chains: how US retailers shape overseas production networks', in G. Gereffi and M. Korzeniewicz (eds), *Commodity Chains and Global Capitalism*. London: Praeger.

Gereffi, G. (1999) 'International trade and industrial upgrading in the apparel commodity chain', *Journal of International Economics*, 48, 1, pp. 37–70.

Gereffi, G., and O. Memedovic (2003) *The Global Apparel Value Chain: What Prospects for Upgrading by Developing Countries?*. Vienna: UNIDO.

Gereffi G., T. Sturgeon and J. Humphrey (2004) 'The governance of global value chains', *Review of International Political Economy*, 12, 1, pp. 78–104.

Gibbon, P. (2002) 'At the cutting edge? Financialisation and UK clothing retailers' global sourcing patterns and practices', *Competition and Change*, 63, pp. 289–308.

Gibbon, P., and S. Ponte (2004) *Trading Down: Africa, Value Chains and the Global Economy*. Philadelphia: Temple Smith.

Gottschalk, P., B. Gustafson and E. Palmer (1997) *Changing Patterns in the Distribution of Economic Welfare: An International Perspective.* Cambridge: Cambridge University Press.

GPN (2003) 'Global production networks in Europe and East Asia: the automobile components industries', *GPN Working Paper 7*, School of Geography, University of Manchester.

Griffith-Jones, S., R. Gottschalk and J. Cailloux (eds) (2003) *International Capital Flows in Calm and Turbulent Times: The Need for a New International Architecture.* Ann Arbor: University of Michigan Press.

Groves, A. S. (1996) *Only the Paranoid Survive.* New York: Doubleday.

Gu, E. (2003) *Labour Market Insecurities in China.* SES papers 33. Geneva: ILO.

Hadden, J. K., and T. E. Long (eds) (1983) *Religion and Religiosity in America: Studies in Honor of Joseph. H. Fichter.* New York: Crossroads.

Hamel, G., and C. K. Pralahad (1994) *Competing for the Future.* Cambridge, MA: Harvard Business School Press.

Hamilton, G., and R. Feenstra (forthcoming), *Emergent Economies, Divergent Path: Organization and International Trade in South Korea and Taiwan.*

Hamilton, G., R. Feenstra and M. Petrovic (2004) 'Demand responsiveness and the emergence of capitalism in East Asia: a reassessment of the "Asian miracle"', <http://www.soc.duke.edu/sloan_2004/Papers/Demand_Resp onsiveness.pdf>.

Hartog, J. (1999) 'Country employment policy reviews: the Netherlands', *Social Dialogue and Employment Success. ILO Symposium, 2–3 March.* Geneva: ILO.

Helleiner, G. K. (1973) 'Manufactured exports from less-developed countries and multinational firms', *Economic Journal*, 83, pp. 21–47.

Hill, T. (1987) *Manufacturing Strategy.* London: Macmillan.

Hira, R. (2004) 'Implications of offshore sourcing'. Mimeo, Rochester (NY) Institute of Technology.

Hoffman, K., and R. Kaplinsky (1988) *Driving Force: The Global Restructuring of Technology, Labor and Investment in the Automobile and Components Industries.* Boulder, CO: Westview Press.

Hummels, D., D. Rapaport and K.-M. Yi (1998) 'Vertical specialization and the changing nature of world trade', *FRBNY Economic Policy Review*, pp. 79–99.

Humphrey, J. (2001) 'Global value chains and local development in the automotive industry', *Background Paper for UNIDO World Industrial Development Report, 2002.* Vienna: UNIDO.

IDS (1997) 'Collective efficiency: a way forward for small firms', *IDS Policy Brief IO.* Brighton: Institute of Development Studies.

IMF (2002) *World Economic Outlook*, <http://www.imf.org/external/ pubs/>.

Jahoda, M. (1973) 'A postscript on social change', in H. S. Cole, C. Freeman, M. Jahoda and K. Pavitt (eds), *Thinking about the Future.* London: Chatto & Windus.

Jaikumar, R. (1986) 'Post-industrial manufacturing', *Harvard Business Review*, November–December, pp. 69–76.

Jefferson, G. H., T. G. Rawski, L. Wang and Y. Zheng (2000) 'Ownership, productivity change, and financial performance in Chinese industry', *Journal of Comparative Economics*, 28, pp. 786–813.

Joffe, A., D. Kaplan, R. Kaplinsky and D. Lewis (1995) *Improving Manufacturing Performance: The Report of the ISP*. Cape Town: University of Cape Town Press.

Jones, C. (1997) 'On the evolution of world income distribution', *Journal of Economic Perspectives*, 11, 3, pp. 3–19.

Kaplan, D. E., and R. Kaplinsky (1998) 'Trade and industrial policy on an uneven playing field: the case of the deciduous fruit canning industry in South Africa', *World Development*, 27, pp. 1787–802.

Kaplinsky, R. (1982) *Computer Aided Design: Electronics, Comparative Advantage and Development*. London: Frances Pinter.

Kaplinsky, R. (1990) *The Economics of Small: Appropriate Technology in a Changing World*. London: Intermediate Technology Press.

Kaplinsky, R. (1993) 'Export processing zones in the Dominican Republic: transforming manufactures into commodities', *World Development*, 21, pp. 1851–65.

Kaplinsky, R. (1994) *Easternisation: The Spread of Japanese Management Techniques to Developing Countries*. London: Frank Cass.

Kaplinsky, R. (1995) 'Patients as work in progress: organisational reform in the health sector', in L. Andreasen, B. Coriat, F. den Hertog and R. Kaplinsky, *Europe's Next Step: Organisational Innovation, Competition and Employment*. London: Frank Cass.

Kaplinsky, R. (1998) 'Globalisation, industrialisation and sustainable growth: the pursuit of the nth rent', *Discussion Paper 365*. Brighton: Institute of Development Studies, University of Sussex.

Kaplinsky, R., and R. Fitter (2004) 'Technology and globalization: who gains when commodities are de-commodified?', *International Journal of Technology and Globalization*, 1, 1, pp. 1–28.

Kaplinsky, R., and J. Readman (2004) 'Globalisation and upgrading: what can (and cannot) be learnt from international trade statistics in the wood furniture sector?'. Mimeo, Centre for Research in Innovation Management, Brighton.

Khan, A. R. (1999) 'Poverty in China in the period of globalization: new evidence on trend and pattern', *Issues in Development Discussion Paper 22*. Geneva: ILO.

Kaplinsky, R., M. Morris and J. Readman (2002) 'The globalization of product markets and immiserizing growth: lessons from the South African furniture industry', *World Development*, 30, pp. 1159–78.

King, R. G., and R. Levine (1993) 'Finance and growth, Schumpeter might be right', *Policy, Research and External Affairs Working Paper No 183*, Washington, DC: World Bank.

Kohl, R., and K. O'Rourke (2000), 'What's new about globalization: implications for income inequality in developing countries', paper presented to 'Poverty and Inequality in Developing Countries: A Policy Dialogue on the Effects of Globalisation'. Paris: OECD.

Krueger, A. O. (1974) 'The political economy of rent seeking society', *American Economic Review*, 64, pp. 291–303.

Kuczynski, P., and J. Williamson (eds) (2003) *After the Washington Consensus*. Washington, DC: Institute for International Economics.

Lal, D. (1983) *The Poverty of 'Development Economics'*. London: Institute of Economic Affairs.

Lall, S., and M. Abaladajo (2004) 'China's competitive performance: a threat to East Asian manufactured exports?', *World Development*, 32, pp. 1441–66.

Lall, S., and M. Teubal (1998) 'Market stimulating technology policies in developing countries: a framework with examples from East Asia', *World Development*, 26, pp. 1369–85.

Lawrence, R. Z., and M. J. Slaughter (1993) 'International trade and American wages in the 1980s: giant sucking sound or small hiccup?', in M. N. Baily and C. Winston (eds), *Brookings Papers on Economic Activity: Microeconomics 2*, <http://www.biz.uiowa.edu/econ/seminars/fall00/ghosh.html>.

Leonard-Barton, D. (1995) *Wellsprings of Knowledge: Building and Sustaining the Sources of Innovation*. Boston: Harvard Business School Press.

Lewis, W. A. (1958 [1954]) 'Economic Development with Unlimited Supplies of Labour', repr. in A. N. Agarwala and S. P. Singh (eds), *The Economics of Underdevelopment*. Oxford: Oxford University Press.

Lipietz, A. (1987) *Mirages and Miracles: The Crises of Global Fordism*. London: Verso.

Little, I. M., T. Scitovsky and M. Scott (1970) *Industry and Trade in Some Developing Countries: A Comparative Study*. Oxford: Oxford University Press.

Liu, X. (2002) 'The achievement and challenge of industrial innovation in China', *Proceedings of the 3rd International Symposium on Management of Innovation and Technology*, Hangzhou, October, <http://www.cma.zju.edu.cn/ismot/>.

Lundvall, B. A. (1992) *National Systems of Innovation*. London: Frances Pinter.

Maizels, A. (1999) 'The manufactures terms of trade of developing countries with the United States, 1981–97', *Working Paper 36*, Oxford: Finance and Trade Policy Centre, Queen Elizabeth House.

Maizels, A. (2003) 'The manufactures terms of trade of developing and developed countries with Japan, 1981–2000', Mimeo, Oxford: Queen Elizabeth House.

Maizels, A., T. Palaskas and T. Crowe (1998) 'The Prebisch–Singer hypothesis revisited', in D. Sapsford and J. Chen (eds), *Development Economics and Policy: The Conference Volume to Celebrate the 85th Birthday of Professor Sir Hans Singer.* Basingstoke: Macmillan.

Malthus, R. (1926 [1798]) *An Essay on the Principles of Population.* London: Macmillan.

Management Review (1996) 'Polishing the apple: has Apple completely lost its luster, or can a new CEO help bring back the shine?' 85, 9, pp. 43–6.

Martin, M. and V. Manole (2003) 'China's emergence as the workshop of the world'. Mimeo, Washington, DC: World Bank.

Martin, W. (2003) 'Developing countries' changing participation in world trade', *World Bank Research Observer*, 18, pp. 159–86.

Mathews, J. A., and D.-S. Cho (2000) *Tiger Technology: The Creation of a Semiconductor Industry in East Asia.* Cambridge: Cambridge University Press.

Mayer, J. A. (2002) 'The fallacy of composition: a review of the literature', *World Economy*, 25, pp. 875–94.

Menzies, G. (2002) *1421: The Year China Discovered the World.* London: Bantam Books.

Milanovic, B. (2002) 'The Ricardian vice: why Sala-i-Martin's calculations of world income inequality are wrong', <www.ssrn.com>.

Milanovic, B. (2003) 'The two faces of globalization: against globalization as we know it', *World Development*, 31, pp. 667–83.

Monden, Y. (1983) *Toyota Production System: Practical Approach to Production Management.* Atlanta: Industrial Engineering and Management Press.

Morris, M., and G. Robbins (2005) 'The role of government in creating an enabling environment for inter-firm cluster co-operation: policy lessons from South Africa', in B. Oyelaran-Oyeyinka and D. McCormick (eds), *Industrial Clusters in Africa: Pattern Practice and Policies for Innovation and Upgrading.* Tokyo: United Nations University Press.

Nadvi, K. (1999) 'Collective efficiency and collective failure: the response of the Sialkot surgical instrument cluster to global quality pressures', *World Development*, 27, pp. 1605–26 [special issue on industrial clusters in developing countries].

Nelson, R. R. (1993) *National Innovation Systems: A Comparative Analysis.* New York: Oxford University Press.

Obstfeld, M., and A. M. Taylor (2004) *Global Capital Markets: Integration, Crisis and Growth.* Cambridge: Cambridge Universtiy Press.

Perez, C. (2002) *Technological Revolutions and Financial Capital: The Dynamics of Bubbles and Golden Ages.* Cheltenham: Edward Elgar.

Pine, J. B. (1993) *Mass Customization: The New Frontier in Business Competition.* Cambridge, MA: Harvard Business School Press.

Piore, M. J., and C. Sabel (1984) *The Second Industrial Divide: Possibilities for Prosperity.* New York: Basic Books.

Pogge, T. W., and S. G. Reddy (2002) 'How not to count the poor', <www.socialanalysis.org>.

Porter, M. E. (1990) *The Competitive Advantage of Nations.* London: Macmillan.

Prebisch, R. (1950) 'The economic development of Latin America and its principal problems', *Economic Bulletin for Latin America 7*. New York: United Nations.

Pyke, F., G. Becattini and W. Sengenberger (1990) *Industrial Districts and Inter-Firm Cooperation in Italy*. Geneva: International Institute for Labour Studies.

Ravallion, M. (2003) 'The debate on globalization, poverty and inequality: why measurement matters', *International Affairs*, 79, pp. 739–54.

Rawski, T. G. (2003) 'Recent developments in China's labor economy'. Mimeo, Department of Economics, University of Pittsburgh.

Readman, J. (2004) 'The competitive advantage of buying networks in wood products value chains', *Upgrading in Small Enterprise Clusters and Global Value Chains*. Geneva: ILO.

Reich, R. B. (1991) *The Work of Nations: Preparing Ourselves for 21st-Century Capitalism*. New York: Simon & Schuster.

Ricardo, D. (1973 [1817]), *The Principles of Political Economy and Taxation*. London: Dent.

Roberts, D., and J. Kynge (2003) 'How cheap labour, foreign investment and rapid industrialisation are creating a new workshop of the world', *Financial Times*, 4 February.

Rodrik, D. (1999) *The New Global Economy and Developing Countries: Making Openness Work*. Washington, DC: Institute for International Economics.

Rodrik, D. (2000) 'Comments on "Trade, growth and poverty" by D. Dollar and A. Kraay'. <http://ksghome.harvard.edu/~.drodrik.academic.ksg/>.

Rodrik, D. (2002), 'After neoliberalism, what?' Paper presented at 'Alternatives to Neoliberalism' conference, 'Coalition for New Rules for Global Finance', Washington, DC, 22–3 May, <http://ksghome.harvard.edu/~drodrik/>.

Rodrik, D. (2004) 'Industrial policy for the twenty-first century'. Mimeo, Cambridge, MA: John F. Kennedy School of Government.

Rowthorn, R., and K. Coutts (2004) 'De-industrialization and the balance of payments in advanced economies', *Discussion Paper No. 170*, Geneva: UNCTAD.

Sala-i-Martin, X. (2002), 'The world distribution of income (estimated from individual country distributions)', *Working paper 8933*. Cambridge, MA: NBER.

Sapsford, D., and J. Chen (eds) (1998) *Development Economics and Policy: The Conference Volume to Celebrate the 85th Birthday of Professor Sir Hans Singer*. Basingstoke: Macmillan.

Sarkar, P., and H. W. Singer (1991) 'Manufactured exports of developing countries and their terms of trade', *World Development*, 19, pp. 333–40.

Schmitz, H. (1999) 'Global competition and local cooperation: success and failure in the Sinos Valley, Brazil', *World Development*, 27, pp. 1627–50 [special issue on industrial clusters in developing countries].

Schmitz, H. (2004) 'Globalized localities: introduction', in H. Schmitz (ed.) *Local Enterprises in the Global Economy: Issues of Governance and Upgrading*. Cheltenham: Edward Elgar.

Schmitz, H., and P. Knorringa (2000) 'Learning from global buyers', *Journal of Development Studies*, 32, pp. 177–205.

Schonberger, R. J. (1986) *World Class Manufacturing: The Lessons of Simplicity Applied*. New York: Free Press.

Schumpeter, J. (1961) *The Theory of Economic Development*. Oxford: Oxford University Press.

Shafaeddin, S. M. (2002) 'The impact of China's accession to WTO on the exports of developing countries', *Discussion Paper No. 160*, Geneva: UNCTAD.

Singer, H. W. (1950) 'The distribution of gains between investing and borrowing countries', *American Economic Review*, 15, pp. 473–85.

Singer, H. (1975 [1971]), 'The distribution of gains revisited', repr. in A. Cairncross and M. Puri (eds), *The Strategy of International Development*. London: Macmillan.

Singer, H. W. (1987) 'Terms of trade and economic development', in J. Eatwell, M. Milgate and P. Newman (eds), *The New Palgrave: A Dictionary of Economics*. London: Macmillan.

Singh, A. (1995) 'How did East Asia grow so fast?', *UNCTAD Review, 1995*. Geneva: United Nations, pp. 91–128.

Smith, A. (1976 [1776]), *An Enquiry into the Nature and Cause of The Wealth of Nations*. 4th edn, ed. R. H. Campbell and A. S. Skinner, Oxford: Oxford University Press.

Streeten, P. (1998) 'Globalization: threat or salvation', in A. S. Bhalla (ed.), *Globalization, Growth and Marginalization*. New York: Macmillan and IDRC.

Sturgeon, T. (2002) 'Modular production networks: a new American model of industrial organization', *Industrial and Corporate Change*, 11, pp. 451–96.

Sutcliffe, R. B. (1971) *Industry and Underdevelopment*. London: Addison-Wesley.

Teece, D., and G. Pisano (1994) 'The dynamic capabilities of firms: an introduction', *Industrial and Corporate Change*, 3, pp. 537–56.

Teunissen, J., J. Joost and M. Teunissen (eds) (2003) *Financial Stability and Growth in Emerging Economics: The Role of the Financial Sector*. The Hague: FONDAD.

Tidd, J., J. Bessant and K. Pavitt (2001) *Managing Innovation: Integrating Technological, Market and Organizational Change*. Chichester: John Wiley & Sons.

Townsend, P. (1979) *Poverty in the United Kingdom: A Survey of Household Resources and Standards of Living*. Harmondsworth: Penguin.

Triplett, J. E., and B. P. Bosworth (2003) 'Productivity measurement issues in service industries: "Baumol's disease has been cured" ', *Federal Reserve Bank of New York Economic Policy Review*, September, pp. 23–33.

Ulrich, K. T., and S. D. Eppinger (2003) *Product Design and Development*. Singapore: McGraw-Hill.

UNCTAD (2002) *Trade and Development Report*. New York: United Nations.

UNCTAD (2003) *World Investment Survey*. Geneva and New York: United Nations.

UNDP (1999) *Human Development Report*. New York: United Nations Development Programme.

UNIDO (1990) *Handbook of Industrial Statistics, 1990*. Vienna: United Nations Industrial Development Organization.

UNIDO (2002) *Industrial Development Report 2002/2003: Competing through Innovation and Learning*, Vienna: United Nations Industrial Development Organization.

USDA Economic Research Service (2000) 'Consolidation in food retailing: prospects for consumers & grocery suppliers', *Agricultural Outlook*, August, pp. 18–22.

USITC (2004) *Textiles and Apparel: Assessment of the Competitiveness of Certain Foreign Suppliers to the U.S. Market*. Washington, DC: United States International Trade Commission.

Wade, R. H. (1990) *Governing the Market: Economic Theory and the Role of Government in East Asian Industrialization*. Princeton, NJ: Princeton University Press.

Wade, R. (1996) 'Japan, the World Bank and the art of paradigm maintenance: the East Asian miracle in political perspective', *New Left Review* 211, pp. 3–36.

Wheelwright, S., and K. Clark (1992), *Revolutionizing Product Development*. Cambridge, MA: Harvard Business School.

Williamson, J. (1990) 'What Washington means by policy reform', in J. Williamson (ed.), *Latin American Adjustment: How Much Has Happened?* Washington, DC: Institute for International Economics.

Williamson, J. G. (1998) 'Globalization, labor markets and policy backlash in the past', *Journal of Economic Perspectives*, 12, 4, pp. 51–72.

Williamson, O. E. (1985) *The Economic Institutions of Capitalism: Firms, Markets and Relational Contracting*. New York: Praeger.

Womack, J. P., and D. T. Jones (1996) *Lean Thinking: Banish Waste and Create Wealth in your Corporation*. New York: Simon & Schuster.

Womack, J., D. Jones and D. Roos (1990) *The Machine that Changed the World*. New York: Rawson Associates.

Wood, A. (1994) *North–South Trade, Employment and Inequality: Changing Fortunes in a Skill-Driven World*. Oxford: Clarendon Press.

Wood, A. (1997) 'Openness and wage inequality in developing countries: the

Latin American challenge to East Asian conventional wisdom', *World Bank Economic Review*, 11, 1, pp. 33–57.

Wood, A. (1998) 'Globalisation and the rise in labour market inequalities', *Economic Journal*, 108, pp. 1463–82.

World Bank (1993) *The East Asian Economic Miracle: Economic Growth and Public Policy*. New York: Oxford University Press.

World Bank (2002) *Globalization, Growth, and Poverty: Building an Inclusive World Economy*. Washington, DC: World Bank; Oxford: Oxford University Press.

World Bank (2004) *World Development Indicators*. Washington, DC: World Bank.

Wrigley, N. (2002) 'Transforming the corporate landscape of US food retailing: market power, financial re-engineering and regulation', *Tijdschrift voor Economische en Sociale Geografie*, 93, 1, pp. 62–82.

WTO (2004) *International Trade Statistics*. Geneva: World Trade Organization.

Yamin, F. (ed.) (2004) *IDS Bulletin*, 35, 3 [special issue on 'Climate change and development'].

Yoffie, D. B. (1983) *Power and Protection: Strategies for the Newly Industrializing Countries*. New York: Columbia University Press.

Zheng, Z., and Y. Zhao (2002) 'China's terms of trade in manufactures', UNCTAD Discussion Paper No. 161, Geneva: UNCTAD.

Index